T. W. (Thomas Welbank) Fowle

The Reconciliation of Religion and Science

Being Essays on Immortality, Inspiration, Miracles, and the being of Christ

T. W. (Thomas Welbank) Fowle

The Reconciliation of Religion and Science
Being Essays on Immortality, Inspiration, Miracles, and the being of Christ

ISBN/EAN: 9783337130299

Printed in Europe, USA, Canada, Australia, Japan

Cover: Foto ©ninafisch / pixelio.de

More available books at **www.hansebooks.com**

THE
RECONCILIATION
OF
RELIGION AND SCIENCE

*BEING ESSAYS ON IMMORTALITY,
INSPIRATION, MIRACLES, AND
THE BEING OF CHRIST*

BY THE

REV. T. W. FOWLE, M.A.
VICAR OF ST LUKE'S, NUTFORD PLACE, LONDON

LONDON: HENRY S. KING & CO.
65 CORNHILL AND 12 PATERNOSTER ROW
1873

TO THE

VERY REV. A. P. STANLEY, D.D.

DEAN OF WESTMINSTER

WHOSE FEARLESS AND CONSISTENT LIBERALISM

MAKES HIM THE FRIEND OF ALL

LIBERAL CLERGYMEN,

𝕿𝖍𝖎𝖘 𝕭𝖔𝖔𝖐

IS DEDICATED.

PREFACE.

SEEING that more than half the differences of opinion in philosophy and theology are due to the use of words in different senses, it may be well to define in what sense the words "religion" and "science" are used in this volume. It is, I may say, the popular, ordinary, and quite intelligible sense which they commonly bear—indeed, in my opinion, the general public has often a better reason for, and more method in, its use of language than the wise men who are for ever setting it to rights. Science is simply the process by which mankind derives knowledge from reasoning about facts. (Occasionally I may have used the word in its more restricted sense of "natural" science—*i.e.*, that department of knowledge which deals with physical facts.) Religion is the word that describes the relations of man with the power or being whom we call God.

Now the quarrel between these two has hitherto consisted in this. Science affirms that nothing is to be regarded as true except that which can be proved by rational arguments addressed to reasonable beings, founded upon facts capable of analysis and verification. I say that science affirms this, because no one who knows anything of the real tendency of positive thought, as seen in its ablest representatives, can permit himself to doubt what the meaning of science is now, and what it will teach the world hereafter. Two things alone it postulates—the existence of mind and the existence of matter—as ultimate incomprehensible facts; why these are, and in what sense they are, incomprehensible, Mr Herbert Spencer will explain to all who care to inquire. Religion, on the contrary, has been made to assert that there are some things which must be taken for granted upon some authority or other, some explanations which must be received although the words which convey them do not represent any actual facts that have been submitted to consciousness. Hence an ill-omened alliance has been struck between theology and the intuitional philosophy; and furthermore, the conclusions of science even in the field of physical fact have been subjected to a rash and irritating opposition in the interests of what was believed to be religious truth. Scientific men, on the contrary, have accepted this view of religion with too great readiness, and taking their opponents at their word, have been content that this antagonism should be regarded as real and permanent. Thus in their minds the two words represented two alien tendencies of thought—the one old, intuitional, theological, and destined to pass away; the other new, positive, founded upon experience, and destined to prevail. And being strong in the growing discovery of law and truth, they have disdained the ill-judged, temporising, and insincere offers of reconciliation which their opponents, goaded from time to time by their fear of the force of facts, have been making to them.

The mode of reconciliation suggested in this book consists in the absolute unconditional surrender of the province of religion to the methods of scientific investigation. And whatever else it may show, this at least is clear, that it is possible for the same man to hold the Christian Creed and yet to belong to the empirical school of thought, and to accept every scientific conclusion which those who are entitled to be heard declare to be established. If the origin of life or the genesis of man seem at all uncertain, it is not because I have the faintest religious partiality one way or another; but because, by common confession, there remains yet much to be explained and accounted for. My only feeling in the matter is to hope that this may be accomplished as soon as possible, in order that religion may have another fact upon which to exercise herself, and so to draw nearer to the mind and will of God.

The way in which this reconciliation is worked out appears in the Essays themselves, but admits, like all simple truths, of being succinctly stated. Knowledge is derived from facts by reason—this is the basis of science. The knowledge of God is derived primarily from historical facts —this is the basis of religion. These facts, it must however be remarked parenthetically, are not the only means, but the first or only *direct* means of knowing God. They give us the clue whereby we may then trace the mind and operations of God in all nature, all history, and all religions. We do not confine (God forbid!) the sphere of the divine working to a few almost isolated (so called) supernatural events, but we take these events, or rather the history that contains them, as helping us to understand how God works in the history of mankind, in the soul of men, in the universe itself. And we affirm that without some such clue, without, that is, facts to go upon, all belief as to the nature, being, and will of God must be and has been the merest guesswork, beautiful indeed and useful, as bearing witness to man's unconquerable instinct to search after God, but never practical to the vast mass of men, and now doomed to extinction before the onward progress of scientific thought.

The kind of demonstration by which facts are proved, varies, of course, in the different branches of knowledge—in religion, being historical, it consists of human evidence. Now, no human evidence taken by itself can prove the intervention of God in history as any natural or ordinary fact of history is proved. The evidence will be received or rejected, according as the knowledge of God which it purports to convey does or does not meet the moral cravings and religious wants of those to whom it is addressed. The time may come, must indeed come, when the minds of men will be made up on the whole in one of two directions; at present every man must do his best to justify to himself the grounds upon which his belief or his unbelief is founded. Meanwhile both parties ought to acknowledge that in the present state of knowledge there is much to be said on both sides; both ought to abstain from irritating and contemptuous language; both ought to rest content with the assurance that truth will ultimately prevail; and finally, both ought to join in cordial alliance against any school of thought or of religion which, by means of intuitions incapable of analysis, or of authority transcending reason, or of facts independent of verification, seeks to hinder rigid scientific method in its inquiry after truth.

It will be observed, I hope, that I have taken pains throughout this volume not to mention (with a mere chance exception here and there) the names of living theologians, and to allude as little as possible to the individual opinions of any of them. I have desired to call attention to a new method of regarding the opposition between religion and science, and not to engage in the passing controversies of the day. Moreover, it is quite possible to entertain the highest esteem for theological writers while utterly repudiating the system of which they are the supporters, and to which they cannot, owing to mere stress of circumstances, avoid belonging. So, while restraining myself from attacking individual opinions, I have put no restraint whatever upon the expression of my dislike for the metaphysical theology which constitutes modern orthodoxy.

The subjects treated are what may fairly be termed the primary elements of religion. These are—God, or that which comes before our experience; immortality, or that which comes after it; and the means, whether actions or thoughts, by which God communicates with man—that is, miracles and inspiration. Subjects like the Atonement, Prayer, the Sacraments, the Church, occupy a secondary or derivative position, and are not therefore touched upon except by occasional allusion. Yet these, too, are susceptible of strictly scientific treatment, which has indeed in one case been successfully employed. Mr Macleod Campbell's book on the Atonement derives its now acknowledged value from the simple fact that its doctrine is based upon the experience of human nature, and upon certain historical events assumed and believed to have actually occurred. Surely it is time, judging from recent controversies, that the great subject of Prayer was similarly treated.

I feel compelled to apologise for the brevity, and consequent obscurity, of the first Essay on Inspiration, the more so as by it more than by any other the success of the "reconciliation" will be tested. It may fairly be said that the very title suggests a book rather than an essay, and requires a large historical induction. I might of course reply that this is a mere sketch to be filled up, or a first attempt to be followed out, as occasion might serve. But apart from personal considerations that are not favourable to any extensive literary undertaking, there is, I think, a very sufficient reason why the time for such an undertaking has not yet come. There are, in point of fact, no scientific data sufficient to carry us much further than I have gone. We are still almost entirely in the dark as to the origin, growth, and nature of the human faculties. What that was in Handel which made him a musician is still as unknown as the inspiration which made St Paul discern the meaning of Christ's religion or St Theresa live its life. But the definite assertion, that religious inspiration is just as much, or just as little, capable of explanation as any other human faculty, is surely a not unimportant step in the right direction. In the same way I have maintained that the actions of God called miracles can be just as much and just as little explained—that is, in their real essential nature—as such ultimate truths as the following : The origin of the universe, the being of God, the nature of law, the correlation of mind and matter. There is nothing whatever specially incomprehensible in any miracle, though there may be much that is incredible. We must therefore remit the case to the tribunal of posterity, that High Court of Appeal in all matters that cannot be verified by absolute demonstration. But it must never be forgotten that we ourselves are not the first court that has tried this cause. However we explain the fact, the fact remains, that Christianity under many disadvantages withstood the first great wave of critical and scientific thought in the eighteenth century. And it withstood it merely because the common-sense of mankind arrived, rightly or wrongly, at the conclusion that the events that give to Christianity its claim upon human allegiance really occurred.

I have added an Essay upon the Church and the Working Classes written some years ago, to remind my readers that the questions started in this book are no mere matters of theological speculation, but concern intimately the future history of this country, and the present welfare and future destiny of the Working classes, to whom that history belongs.

The publication of this book coincides with the period at which the fortunes of Liberal Christianity in the Church of England seem to have declined to their lowest ebb. It is not that there are no Liberal writers and workers, but that, to all outward appearance, they have failed to reach the mass of religious thought, sentiment, and action that lies embedded in the heart of the "common people." Not to mention the names of living men (in speaking of whom I could not claim the grace of impartiality), the Church of England has within one generation produced three men who, if nobility of spirit and originality of mind go for anything, might have been expected to have begun the new reformation by bringing home to the hearts of men the new truths that are in the air around us. Seldom, indeed, has reform been presented to mankind in a guise so attractive, by men so indescribably winning, as by these three, Arnold, Robertson, and Maurice. Differing in much, they were alike in this, that they were Englishmen to the backbone. Side by side with them was started the Catholic movement. It was alien to all dominant English traditions and sentiment; it has produced no great names since the first generation, the leading minds of which showed their appreciation of their position by deserting the Church of their fathers for the communion held in the utmost dislike by the English nation. Yet at this moment it has absorbed to itself all that is most vital and practical in the religion of English Churchmen, and dominates within the Church of whose traditions and history it does not now seem capable of forming a conception. The reaction triumphs all along the line.

The causes of the success of the Tractarian movement are easily discovered, as must always be the case with movements essentially superficial, retrogressive, and non-permanent. I am not concerned with them further than to observe that they are to be traced more or less directly to the decay of Evangelical religion, while as yet there was nothing to satisfy the hunger of men's souls for a definite system of religious belief and practice. But the question, Why has Liberal theology hitherto failed to all outward appearance, and in all outward operations? requires a single word of explanation.

To begin with, no Liberal can possibly admit that the failure is anything but in appearance and not in reality. Sooner or later, whether by slow approximation or by sudden convulsion, the Christianity of England will be drawn towards those views of God's will, His relations with man, man's duty to God and to his fellows, which these three writers were among the first to teach. This at times seems evident even to the most determined of the Reactionists; it accounts for that strange uneasiness, that defiant obstructiveness, that vehement passionateness, which they are wont to display even in the hour of seeming victory. Nor is it difficult to perceive the causes which have hindered hitherto the outward success of the Liberal movement. The time is not yet fully come. The really important and interesting thing is, however, to realise clearly in what sense these three men have not failed but succeeded, and how they have accomplished the work to which they were sent.

The process through which those vital religious changes called reformations seem in part to pass is something of this sort. Prescient minds discern something false, contradictory, non-human, immoral, in the opinions or practices of contemporary religion; they see that the best life of the world is becoming alienated from religious belief. Tokens of a coming storm are everywhere in the air, and yet none can tell from what quarter it will burst or what direction it will take. Then these minds set themselves, by a necessity arising from their personal reaction from popular religion, to re-state and re-establish for themselves and for the world the primary truths of all religion. This was accomplished by the first generation of Liberal English Churchmen, the popular mind meanwhile, as was only natural, going back, in the general break-up of traditional opinions, to the oldest and most positive authorities it could find. It was not the business of men like the three I have mentioned to lay down the exact relations of religion towards that spirit of the age called science, which was beginning to assail almost like an intellectual storm the oldest convictions, traditions, and institutions of the world. To them, as to Samuel, Savonarola, and above all Wickliffe, belonged the far nobler task of laying the roots of religion so deep in the heart of man, of recommending it so forcibly to his intellectual and moral needs, that when the storm burst and beat upon the house it should stand and not fall, because it was founded upon a rock.

If, then, at this moment everywhere men are yearning for a religion, are admitting that it is essential to humanity, are seeking for it by every available and unavailable route, —if, moreover, religion is able to hold her own as a power that must be acknowledged and that cannot be destroyed, —it is due to the writings of these three Englishmen, and others like them. They are doing the work of Wickliffe over again; for England, let her detractors say what they will, is ever the "mother of originality." I declare, after attentive study, that there is more of the vital essence of religion, more to convince us of its spiritual necessity, more life, hope, spiritual brightness, and energy in Mr Maurice's commentary on St John, than in all the German commentaries on the same book—with which at any rate I am acquainted—put together. To the High Church party belongs the immense credit of having kept religion as a power and a reality before the mass of the people, alike by what they have done and have stimulated others into doing. To the Liberals, who are not a party but a school of thought, belongs the more abiding credit of having implanted even in the scientific intelligence of mankind the idea of the indestructibility of the worship of the Lord God Almighty.

For a guess at the future course of events let us go to a parable taken from history. Never was failure more absolute, never did extinction itself seem more close at hand, than when the last man of the last English army died round the last of the English kings upon the fatal field of Hastings. And in a sense this was true; the old England lay dead with those dead warriors, the new England was yet to rise from their graves. Pass a few years, and the old saying is found once more to be true, " Anglia victa cepit victores." Not by victories, nor revolutions, nor heroic actions, but merely by the process of gradual absorption, by the strength and flexibility of the English nature, nay, by the very act of submitting to the inevitable and acknowledging the supremacy that could not be gainsaid—in short, by treating facts and laws as though they were facts and laws, the English character leavened, transformed, and finally assimilated the vital elements in the character of the conquering race. Through what years of patient suffering, through how prolonged an agony of silent evolution, this took place, there are few records to explain to us. But the genius of historical insight has flashed a ray of light upon the lives of Englishmen during this period, and in the character of Cedric the Saxon (to me, for reasons that I now comprehend, always specially attractive) we catch a glimpse of the process by which England in the hour of defeat was slowly becoming England once more. And that the ancient spirit lived on, producing new hopes without itself daring to hope, is due to the men whose memories kept alive the pride and name of the English race, and whose glory and whose works became the property of vanquished and vanquisher alike. The men who fell at Hastings were in sober truth the spiritual ancestors of the ENGLISH barons who confronted the tyrant on Runnymede, of the archers who let fly their shafts at Agincourt, of the sailors who "did their duty" at Trafalgar, of the grey horsemen who "rode so terribly" at Waterloo. Ah ! but the story of the Cross, in all its essential meaning, has been repeated in the lives of may a warrior, whether of the sword or of the pen, who has fallen on the field of battle as defeated but not destroyed, as dying and behold he lives.

The application of our parable is easy. The hour is coming when upon the field of intellectual controversy the army of science will storm the last stronghold of religion regarded from the intellectual side. Reason will conquer for herself the kingdom which, even in the act of admitting the inevitable result, it seems so hard to believe can really belong to her. But "magna sunt facta et prævalebunt." The methods, the assumptions, the opinions, the dogmas, the creeds of Christendom, will pass under the yoke of scientific inquiry, and will continue to exist only so far as science permits and approves. And with the death of the old theology will begin the new religion, just as when the Norman soldiers sat down on English soil to eat their meal on the night of victory, there began then and there that process which was to make them more English than the English themselves. In this sense, and this is what men really mean by the assertion, there can be no permanent contest between religion and science : at the moment of victory the spell of the spiritual power of religion begins to weave its influence round minds that have been forced by circumstances into an intellectual antagonism. Once again, by mere process of assimilation, by the spirit of patient endurance, by the memory of great names and deeds, by the instinctive clinging to the essential ideas of religious humanity, by breathing the old spirit into words that sound so harshly in the ear of the vanquished, by sheer strength of character and positive determination to exist, by the power of numbers, by the grace of prayer, by the imperious craving for unity, religion will live again amidst the forms, the methods, and the dogmas of science. How this Reconciliation of Religion and Science will come about we know not, any more than we know how a corn of wheat if it fall into the earth and die brings forth much fruit. It may be in this way or in that way, by this man or by that man, or by no way at all that we can see, and by no man of whose name we could make special mention; all we can say for certain is, that it will be accomplished by the application of rigorous scientific method to the subject of religion in the first instance, and the infusion of religious spirit into the mind and method of science in the second.

To have made an attempt in this direction is the claim of this otherwise unpretending book. It is an endeavour to carry on the traditions received from the founders of Liberal Theology in England, and to harmonise the religious truths they derived from nature, history, the Bible, and the soul of man, with scientific thought. And if there be nothing in its arguments to bring about, there is, I will venture to say, nothing in its spirit to retard, that reconciliation which every man desires who believes that because Unity is the Being of God, it is therefore the prize of reason and the crown of humanity. May I add that some such thought as this crossed my mind as, a year ago, I turned aside from the grave of Maurice? Therein had just been laid all that was mortal of my dear friend and teacher; but the immortal spirit was stirring in the hearts of those who stood around, so that one of them was fain to exclaim, "What life there is here!"

CONTENTS.

	PAGE
THE DIVINE CHARACTER OF CHRIST,	1
SCIENCE AND IMMORTALITY,	22
MORALITY AND IMMORTALITY,	48
CHRISTIANITY AND IMMORTALITY,	86
RELIGION AND FACT,	118
THE MIRACLES OF GOD,	151
THE MIRACLES OF MAN,	183
A SCIENTIFIC ACCOUNT OF INSPIRATION,	220
THE INSPIRATION OF THE JEWS,	256
THE INSPIRATION OF THE BIBLE,	288
THE DIVINITY OF CHRIST AND MODERN THOUGHT,	325
THE CHURCH AND THE WORKING CLASSES,	360

THE RECONCILIATION OF RELIGION AND SCIENCE.

THE DIVINE CHARACTER OF CHRIST.

NO one, I think, can doubt that the question of the historical truthfulness of the New Testament—that is, of the personality of Jesus Christ—is being tried before us, and will be decided by our children ; nor is it possible for any candid person to say what the result of the conflict may be, no matter how firm his own persuasion and faith. We cannot foresee the exact influence of the result of scientific discovery upon the religious faith of the future ; it may quench the possibility of belief in the divine interposition under the overwhelming pressure of a changeless law of evolution, from the time when this globe was a chaos of nebulous matter, or it may compel men to fall back upon the belief in the divine mission of Christ as the one means of escape from a law more horrible than anarchy itself. But it is clear that once more men will be brought face to face with the deepest questions of religious belief; and it is melancholy, indeed, to notice the absolute ignorance of popular religionism, and its popular leaders, as to the true nature of the approaching crisis. That Mr Darwin's last book should surprise the religious world in the midst of a hot fight about articles and rubrics, disestablishment and vestments, is sadly ominous of the result of the battle.

Now, one advantage—at any rate, one consequence—of a real crisis, is that it clears the ground, divides men into two distinct armies, sets before them a worthy object of contention, appeals to manly virtues, and calls forth a robust and clear-sighted faith. Such a time is especially fatal to a class of thinkers whom I shall not attempt to describe, because I am conscious that I have not sufficient sympathy with them to enable me to do them justice. These are sentimentalists, idealists, moralists, to whom the goodness or the beauty of Christianity are dear, but who emancipate themselves from the necessity of believing it as a record of actual events displaying a divine purpose. They act the part of neutrals in keeping well with both parties—and, like neutrals when war breaks out, they run no small risk of being effaced. Their voice is silenced when once the great debate is opened, and men demand with vehement determination a simple answer to a plain question—"Are these things true, or are they not? Did they happen, or did they not? Answer, yes or no."

Now the purpose of this essay is to examine one of the pleas by which, as it seems to me, honest men desire unconsciously to evade answering this question either to their own minds or to those of other people. We are constantly told that the character and teaching of Christ, even if everything else perished, would be a sufficient basis for a distinctive Christian creed, and, I suppose, for a defined Christian Church. Everything is staked upon His moral perfection. I propose, therefore, to examine, by an appeal to the facts of the case, how far this is true. Without attempting to establish distinct propositions, the general course and tenor of my argument will be as follows :—That the biography was never intended, and is manifestly inadequate, for the purpose of setting forth a character merely for criticism, admiration, and imitation : that there is in this character itself a distinctly divine or non-human element, as much so as are the miracles among His actions, the personal claims amidst His teaching, and the Resurrection in His life : that this element, both as a matter of fact and of right, calls for worship on our part, as well as, or rather than mere imitation : that it is far more difficult to believe in the possibility of a perfect character existing in an ordinary man, than to believe in the historical personality of Jesus Christ: that the character is not separable from, and can only be explained by, or be possible to, His personality, and *vice versâ ;* and that thus the two are not distinct inlets to the Christian faith, the one prior in time or in experience to the other, but, as it were, folding-doors, giving us a wide, easy, and simultaneous access thereunto.

At the outset, however, I am confronted by an enormous danger. Although it is clear to myself that my argument, though close to, is nevertheless entirely outside the limits of the well-worn controversy as to the identity of divine and human morality, yet I am equally sure that there will be an almost irresistible tendency in the mind of my readers to raise that question. In the hope, then, of somewhat stemming this tendency, I hasten to affirm my belief that the life of Christ is the revelation of divine goodness in man ; that the idea, though not the capacity of goodness, is everywhere the same : that man has therefore an inherent power of judging goodness, call it divine or human, wherever it appears, by the unchanging laws of right and wrong. But then it seems to me self-evident that a divine being conscious of himself will, by virtue of the very same laws, act differently and have some different qualities from ordinary men. Given the same laws and forces of morality, *and* a different person in his origin and self-consciousness, and the result must be a variation in character and conduct. Hence, too, it follows that this variation may be the object, as I have said, of worship rather than of imitation. Only I must here seize the opportunity of pointing out how desirable it is to remember that words such as divine, superhuman, worship, perfection, goodness, and the like, from seeming to explain and to signify more than they really do, have a most confusing tendency, against which it is necessary to guard by keeping steadily before our minds facts, and things, and events. Two instances showing the need of this have already occurred in this present essay. I use the word Personality in respect of Christ, as wishing to avoid all controversy upon His essential divinity or relations to the Father, and simply as expressing that historical account of Him in which He is represented as being free from human sin in His birth, and from human corruption in His death. Personality would thus mean what a man is by virtue of powers, such as the paternal, apart from himself; and character what he is by virtue of his own self-determination inherent in himself. And, again, when I speak of a character as calling for worship rather than imitation, I define worship to be the desire of the creature to be like the Creator, accompanied by the consciousness of its own imperfection and powerlessness. We turn now, then, to see what the character of Christ really is in the light of simple facts.

The essence of the revelation of God to us has come in the form of a biography—beyond all doubt the most suitable for teaching morality. The history of a life affects most powerfully our moral nature by the example proposed, the sympathy evoked, the light shed upon the inner workings of humanity, above all, by the necessity imposed of using our moral discernment to decide upon the character and conduct of its hero. Now it is surely a mere matter of fact that the life of Christ is presented to us in a form very different from those of other men, and very imperfectly fulfilling these conditions, though certainly fulfilling them in part. We may throughout this argument usefully compare the history of St Paul, though I shall leave it for the most part to be done mentally. That history resembles the history of Christ in being to a large extent in its materials autobiographical, and in having been compiled by the same man. And it must be a source of unceasing wonder that St Luke should have been able to draw two portraits of two—on any view—of the greatest persons that ever existed, without for one moment confusing the outlines, or portraying the smallest essential resemblance, or leaving upon his readers the least identity of treatment and effect, or placing them for one moment upon a level of power and goodness.

The character of Christ is a mere outline. Though, by the hypothesis which I am controverting, His character as a human being is the sole ultimate evidence for His divinity, or for whatever view men take of His person; yet the account of it is so short and undefined as to be proof against ordinary criticism. There are no letters, nothing about His personal appearance, next to nothing of His inner feelings and thoughts, no record of His opinions upon science, art, philosophy, history, literature, and metaphysics. St Paul, on the contrary, lives before us, his bodily presence weak and contemptible, his letters weighty and powerful, the agitations of his inner life, loves, hopes, fears, plans, speculations, all engraven in living characters. Painting St Paul, you paint a real man; painting Christ, you reproduce the ideal of the artist, or the age, or the nation. And His life appears to have had just the same effect upon those who saw it as upon those who read it. With an exception to be mentioned, they make no direct allusions to His character as an object of imitation. What possessed their souls and filled their imagination was not sympathy with His character, but admiration and worship of His person. They built their faith, not upon His perfection, but upon His birth, which was to them the love of God; His death, which was to them the goodness of the Son of God; His Resurrection, in which they saw the power of God over evil; the Ascension, in which they felt the power of the Son of God for good over the world. They never attempted to prove that He was perfectly good by explaining His actions or defending His conduct, nor have they left any materials by which we can do so. They took all this for granted, and thus gave to His life that divine suggestiveness by which we can, and must, attach all our ideas of moral perfection to Him, not find them complete in Him. This is that perfection which He too claimed—"Which of you convinceth me of sin?" which, the moment we begin to think of it, fades away into infinity, loses itself in God. It presents to us not a character to be analysed, but a life to be lived, and that lives in us. It is not merely that He is far removed from us and above us; so also is St Paul, who seems nearer to Christ than we to him. But then we are, so to speak, in the same plane as St Paul, and can see the steps that lie between us and him; whereas, around Christ there is a vacant space, across which no man may in this life tread, and in which the desire for mere imitation ceases and dies; and an instinct of His greatness and our weakness constrains us to cry, "My Lord and my God!"

And this is on the whole a description of the effect of His life upon those who knew Him best. Not, certainly, that it found vent in the mere bare assertion that He was God—for that in so many words they never said. But they spoke of Him with reverent reticence, as men who struggle with thoughts too big for them, tending to conclusions that defy the power of language. Contrast, for instance, the awkward, incoherent utterance of St Paul—"He thought it not robbery to be equal with God;" or again, the prophetic ecstasy which exclaimed, "Then shall the Son also Himself be subject unto Him that did put all things under Him, that God may be all in all," with the precise, logical, but hollow-sounding definitions of the Athanasian Creed. And they felt sure of this, too, that He was alive still, and had distinct personal relations with each of them; and further, that His works and death affected them, not as others do, historically and indirectly, but directly and spiritually, and that He had not died for the Jews, or for the disciples, or for truth, or even for humanity, but for each individual soul.

Now all this may be consistently and plausibly explained by the theory of a myth growing up about an unusual life crowned by a very remarkable death. But to abandon historical certainty, and then attempt to construct out of shifting shadows of myths, or the doubtful utterances of an ingenious fanatic, a morality which shall satisfy the conscience of men, or abide their criticism, or create a faith, or found a church, appears to me the most singular delusion ever imagined. The world has seen the result of one such attempt, and has grown very impatient of Niebuhrism. Did He believe Himself able to work miracles? If not, then the very ground of the history is taken from us, and we are launched into chaos. If He did, then, *ex hypothesi*, the morality by which men are to live and die rests upon the words of one whom impartial judgment must pronounce to be on the whole below Socrates, who neither claimed supernatural gifts, nor died believing that he should rise in triumph. Or how can we say of such an one that He was perfectly or even unusually good, in the absence of all real evidences as to much of His conduct, such evidences as we have being furnished by devoted, not to say deluded followers? Who can affirm that He was or was not unduly angry with the Jews, that He acted harshly towards Judas, that His expressions were always modest and truthful? Renan's Life gives an absolute negation to the possibility of returning any answer whatever, and leaves us face to face with the true alternative—either myth altogether or history altogether.

So much for the way in which the character is presented to us; let us now try, by a simple analysis of the history itself, to discover whether there is not in it a distinctly divine element as clearly separating it from that of ordinary men, as the raising of Lazarus separates the (recorded) actions from ours. I might lay stress upon the difficulty of discovering any special point of view from which to regard it, or of discerning the leading features, or of classifying and labelling the phenomena it presents. But, endeavouring to deal with it as with that of ordinary men, I will assume its essence and foundation to consist in three qualities: unselfishness, or His attitude towards Himself; meekness, or His attitude in receiving treatment from men; humility, or His attitude in dealing with men.

1st. Beginning, then, with His unselfishness, there is, I venture to think, an element in it suitable only to God, possible only to God, intelligible only in God, and an object of worship to imperfect beings like ourselves during this our progress to perfection. We distinguish between selfishness and self-love. By the former we mean sinful excess in regard to self, and to it we know that He was tempted in both of its two forms. At the beginning of His life, by the desire of power, pleasure, and success in its most subtle manifestations; at the close, by the fear of pain and death in its most overwhelming force. In all this He has left us something which we can hope to follow; and yet even here we cannot fail to notice that nearly all that is valuable for mere imitation is omitted. Of the inner shades of thought and feeling, the varying moods, the little details, we learn on the first occasion nothing, and on the second as much as can be told in two or three verses. Our attention is fixed upon the fact of Jesus victorious over sin and death, although, of course, we are bidden to walk in His steps, taking up our cross and following Him. But granting, as I am quite willing to do, that unselfishness or self-sacrifice, in its ordinary human sense, is a perfectly adequate word to describe His life at these epochs, yet we see, besides this, another element which is not merely the perfect negation of selfishness, but the entire absence of self-love. By this we mean, that rational, reasonable, and righteous care of self, which is practically admitted into all systems of moral philosophy, and certainly into His teaching, "Thou shalt love thy neighbour as thyself, and do to him as thou wouldest he should do to thee." Now, is it not obvious that, while Christ laid down this rule for others, He lived Himself by a higher law which included, and, for Him, abolished the former? We cannot, I think, describe His conduct in these words, or assign it to these motives. He never cared for what men did to Him, or thought of Himself at all. Moral perfection, that is God, made for itself a new law, a law impossible for imperfect beings, though distinctly apprehended by them as the goal to which they tend in the eternal life. I speak with great diffidence, but I am inclined to think that this consideration enables us to answer a charge urged by Positive philosophers against Christian morality, the stress of which has always appeared to me undeniable. They urge that self-love is not so true or deep a basis for morality as the loving humanity better than ourselves. To which it may be answered, that Christ lived Himself by the latter law, but was obliged to recognise a necessity for self-love in beings as yet imperfect, in course of training for a higher, though in noways different, manifestation of goodness—that is, of moral perfection. At any rate, let us now examine whether He was not free essentially from those self-limitations and regards, from which, as a mere matter of fact, no man has ever, actually or in consciousness been able to free himself.*

We cannot imagine God as conscious of self, or having self-interest, or needing self-justification. He is, and lives, and is recognised in the works of His creative power and love. Man, on the other hand, cannot divest himself of self; he must remember that he has a soul to save, a character to justify. The true saving of the soul may lie, as of course it does, in the triumph over all self-interest; but the consciousness of the soul and of its salvation cannot be got rid of. How, then, stands the case with Christ?

(*a.*) Self-consciousness. What is with us the obtrusion of self into our works, not at all in a sinful, but simply in a necessary form, corresponds in Him to the consciousness of the Father doing all the works. His meat or drink was to finish that work; His glory, in having finished it. And it is remarkable that this consciousness of self, this reflection upon our motives and successes, this almost agonising survey of our work and life, is particularly strong in religious reformers. The men who have most moved the world in religion have been those to whom the movements of their own souls have been most painfully clear; for instance, St Paul, Luther, and Milton. Consider the former painfully conscious of his bodily appearance, his reputation, his conversion, his very hand-writing, his labours; consider the latter brooding over his blindness, his treatment, his failure, the evil days on which he had fallen. And these men powerfully affected the world in

---

* That is, as a being who stands in need. In another sense, as will be seen further on in this book, self-consciousness is necessary to our conception of God as a personal Being.

which they lived, whereas Homer and Shakespeare, of all men the most destitute of self-consciousness, fade away from history, and are spirits, voices, rather than distinct human beings. But in Christ we have an element of self-forgetfulness, so to speak, combined with a power to move humanity, which renders Him unique in history. But then, to be unique in history, what is it but to be divine?

(*b.*) Notice, again, the absence of self-interest, which is, indeed, entirely human, and therefore imitable, though rarely imitated, in His refusal to yield to that last temptation of noble souls, and be made a king. But in the great and crowning sacrifice upon the cross there appears another element distinguishable from the former. We have, indeed, the perfectly human spirit, the half-concealed but quite overcome reluctance, the unavailing protest against might, the yielding as to a superior power, which all combine to give their true beauty to human martyrdoms, and shine in the humour of Socrates, the wit of Raleigh, the impulsive courage of Cranmer, and the hapless submission of Lady Jane Grey. But then, side by side with this, we have words and conduct which are, upon any human ground, neither intelligible nor defensible. All the beauty of mere martyrdom dies out in the words of One who lays down His life of Himself, and will let no man take it from Him. All the rules by which we can judge of ordinary men are set at defiance by One who, after carefully guarding Himself because His hour was not yet come, suddenly refused the most ordinary precautions, courted death, allowed—nay worse, commanded—the foreknown treachery of Judas to do its work, and died with the certainty of rising again. Such an one may be as far below men as a mistaken fanatic, or as far above them as a Being conscious of a divine origin and mission. He may be the Christ of Renan or of St John, but hardly of those who acknowledge no other claims upon their allegiance than His character and conduct.

(*c.*) Lastly, self-justification. To take all necessary steps to justify ourselves, and then to leave the issue in the hands of God, is our rule of conduct, not merely for our own sakes, but in the interests of truth and public morality. And it was His, as when He said, "In secret have I said nothing," and "If I have done well, why smitest thou me?" But once more a different element asserts itself, indicating a different source of motive and action. Thus the words, "Many good works have I shown you," standing by themselves, are, though somewhat arrogant, entirely human; but the addition, "from my Father," gives an absolutely different colour to His defence, and takes every idea of self out of it. He was but an instrument in the hands of God. And again, I remember no instance of the smallest anxiety to know what men thought of Him, that anxiety of the noblest and highest kind, indeed, which breathes in every word of St Paul's, whose whole life and work was bound up with the necessity of vindicating himself. Christ's question is not, "What do men think of me?" but, "Whom do men say that I, the Son of Man, am?" A question once more, either the height of human arrogance or the depth of divine humility, conscious not of itself, but of its origin and work from God.

2d. Passing on next to His meekness and humility, by which I have ventured to describe the laws which guided His attitude towards men, we shall, I think, find the same divine element. It may be well to remark here that I have not chosen these arbitrarily, but because they describe the two qualities expressly claimed by Himself, "I am meek and lowly in heart," and therefore, so far as I remember, the only two expressly attributed to Him by St Paul, and used as a moral persuasive to goodness, that is, as an example. It might seem, indeed, almost treasonable to say that there is in these an element which we cannot imitate, for the remembrance of the cross prefigured, foretold, and typified in countless passages of the Old Testament, is exactly that in which the example of Christ speaks most powerfully to our souls just when those souls are at their weakest, and stand most in need of support from without. Yet how can we fail to see that Christ Himself does not use them as an example, but as the ground of an invitation to all weary and heavy-laden souls to come to Him and take His yoke upon them and learn of Him? The divine consciousness speaks out in the very words that claim human meekness, and asserts for that meekness a more than human power. What a strange mixture of humility and pride would this invitation appear in any ordinary human being! With what jealousy should we not scan such pretensions! Let us, however, consider these two qualities separately.

There are two aspects of meekness: one, that of receiving favours; the other, injuries—the one, for instance, reminding us of Palm Sunday; the other, of Good Friday. Now, belonging to the first of these is the feeling of dependence which is not too proud to ask a favour, or to be thankful for it when received; and of any one who did not ask we should be inclined to say that he was hardly a human being at all, whereas the absence of gratitude is conceivable in one who knew himself to be something more than man.

Precisely these phenomena present themselves in the life of Christ. There is, indeed, nothing of that continual or recurring dependence so touching in great souls, and binding them so close to our frail humanity; but there is one request for help, and, so far as I remember, only one, which vindicates His perfect sympathy with our nature. In that hour when most that weak nature asserted its weakness, we find Him entreating the disciples to watch with Him—with what result we know, a result that almost, more than anything else, attests His awful solitariness. But though He could thus once ask for help, yet He never expressed gratitude for what He received unasked, or even thanks for the obedience paid to His regal requests; for instance, for the ass's foal, or the upper room at Jerusalem. He defended, indeed, as in the case of the women, those who had done Him a kindness from ungenerous misrepresentations, and He rewarded them after a divine fashion, but their works He accepted as due to Him. But how can a character, in which dependence appears but once and gratitude never, be presented as a perfect model, except upon the supposition of a divine consciousness which explains and harmonises these traits at once?

Once more, in the meekness with which He endured injuries there is nothing of that righteous anger on His own account which is at once essential and unavoidable in man. Anger plays the same part in moral economy that pain plays in physical; it is the instinctive attitude of self-preservation, of which, having no self-love, He had no need. The idea that He resented the treatment He received, and died praying, not for His enemies, but for the mere ignorant agents of their cruelty, is false to all true conceptions of His character, to the testimony of the narrative, and to the instincts of Christianity. Such a self-sacrifice as His, the free laying down of His life with views that embraced the vast future, the refusal to use any means of escape, is incompatible with anger for personal outrages, and would, indeed, degrade it below our human level. How can the conscious master of more than twelve thousand legions of angels be indignant at the wrongs to which He voluntarily submitted? But then this absence of anger on one's own account answers precisely to our—not the Jewish —conception of God.

3d. His humility must be discussed in very few words. By humility is meant freedom from that pride which is the fatal curse of men conscious of great and unusual powers, especially, *e.g.*, Napoleon, in dealing with their fellow-creatures. Now at once occurs the temptation to say that His humility was all the more wonderful because it was consistent with perfect freedom from the sense of sin. But surely to argue thus would be to fall into the error from which I have been painfully endeavouring to keep clear— of drawing a distinction in kind between divine and human morality, as though humility in us sprang from a different source, and meant something different from His. Sin does not cause humility, but humiliation, and our humility, so far as we can attain unto it, is the result of Christ's spirit working in us, and not of our conviction of sin. He was conscious of kingship, messiahship, miraculous powers, and that perfect self-command and knowledge and control of others which is the secret of power among men. Yet we see Him without one word of pride, never intoxicated with success, shunning earthly honour, consorting with the humblest, refusing to lift a finger to stir the crowd which on Palm Sunday were ready for anything He desired, washing the disciples' feet, careless of what kind of death He died—that last weakness of poor human pride. In all which there is a humility to which our whole nature responds. But then there is something more. Where in Christ's life is there any trace of that self-respect, the reasonable and righteous form of pride, which is an essential part of our being? The root of this lies, perhaps, in the necessity which, as a mere fact of history and of consciousness, is incumbent upon every man, of comparing himself with others. This trait once more is especially prominent, nay, even predominant, in St Paul, who in one memorable passage descends to comparison of himself with others in mere personal advantages. True, he does so with an air of proud humility, and with a protest against his own folly; but that does not take away the fact that the comparison, after all, was made, and was felt to be necessary. How absolutely and entirely different is the whole aspect and attitude presented in the life of Christ, who never spoke of others, except in one or two difficult passages, in the way of denying the possibility of any comparison at all. One who could say, "It is the Father that doeth the works," could not compare Himself with others. To such an one it is possible to have all power and no pride. And this is our very idea of God, who rejoices in the works of His hands, who cannot be proud of them.

At this point I bring my argument to a close, though it might be pursued into endless details. It would be possible to point out in Him a power of self-assertion, culminating in what we should call in any other man the most absolute sectarianism, of that very kind from which St Paul and Luther on the whole succeeded, and Calvin and Wesley failed in guarding themselves. We should have to inquire into the true significance of a character to which the expression of joy and wonder was never ascribed by His biographers, save once in the first instance, and twice in the second; in each case at the contemplation of the moral and spiritual effects of belief or of unbelief. We should have to account for, and possibly upon any ordinary view of His character to explain away, His excessive indignation at the Jews, resulting in a condemnation of them that regarded no pleas of excuse, palliation, or even of explanation. The forms, again, in which His knowledge was displayed; His assertion of personal liberty from all domestic and social and patriotic ties; His claim to know the truth, and the foundation upon which that claim was based, would require minute investigation. Finally, we should have to consider carefully the exact meaning in Him, and the real power over us, of that trait which most of all speaks to our spirits now, as summing up the Revelation that He made from heaven—namely, the profound, unbroken consciousness of the Fatherhood of God. And apart from His personality, we should probably have to conclude with an assertion no stronger than this—That having regard to the testimony of a very wonderful Jewish enthusiast, this attitude of Sonship is, on the whole, the highest, the most comfortable, and the most profitable that imperfect creatures like ourselves can assume towards a God, who, nevertheless, it would have to be admitted, has never done a fatherly act towards us since the day when He created, if create He did, the nebulous matter from which all life has proceeded.

And the further we inquired, the more apparent it would become that the character suits and implies the personality, that the personality explains and vindicates the character, and that both together present a foundation ample enough for the moral being of man to repose upon.

I must crave the indulgence of my readers for a moment longer, in order to answer two objections, which, if unanswered, would be fatal to my argument.

1st. In predicting a crisis in which there shall be two hostile camps, divided by a sharp line from each other, I am not to be supposed to be intolerant of those who cannot make up their minds one way or other; for the dividing line is not drawn between separate men, but in the soul of each individual man, so that he doubts to which side he belongs, and in a way belongs to both. I do not, indeed, profess to sympathise with, because I do not understand, the doubts of those who do not feel themselves compelled to face the facts of the case, or to decide upon the truthfulness of the revelation presented to them. Nor is, indeed, doubt quite the right word to apply to them; let us rather reserve it with all its (remembering Gethsemane) sacred associations for those who have distinctly realised the plain conditions of the question, to whom God seems to be saying, "Trust me all, or not at all;" whose minds range from the highest ecstasies of faith, to the sharpest agonies of despair; whose doubts are as manly as their sufferings are great. Let such be consoled by the reflection that in their doubts the intellectual, and in their sufferings the moral, future of the Christian religion lies concealed.

2d. A protest, hitherto silent, may have arisen in the minds of many, to the effect that the longing to imitate

Christ perfectly, the conscious determination to be like Him, is sufficient to break through all the cobwebs of such an argument as the preceding. And so it would be, if there were a syllable in that argument which thwarted it, or opposed it, or did it violence in any way. But if we adhere to the definition of worship as the desire for imitation, coupled with the consciousness of inability to imitate perfectly in the present life, we leave the amplest scope for the satisfaction of this desire, and provide, what is in these days much wanted, one of the strongest possible arguments for immortality. A little consideration will make this clear. If men become here or hereafter (it makes no matter which, both alike would be heaven) Christlike, then the necessity, and indeed the possibility, of such a life as His in the flesh ceases; there can be none of the distinctive virtues which suffering produces, when there are none to inflict suffering. Consequently, as has always been the case with simple Christian instincts, the desire for imitation fastens ultimately upon the essential and fundamental qualities of the divine nature, which assumed certain forms when brought into contact with human sin and sorrow, in the life of Christ, and which will abide in those forms wherever there is sin to be healed or sorrow removed; but which, apart from the sin and sorrow, we dimly foresee, and in half-intelligible language try to describe, as the eternal life of self-sacrifice, in which the self is somehow dropped out of it, that God may be all in all. At any rate, nothing that has been said places the smallest barrier whatever to the boundless desire to imitate the divine character, though with St John I may have ventured to postpone the satisfaction of the desire to the time when He shall appear, and we shall *then* be like

Him, for we shall *then* see Him as He is. Words which, however expressive of defective knowledge of His character, and therefore of defective imitation now, do not, nevertheless, prevent him from adding, with an apparent contradiction, which I have tried in this essay to explain, but which is, perhaps, more truly described as the self-contradiction of the soul when gazing upon ultimate truths of God— "And every man that hath this hope in him, purifieth himself, even as He is pure."

SCIENCE AND IMMORTALITY.

HE who pretends to have anything new to say upon so old a subject as the immortality of the soul, must expect to arouse certainly opposition, and probably contempt. Nevertheless, this at least is certain, that the tendency of science, which has powerfully affected every domain of thought in new and unexpected ways, cannot but place the old doctrine of immortality under new, and, it may be, unexpected lights, abolishing old arguments, and suggesting new ones that have not yet obtained the consideration they deserve. My object in this essay is, to endeavour, by the aid of all-victorious analysis, to throw some little light upon the relations of the belief in immortality with scientific thought; and at the outset, I wish distinctly and positively to affirm, that it is not my intention to construct any argument for the belief against science, but merely to explain the conditions under which, as it seems to me, the question must be debated. Those conditions, though in themselves plain and simple, are, I believe, very imperfectly understood, and much bewildering nonsense is talked upon both sides of the question by men who have not clearly realised the nature of evidence, the amount of proof required, or the sources from which that proof must be derived. I think it possible to lay down a series of propositions with which, in principle at any rate, most reasonable minds would agree, and which would have the effect of defining the area of debate and the true point of conflict. This may sound presumptuous; whether it be really so or not, the event alone can prove.

Now, the first demand of science is for an accurate definition of the object of discussion, that is, that both religious and scientific thinkers should be quite sure that they are discussing the same thing. Immortality is bound up in the minds of religious people with a vast amount of beautiful and endearing associations, which form no part of the hard, dry fact itself. The definition of immortality, viewed scientifically, is, I take it, something of this sort: the existence of a thinking, self-conscious personality after death, that is, after the bodily functions have ceased to operate. This personality may or may not exist for ever; it may or may not be responsible for the past; it may or may not be capable of rest, joy, and love; it may or may not be joined to its old body or to a new body. These, and a hundred similar beliefs with which religion has clothed the mere fact of existence after death, form no essential part, I must again affirm, of the fact itself. And throughout the argument, this, and no other than this, will be the sense in which I use the word immortality; because it is the only one that I have a right to expect that the scientific mind will accept.

It may be well, also, before going further, to make it clear to ourselves in what sense we use the word religion. Men who would be very much ashamed of themselves if they were detected using scientific words inaccurately, do, nevertheless, attribute meanings to the word religion which it is difficult to hear with patience. Without, however, entering into verbal discussions, it will be, surely, enough to define religion as a practical belief in and consciousness of God and immortality; and as the latter is now absolutely essential to the idea of religion as a motive moral power, and as, moreover, it includes, or at any rate necessitates the belief in the existence of God, we may fairly conclude that, for all practical purposes, and certainly for the purpose of this argument, religion is synonymous with a belief in immortality. And if, for any reason, mankind does at any time cease to believe in its own immortality, then religion will also have ceased to exist as a part of the consciousness of humanity. To clear up, therefore, the relations between immortality and science becomes a matter of the utmost importance.

It will be well next to analyse briefly the effect which science has upon the nature of the proofs by which this, like all other facts, must be demonstrated. Let us, for convenience sake, regard the world as a vast jury, before which the various advocates of many truths, and of still more numerous errors, plead the cause of their respective clients. However much a man may wrap himself up in the consciousness of ascertained truth, and affirm that it makes no matter to him what the many believe, yet nature is in the long run too powerful for him, and the instinct of humanity excites him to plead the cause of what he knows to be truth, and to mourn in his heart and be sore vexed if men reject it. Truth is ever generous and hopeful, though at the same time patient and long-suffering; she longs to make converts, but does not deny herself or turn traitress to her convictions if converts refuse to be made. There is a sense, indeed, in which it may be said that truth only becomes actual and vital by becoming subjective through receiving the assent of men. What then must the advocate for the fact of the immortality of the soul expect that science will require of him, when he pleads before the tribunal of the world for that truth which, because it is dear to himself, he wishes to enforce on others?

The alterations in the minds of men which the tendency of modern thought has effected in respect of evidence, may be summed up under two heads. First, the nature of the evidence required is altogether altered, and a great many arguments that would in former days have gone to the jury, are now summarily suppressed. Fact can only be proved by facts, that is, by events, instances, things, which are submitted to experience and observation, and are confirmed by experiment and reason. And secondly, the minds of the jury are subject to *a priori*, and, on the whole, perfectly reasonable prepossessions before the trial begins. The existence of changeless law, the regular, natural, and orderly march of life, the numerous cases in which what seemed to be the effect of chance or miracle have been brought within the limits of ascertained causation; all these things predispose the mind against pleadings for the supernatural or the divine. Most true of course it is, that there are most powerful prepossessions on the other side as well; but the difference is, that these are as old as man himself, while the former have only been of later times imported into the debate, and if they have not been originated, have at least received their definite aim and vivid impulse from the results of scientific research.

Now, the first result which flows from these alterations is the somewhat startling one, that all the arguments for immortality derived from natural religion (so-called) are, in the estimation of science, absolutely futile. To put this point in the strongest form, all the hopes, wishes, and convictions of all the men that ever lived, could not, and cannot convince one single mind that disbelieves in its own immortality. Unless the advocates of religion clearly apprehend this truth, they are, it seems to me, quite disabled from entering into the discussion upon conditions which their opponents, by the very law of their opposition, cannot but demand. It is true, indeed, that this temper of mind is confined at present to a comparatively few persons, as in the last century it belonged to the philosophers and to their immediate followers. But then it is as clear as the day that, as science is getting a more and more practical hold upon men's minds by a thousand avenues, and mastering them by a series of brilliant successes, this temper is rapidly passing from the few into the popular mind; that it is becoming part of the furniture of the human intellect, and is powerfully influencing the very conditions of human nature. Sooner or later we shall have to face a disposition in the minds of men to accept nothing as fact, but what facts can prove, or the senses bear witness to. In vain will witness after witness be called to prove the inalienable prerogative, the intuitional convictions, the universal aspirations, the sentimental longings, the moral necessity, all which have existed in the heart of man since man was. Nor will the science of religion help us in the hour of need.

There can be a science of religion exactly as there can be a science of alchemy. All that men have ever thought or believed about the transmutation of metals may be brought together, classified as facts, and form a valuable addition to our knowledge of the history of the human mind, but it would not thereby prove that the transmutation had taken place, or that the desire for it was anything more than man's childlike strivings after that which could only be really revealed by the methods of natural science. So also the science of religion can prove what men have held, and suggest what they ought to hold. It can show that they have believed certain things to be true; it is utterly powerless to prove that they are true. It can strengthen the principle of faith in those who do not require positive demonstration for their beliefs; it cannot even cross swords with those, soon to be the majority of thinking men, to whom positive demonstration has become as necessary to their minds as food to their bodies. Nay, they will resent rather than welcome the attempt to put a multitude of hopes and myriads of wishes in the place of one solid fact, and will soon confirm themselves in their opinions, by the obvious argument that these hopes and wishes are peculiar to the childhood of the race, and form only one out of many proofs, that man is liable to perpetual self-deception until he confronts fact and law. Not, indeed, that they will indulge in the equally unscientific statement that there is no such thing as immortality. The attitude of mind which they will assume will be that of knowing nothing, and of having no reasonable hope of ever discovering anything about man's future destiny. And while they will think it good that man, or at any rate that some men, should allow themselves to hope for life after death, yet they will steadily oppose any assertion that these hopes ought to guide men's conduct, influence their motives, or form their character.

Now if this be true, it is difficult to overrate the importance of thoroughly and distinctly realising it. That the evidence for the truths of natural religion is overwhelming, is one of the statements that are accepted as truisms, at the very moment that science is slowly leavening the human intellect with the conviction that all such evidence is scientifically worthless. Nevertheless, the opposite idea has taken firm hold of the religious mind, and forms the basis of many an eloquent refutation of the "presumptuous assurance" and "illogical obstinacy" of modern thought. Men must have smiled to hear themselves alternately refuted and rebuked by controversialists who did not understand the tone of mind against which they were arguing, or who assumed as true the very things which their opponents resolved to know nothing about, either in the way of belief or rejection. It is very certain, however, that this error will not yield to the mere statement that it is an error, and therefore I will go on to examine a little more minutely the various arguments by which men seek to prove the doctrine of immortality. These are mainly fourfold :—

(1.) That it is an original intuition, and arising from this—

(2.) That it is an universal belief.

(3.) That it follows necessarily from the existence of God.

(4.) That it is essential as a motive for human morality.

(1.) I take the statement of this argument from the words of one, than whom no man has a better right to be heard on such a subject. Professor Max Müller, in his preface to the first volume of his "Chips from a German Workshop," writes as follows:—"An intuition of God, a sense of human weakness and dependence, a belief in a divine government of the world, a distinction between good and evil, and a hope of a better life, these are the radical elements of all religions. . . . Unless they had formed part of the original dowry of the human soul, religion itself would have remained an impossibility." Now I am not quite sure that I understand in what sense the writer means to assert that these intuitions, which, for practical purposes, may be limited to three—God, sin, and immortality, are part of the original dowry of the human soul. If it is meant that there was a special creation of the human soul, furnished from the beginning with these three intuitions, then science will resolutely refuse to admit the fact. There can be no mistake about the position held by the bulk of scientific men, and little doubt, I should think, as to its reasonableness. If there is anything that is in ultimate analysis incomprehensible, or any fact that cannot be accounted for by natural causes, then the possibility of special creation and original intuitions must be candidly allowed, but not otherwise. There is just a chance, for instance, that the difference between the brains of the lowest man and the highest animal, may ultimately be regarded as a fact inexplicable upon any theory of evolution, more, however, from a lack of evidence than from any other cause. Be this as it may, the possibility of special creation finds a distinct foothold in the acknowledged fact that the connection between thought and the brain of animals as well as of man, is an ultimate incomprehensibility, a mystery which the law of man's intelligence prevents his ever even attempting or hoping to understand. The famous saying, "*Cogito, ergo sum*," the foundation of all modern metaphysics, may come to be a formula under which religion, philosophy, and science may all take shelter, and approach each other without ever actually meeting.

But the three intuitions of God, sin, and immortality, can all be accounted for by the growth of human experience, as every one knows who has at all studied the subject. At some period of the world's history, science will answer, an ape-like creature first recognised that it or he had offended against the good of some other creature, and so became conscious of sin, or was created as a moral being. Thus Mr Darwin has affirmed, but (speaking from memory) I do not think he has called very special attention to that still greater epoch (or was it the same?) in man's history, when this ape-like creature, seeing one of its own species lying dead, recognised as a fact, "I shall die." This is what we may term the creation of man as an immortal being; for in the very conflict of the two facts—one, the reflecting being, the self-conscious I; the other, death, the seeming destroyer—lies embedded all man's future spiritual cravings for eternity. And the idea of God would come in the order of nature, before either of these, to the creature which first reflected upon the source of its own existence, and recognised a "tendency in things which it could not understand." This is, in brief, the scientific account of man's creation, and of the growth of the ideas of natural religion within his mind; and we may remark in passing that it must be a singularly uncandid and prejudiced mind which does not recognise that the book of Genesis, which, upon any theory, contains man's earliest thoughts about himself, expresses in allegorical fashion, exactly the same views.

The same views are also apparently expressed by Professor Max Müller, in a very beautiful passage in the article on Semitic Monotheism, in the same volume :—

"The primitive intuition of God and the ineradicable feeling of dependence upon God could only have been the result of a primitive revelation in the truest sense of that word. Man, who owed his existence to God, and whose being centred and rested in God, saw and felt God as the only source of his own and all other existence. By the very act of the creation God had revealed Himself. Here He was, manifested in His works in all His majesty and power before the face of those to whom He had given eyes to see and ears to hear, and into whose nostrils He had breathed the breath of life, even the Spirit of God."

The first impression made by this passage may be, that, in speaking of a "revelation in the truest sense," it affords an instance of that hateful habit of using religious words in a non-natural sense. But a little deeper consideration will show that no possible definition of a revelation, accompanied and attested by miracles, can exclude the revelation made by nature to the first man who thought. In fact, we have here a description of creation, which science, with possibly a little suspiciousness at some of the phrases, may accept, while, at the same time, natural religion is carried to its utmost and highest limits; and along with this a foundation is laid for a truer theory of the miraculous. But while gladly admitting all this, the fact remains that these intuitions, following upon a revelation in which nature herself was the miracle, are still plainly only the expressions of man's inward experiences, and that, however old and venerable and exalted, they are still only hopes, wishes, and aspirations, which may or may not be true, but which are incapable of proving the actual facts towards which they soar. It is open, therefore, to any man accustomed to look for positive demonstration, to dismiss them as dreams of the infancy of man, or to relegate them into the prison-house of the incomprehensibilities, or to content himself with a purely natural theory of human life, which rejects and dislikes the theological.

(2.) But when we come to inquire how far these primary intuitions have been universal, and whether they can be fairly called ineradicable, we are met by some very startling facts. The dictum, ὃ πᾶσι δοκεῖ τοῦτο εἶναί φαμεν, is so reasonable in itself, that no serious attempt would be made to question a belief that even approached to being universal, even if it could not be shown to be part of the original furniture of the mind. But the real difficulty lies in finding (apart from morals) any beliefs of which this universality can be predicated, and assuredly the immortality of the soul is not one of them. The mind of man at its lowest seems incapable of grasping the idea; and the mind of man at its highest has striven to emancipate itself from it altogether. The evidence for this statement lies within the reach of all, but I will just adduce three names, whose very juxtaposition, by the sense of incongruous oddity stirred up, may make their joint testimony the more important. I mean Moses, Buddha, and Julius Cæsar, all of whom, though widely separated in time, race, and character, representing absolutely different types of human nature, approaching the subject from widely different points of view, do, nevertheless, agree in this, that the consciousness of immortality formed no part of the furniture of their minds.

Moses lived one of the most exalted lives, whether regarded from the religious or political side, that has ever been lived on earth, and yet, as is well-known, there is not a shadow of a trace to prove that he was moved by the hope of a reward after death, or that the idea of existence after death was ever consciously presented to his mind. He may be, on the whole, claimed by modern science (the miraculous element being by it excluded) as an example of those who perform the greatest practical duties, and are content to stand before the mystery of the Unknowable without inquiry and without alarm, so far as the doctrine of man's immortality is concerned. Here is another of those strange links that unite the earliest thinker and legislator with so much of the spirit of modern thought and law. Buddha, on the contrary (or his disciples, if it be true that his original teaching is lost to us), cannot be quoted as one who did not realise the possibility of life after death, nor is any scheme of philosophy that is practically Pantheistic inconsistent with immortality, if we limit the word to the bare idea of existing somehow after death. But I rather quote him as one of those who show that the very consciousness of undying personal life, the existence of a self-reflecting ego, which gives all its shape and force to the desire for life after death, may come to be regarded as a positive evil, and painless extinction be maintained as the ultimate hope and destiny of man. And the case of Julius Cæsar is, in some respects, stronger still. He is one of the world's crowning intellects, and he lived at a time when men such as he were the heirs of all the ages, the possessors of the treasures of thought, in which, for generations past, the greatest men had elaborated doctrines concerning religion, duty, and life. And he represents the views of those whom the truest voice of science now repudiates as running into unscientific extremes. With him non-existence after death was a matter of practical belief. It coloured his opinions upon politics, as really as Cromwell's religion affected his. He spoke against the infliction of the penalty of death upon the conspirators in Catiline's case, because death was a refuge from sorrows, because it solved all mortal miseries, and left place for neither care nor joy. And Cato expressly applauded his sentiments, though with a touch of reaction from popular theology, which sounds strangely modern. To this then all the original intuitions of the human mind, all the glowing aspirations enshrined in Greek poetry, legend, and art, all the natural theology contained in the words of Socrates and Plato, had come at last. Will any reasonable man affirm that an age, which breathes the very air of materialism, and whose children suck in the notions of changeless law with their mother's milk, can arrive at anything better if it has no facts upon which to rely, as proofs that its hopes are not unfounded? And how can that be called a truth of human nature, or be allowed to exercise a real influence upon men's minds, which is capable of being either entirely suppressed, or earnestly striven against, or contemptuously rejected?

(3.) The remaining two arguments need not detain us long; indeed, I should not have mentioned them were it not that very eminent divines have based the belief in immortality upon the existence of God or the necessities of man. Let it once be granted that we are the creatures of a personal, loving, and sustaining God, concerning whom it is possible to form adequate conceptions, and then doubts as to our immortality would be vain indeed. But the rejoinder from the scientific view is plain enough. This, it would be said, is a mere *obscurum per obscurius*. The belief in God is simply the working of the human mind, striving to account for the beginning of its own existence, exactly as the belief in immortality is the result of the attempt to think about the end thereof. If the definition of God be a stream or tendency of things that we cannot otherwise account for, then it will not help us to a belief in immortality. It is surprising indeed to see how the plain conditions of the case are evaded by enthusiastic controversialists ; and I am almost ashamed of being obliged to make statements that have an inevitable air of being the baldest truisms.

(4.) The idea that immortality is essential to the moral development of man, and that therefore it is demonstrably true, seems to receive some little countenance from Professor Max Müller in the close of his article on Buddhism, in which he thinks it improbable that—

> "The reformer of India, the teacher of so perfect a code of morality, . . . should have thrown away one of the most powerful weapons in the hands of every religious teacher, the belief in a future life, and should not have seen that, if life was sooner or later to end in nothing, it was hardly worth the trouble which he took himself, or the sacrifices which he imposed upon his disciples."

The true bearing, in all its immense importance, of human morality upon the belief in immortality, will have to be considered hereafter ; but when used as a demonstration, it is at once seen to belong to a class of arguments, which science resolutely rejects. The moral development of man depends upon a right recognition of ascertainable facts, never upon beliefs which may or may not be fictitious. A much more fatal answer, however, is found in a simple appeal to history, from which it will be found that, in Mr Froude's words, no doctrine whatever, even of immortality, has a mere "mechanical effect" upon men's hearts and consciences, and that noble lives may be lived, and exalted characters formed, by those who are brave enough to disregard it. Nay, what is worse, immortality may be a powerful weapon for evil as for good, if it chime in with a perverted nature. The Pharaoh before whom Moses stood believed it, and we know with what results. Only that, once more will science retort, which can be proved to be true upon sufficient evidence, can be positively known to be useful.

To sum up, then, what has been said, we have seen that, however strong may be the wishes of man for immortality, however ennobling to his nature and true to his instincts the belief in it may appear to be, there is nothing in natural religion to answer the demands of modern thought for actual proof, and nothing therefore to impugn the wisdom or refute the morality of that class of persons, representing, as they do, a growing tendency in the human mind, who take refuge in a suspense of thought and judgment upon matters which they declare are too high for them. Occasionally we may suspect that the garb of human weakness does but conceal the workings of human pride, never perhaps so subtle and so sweet as when human nature meekly resolves to be contented with its own imperfections, and to bow down before its own frailty; but denunciations of moral turpitude only harden the hearts of men who ask for the bread of evidence, and receive stones in the shape of insults.

We turn next to consider the effects of modern thought upon the evidence for immortality derived from Revelation. And here the difficulty of obtaining assent to what seem to me obvious truths will be transferred from the advocates of religion to those of science. Nevertheless, I maintain an invincible conviction that it is possible to state the terms of debate in propositions which commend themselves to candid minds, and which do not, as I have said, pretend to solve the controversy, but merely to define its conditions.

Now the first proposition is: That the Resurrection of Jesus Christ, if assumed to be true, does present actual scientific evidence for immortality. An illustration will make my meaning clear. Whether or not life can be evolved from non-living matter is a subject of debate; but it is admitted on all hands, that if a single living creature can be produced under conditions that exclude the presence of living germs, then the controversy is settled, and therefore Dr Bastian sets himself to work with the necessary apparatus to prove his case. So, in the same way, if any man known to be dead and buried did rise again (as for the moment is assumed to be the case), and did think and act and speak in his own proper personality, then immortality (in the scientific sense of the word) is thereby proved. Accordingly, those who wish to prove their case, betake themselves to history for the required evidence, which they may or may not find, but which, such as it is, must be allowed to go to the jury. Science may refuse to listen to arguments for facts derived from men's hopes and beliefs; it ceases to be science if it refuses to listen to arguments which profess to rely upon facts also. Were there to happen now an event purporting to resemble the Resurrection, it would be necessary to examine the evidence exactly as men are commissioned to investigate any unusual occurrence, say, for instance, the supposed discovery of fertile land at the North Pole. All this is plain enough, and leads to no very important conclusions, but it is, nevertheless, necessary that it should be stated clearly, and distinctly apprehended.

Two other propositions may also be laid down as to the nature of the evidence for the Resurrection, both of them once more sufficiently obvious; but still not without their value in leading to a fair and reasonable estimation of the exact state of the case, and tending also, as we shall see presently, in one direction. It may be taken for granted, in the first place, that nothing can be alleged against the moral character of the witnesses, or against the morality which accompanied, and was founded upon the preaching of the Resurrection. Mistaken they may have been, but not dishonest; enthusiasts, but not impostors. Furthermore, the deeper insight into character, which is one of the results of the modern critical spirit, enables us to see that they numbered among their ranks men of singular gifts, both moral and intellectual, who combined in a wonderful degree the faculty of receiving what was, or what they thought to be, a miraculous revelation, and the power of setting it forth in a sober and measured manner. All this is candidly admitted by the best representatives of modern thought.

Again, it may safely be asserted that, judged by the critical standards of historical science, the evidence is abundantly sufficient to prove any event not claiming to be miraculous. Let us suppose such an event as an extraordinary escape from prison related in the same way, though I admit that it requires a considerable intellectual *tour de force* to eliminate, even in imagination, the supernatural from the narrative. It is not going too far, to say that no real question as to its truth would in that case ever be raised at the bar of history, even though a powerful party were interested in maintaining the contrary. A strictly scientific investigation, for instance, has brought out in our own days the absolute accuracy, and consequent evidential value, of the account of St Paul's voyage to Malta. On the whole, then, we may conclude that the testimony is really evidence in the case, that it proceeds from honest and capable men, and that no one, *apart from the existence of the supernatural element*, would care to deny its truthfulness, except upon grounds that would turn all history into a mass of fables and confusion.

There remains, then, the old argument, that it is more easy to believe the witnesses to be mistaken than the fact itself to be true, and that we cannot believe a miracle unless it be more miraculous to disbelieve it. To this argument I avow my deliberate conviction, after the best thought I can give the subject, that no answer can be given regarded from a merely intellectual point of view, and subject to the conditions which modern thought not only prescribes but is strong enough to enforce. It goes by the name of Hume, because he was the first to formulate it; but it is not so much an argument as a simple state ment of common experience. All men who, from the days of St Thomas, have disbelieved in miracles have done so practically upon this ground. And to the "doubting" Apostle may be safely attributed the first use of the now famous formula, "It is much more likely that you, my friends, should be mistaken than that He should have risen." Now, to such a state of mind, what answer short of another miracle could be given then, or can be given now? True, you may point out the moral defects in the mind of Thomas which led him to disbelieve, but these are immediately counterbalanced by a reference to the intellectual defects of Mary Magdalene, which prompted her to accept, the miracle. There is no real room for weighing the evidence on both sides, and pronouncing for that which has the greatest probability, when your opponent, by a simple assertion, reduces all the evidence on one side to zero. Once more let me ask Christian apologists to realise this, and having realised it, no matter at what cost to the fears and prejudices of theology, let us then proceed the more calmly to examine what it precisely means, and to what conclusions it leads us.

We observe, first, that this argument is derived not from the first of the two ways in which, as we saw, science influences belief,—namely, by altering the nature of the evidence required, but from the second,—namely, by predisposing the minds of men against belief upon any attainable evidence whatever. We have seen that the evidence is that of honest men, that it is scientifically to the point, and sufficient to prove ordinary historical events. More than this cannot be demanded in the case of events which do not come under law or personal observation. But the minds of men are so predisposed by their experience of unchanging order to reject the miraculous, that, first, they demand more and more clear evidence than in other cases, and, secondly, they have recourse at once to the many considerations which weaken the force of evidence for things supernatural, and account for men's mistakes without impugning their veracity. Any one who reads Hume's essay will be struck at once with the, so to speak, subjectivity of the argument. Upon this very point he says, "When any one tells me he saw a dead man restored to life, I immediately *consider within myself,*" &c., &c. We ask then, at once, "To whom is it more likely that evidence of a miracle should be false, than that the miracle should be true?" and the answer must of course be, "Those who, rightly or wrongly, are predisposed in that direction by their experience of a changeless law, growing ever wider and more comprehensive." Nor is Paley's answer, which assumes the existence of God, at all available as against Hume, who, in his next section, puts into the mouth of an imaginary Epicurus all the arguments against such a belief. But it is a most just and reasonable remark that this predisposition does not exist in the case of those who—again rightly or wrongly—are wishing to know God and hoping to live after death. It is at this point that natural and revealed religion, weak when divided, becomes strong by combination. The Resurrection would certainly never be believed, if it did not fall like a spark upon a mass of wishes and aspirations, which are immediately kindled into life. Granted a man (and this is no supposition, but a fact), whose whole nature craves, not to die, and whose mind is occupied by the standing miracle of its own immortality, and then the Resurrection, so far from being improbable, will be the very thing which gives life to his hopes. The more he sees that natural religion cannot give him facts, as proofs, the more he will welcome Revelation which does, just because it will satisfy the rational desire which science is creating in the human mind. And just as there is no answer to Hume's argument for one predisposed as Hume was, so is there none to one predisposed as this supposed (but very actual) man is. The one is as incapable of disbelief as the other of assent. Hume and Paley do not really grapple with each other, but move in parallel lines that never meet. As Hume himself said of Berkeley, "His arguments admit of no answer and produce no conviction," so might each of the two say of the other. On the one hand we have all the results of human experience, a severe standard of intellectual virtue, a morality which confines itself to its duties towards humanity, and the power of being able not to think about ultimate incomprehensibilities. On the other hand, we have intense longings after the infinite, which science, admitting, as it does, the existence of the Unknowable, cannot possibly deny to be legitimate in those who feel them sincerely; also a body of evidence, sufficient to prove ordinary events, for a fact, that gives certainty and power to all these longings; a morality, which has reference to a Supreme Judge, and an absolute incapacity for life and duty, until some sort of conclusion has been arrived at concerning the mysteries of our being and destiny. Both of these represent tendencies of human nature with which the world could at this stage very badly dispense; both may have their use and their justification;

either may be true, but *both* cannot, for the Resurrection either did or did not happen.

From this account of things some very important considerations follow, a few of which I will endeavour to sum up in three heads. The scientific value of Revelation as a necessity, if there is to be any vital and practical religion at all, will, I hope, have been sufficiently indicated already.

(1.) The lines of a long, and, perhaps, never-ending conflict between the spirit of Religion and what, for want of a better word, I will call the spirit of Rationalism, are here defined. Neither of the two being able by mere argument to convince the other, they must rely upon gradually leavening the minds of men with prepossessions in the direction which each respectively favours. The time may come when Rationalism will have so far prevailed that a belief in the miraculous will have disappeared; the time may also come when the Christian Revelation, historically accepted, will everywhere be adopted as God's account to man of ultimate incomprehensibilities. Surely, no man who has ever fairly examined his own consciousness can deny that elements, leading to either of these two conclusions exist within his own mind. He must be a very hardened believer to whom the doubt, "Is the miraculous really possible?" never suggested itself. And he must, in turn, be a very unscientific Rationalist who has never caught himself wondering whether, after all, the Resurrection did not take place. Nor, so far as we may at this epoch discern the probable direction of the contest, is it possible to estimate very accurately the influence which science will exercise upon it. On the one hand, it will certainly bring within the mental grasp of common men that view of law and causation, which, in Hume's time, was confined to philosophers and their followers, and was attained rather by intellectual conceptions, than by such common experiences of every-day life and thought as we have at present. On the other hand, it will purge religion of its more monstrous dogmas, and further, by calling attention to the necessity of proving fact by fact, and again, by clearing up the laws of evidence, will tend to deepen in the minds of religious people the value and meaning of Revelation; while, at the same time, by its frank admission of hopeless ignorance, it will concede to faith a place in the realm of fact. Every man will have his own views as to the issue of the conflict: for the present it is sufficient for him, if he can be fully satisfied in his own mind.

(2.) The predisposition in men's minds in favour, whether of Religion or Rationalism, will be created and sustained solely by moral means. This is the conclusion toward which I have been steadily working from the beginning of this Essay to the end of it. The intellect of both Christian and Rationalist will have its part to play; but that part will consist in presenting, teaching, and enforcing each its own morality upon the minds of men. I need not say that I use the word morality, as expressing in the widest sense all that is proper for and worthy of humanity, and not merely in the narrower sense of individual goodness. Rationalism will approach mankind rather upon the side of the virtues of the intellect. It will uphold the need of caution in our assent, the duty of absolute conviction, the self-sufficiency of man, the beauty of law, the glory of working for posterity, and the true humility of being content to be ignorant where knowledge is impossible.

Religion will appeal to man's hopes and wishes recorded in nature and in history, to his yearnings for affection, to his sense of sin, to his passion for life and duty, which death cuts short. And that one of the two which is truest to humanity, which lays down the best code of duty, and creates the strongest capacity for accomplishing it, will, in the long run, prevail; a conclusion which science, so far as it believes in man, and religion, so far as it believes in God, must adopt. Here, once more, it is well nigh impossible to discern the immediate direction of the conflict, whatever may be our views as to its ultimate decision. Science is almost creating a new class of virtues; it is laying its finger with unerring accuracy upon the faults of the old morality; it is calling into existence a passion for intellectual truth. But then religion has always given the strongest proofs of her vitality by her power of assimilating (however slowly) new truths, and of rejecting (alas ! how tardily) old falsehoods at the demands of reason and discovery. A religious man can always say that Christians, and not Christianity, are responsible for what goes amiss. It is because religious practice never has been, and is at this moment almost less than ever, up to the standard of what religious theory exacts, that we may have confidence in gradual improvement and advance, until that standard, towards the formation of which science will have largely contributed, be attained.

(3.) Closely connected with the above, follows the proposition that all attempts on the part of religion to confute the "sceptic" by purely intellectual methods are worse than useless. There is no intellectual short cut to the Christian faith; it must be built up in the minds of men by setting forth a morality that satisfies their nature, consecrates humanity, and establishes society. It is not because men love the truth, but because they hate their enemies, that in things religious they desire to have what they call an overwhelming preponderance of argument on their side of the question, the possession of which enables them to treat their opponents as knaves or fools or both. Religion may have been the first to set this pernicious example, but, judging from the tone of much modern writing, Rationalism has somewhat bettered her instructions. No doubt it is a tempting thing to mount a big pulpit, and then and there, with much intellectual pomp, to slay the absent infidel—absent no less from the preacher's argument than from his audience. Delightful it may be, but all the more dangerous, because it plunges men at once into that error, so hateful to modern thought, of affirming that intellectual mistakes are moral delinquencies. No one, least of all science, denies that men are responsible for the consequences of their belief, provided these consequences are limited to such as are capable of being recognised and foreseen, and are not extended to comprehend endless perdition in a future state—an idea which is supposed, rightly or wrongly, to lurk beneath the preacher's logical utterances, and which religion has done next to nothing to disavow. And so we come to this conclusion: to build up by precept and example a sound and sufficient morality; to share in all the hopes and aspirations of humanity; to be foremost in practical reforms; to find what the instincts of mankind blindly search for by reference to the character of God finally revealed in Christ, and to the hope of immortality which His Resurrection brought to light; to endeavour to clear religion from the reproach of credulity, narrowness, timidity, and bitter sectarian zeal;—these are, as our Master Himself assured us, the only means of engendering in the hearts of men that moral quality which we call Faith : for " HE THAT IS OF THE TRUTH HEARETH MY VOICE."

MORALITY AND IMMORTALITY.

THE general result arrived at in the previous Essay may be summed up as follows :—

1. The desires and opinions of men upon the subject of their ultimate destiny do not amount to such an absolute demonstration of the truth of immortality as science demands, whereas the Resurrection of Jesus Christ, *assumed to be true*, is an actual instance of the fact requiring to be proved, *i.e.*, that men can live after death.

2. There is enough evidence to satisfy a reasonable man of the truth of the history of the Resurrection, provided there was nothing miraculous in that history.

3. Minds that are already deeply concerned with the miracle of their own immortality will find no difficulty in accepting the narrative, even though it includes a miraculous element, whereas minds that are not so concerned will find no difficulty in rejecting it.

4. Hence it follows that the controversy will ultimately turn upon the question, whether the doctrine of immortality can or cannot be recommended to the minds of men as necessary to, and necessitated by, human morality in its widest sense. If it can, then men will continue to believe the Resurrection, the evidence of which is, apart from the

miraculous, sufficient, and reasonable; if it cannot, then they will cease to believe that which has no moral value for them.

It now becomes my duty to abandon the neutral position I have hitherto endeavoured to maintain, and to assume that of an advocate for Christianity. But it is necessary to observe that this does not imply either that I should advocate Christianity as it now is, or find fault with science for holding aloof from it. On the contrary, the best hope for religion lies in the fact of science continuing to utter a clear and outspoken protest against the errors that are bringing discredit upon her name, and sensibly, though gradually, weakening her influence for good. Assuredly, if Christianity is to prevail by being morally attractive to all that is best in humanity, then there is nothing in the modern forms it has assumed to attract minds trained in the severe love of truth, and in the search for facts whereon truth may repose. Christian apologists are too apt to speak as though the ideal Christianity which they represent had any real hold upon the minds of the mass of men, and to forget that practically it means ultramontanism and sectarianism, the infallibility of the Pope, balanced by the infallibility of the Bible. Its moral value in special departments of life is not denied, but it is contended that these gigantic sins against humanity and truth do at this present moment, on the whole, outweigh its claims in other respects. This is not, however, a very practical question, nor one into which I greatly care to enter; it is enough to point out that unless (what I fully expect) science reforms religion in the same way as did the revival of classical learning, religion will cease to be the custodian of man's deepest thoughts upon morality and eternity.

D

My business is simply to call attention to facts, which seem to show that a belief in immortality is essential to the highest powers, as well as to the most general needs of human nature. This inquiry belongs to the science of religion, and is strictly scientific in its methods and results. Let me once more state what the proofs thus obtained really amount to. It is quite possible to examine the facts of human nature and of history, and from them to discover whether or not they lead, and will continue to lead, to a desire for immortality; but such a desire amounts to no scientific proof of the fact itself. That the desire for immortality is natural to man, and in accordance with his instincts and circumstances, is what I believe, and am about to endeavour to show. But then, why should I have to do it at all? Surely it might be thought that so obvious a duty would be discharged more than sufficiently in all the sermons and writings produced by a fertile and laborious theology. Yet, so far as my own reading of modern religious books goes, I have met with no systematic attempt in this direction, indeed, with nothing but an occasional remark occurring amidst a crowd of other and irrelevant topics. Christian literature, taking its tone from Dr Newman, may be said, on the whole, to attempt to answer these questions by an evasion of the law of evidence. This is, indeed, a just and fitting punishment. If men choose to return to scholastic subtleties and verbal definitions, if the minds and pens of Catholics and Evangelicals alike are occupied with questions about the methods and meaning of Regeneration, Justification, The Real Presence, Church Government, and Ritual Observance, then they must be content to leave the weightier matters of humanity to those who stand outside of Christianity altogether, and who watch them with malicious amusement paying tithe of mint and cummin, enlarging the borders of their garments, and compassing sea and land (not to say the law courts) that they may make one proselyte—with what result let the tone and temper of the religious press declare.

We are now to consider some plain facts of man's nature as bearing upon his wish for immortality. And first, I avail myself of the old truth that men must seek their own happiness, only substituting for that much-abused word one that Christianity has sanctioned and science will accept,—the joy of existence. Of what elements is this composed? What are the things by which men live, and to which they have, as it were, a personal and inalienable right? What, when we examine the wonders of our own being, can we claim of God, who has made us what we are, and therefore made us to wish for that which we find ourselves incapable of not wishing for? I have worded this last sentence so as to include both the Christian and scientific conception of God, but in future I shall speak of the facts of life and nature under the terms which religion has given them. Now the answer to these questions may be summed up under these three words, power, reputation, and rest, to which, though in a somewhat different category, may be added love. I do not put these forward as a scientific classification, though it is obvious that they may be taken to cover the joy of existence regarded as present, past, and future. But I state them as simple facts of human nature, which history and consciousness assure us to be true, and I propose to take them in order, and see what they teach us concerning man's desires for immortality.

I might, of course, trace the sense of power to man's consciousness of being a free agent, that is, a creative and originating being, but as this would lead us straight to thorny metaphysical discussions, I prefer to rest it upon the simplest fact of observation and experience. Every human soul is different from every other, and the further we ascend in the scale of civilisation, grows more widely different. Life, when regarded from the stand-point of the doctrine of evolution, may be compared to a cluster of mountains crowded together at their base, but whose peaks shine far apart in solitary splendour. Every man has a character of his own, a part of his own to play, duties which none but he can discharge, persons dependent on him for love and help. God (it would be equally true if we said law or nature) cannot consistently with Himself create two moral beings exactly alike, to each is given a special spark of the divine life; when we realise this, then the whole astonishing conception of man's essential divinity rushes into the mind. And therefore every true soul cannot but demand the power to live out its life, and to fill its place in the universe of God. To learn more of that knowledge which is open to all, to perform better those duties which are common to all and yet special to each, to become more useful in our place and calling, this is power, and right, and life. But this consciousness of individuality and of progress pleads for a life to come; it is the combination of the two that makes the desire irresistible. Men resent the idea of final death because they have learnt to feel that humanity progresses by the progress of individuals, and death interferes just when the moral being is developing towards perfection. It is of course tempting to adduce the case of those who die in the prime of strength and usefulness as filling mankind with an inextinguishable desire for completion in a future state; but in truth the argument is far stronger if we take, not the exceptional, but the typical case, that of men who depart in the fulness of age. On the one hand, there is a sense of departed power, a consciousness of thwarted labour, a faintly sad smile as of those to whom work has become impossible; on the other, there is a tender sagacity that has ceased to strive here, and is preparing for work hereafter, a special and anxious care for those around as though they could never cease to be objects of love and care: in a word, the decay of autumn, when the flower is fading and the seed within is ripening. Such is the old age of men who have worked and hoped, and such is the life which, if any one has ever possessed it, or rather been possessed by it, he will not lightly part with it, or cease to wish that it may be continued in a world to come. The *onus probandi* is as it were changed, and he insists on desiring immortality unless it can be shown that death is final. His desire may be destroyed by contradictory evidence, or rather it may be shown to rest upon no evidence at all, for to adduce evidence that we are not immortal is a contradiction in terms, and requires immortality to do it. But assuredly it will welcome any fact which throws light upon its own yearnings, and gives force and power to its own convictions; and thus it fastens upon such an event as the Resurrection, supported as it is by reasonable evidence, with a tenacity that will defy the assaults of persons otherwise minded and in other ways supported. Nor can it be blamed upon moral grounds for so doing; much less can it be shown to be contrary to scientific conceptions. Natural development is carried on by means of minute physical variations in each successive generation, but when we ascend to man, the moral variations in descendants are so great and so complex that they do not form, and cannot be classed under a new species, but become separate individuals, which, just because they are separate, lay claim to an eternity, in which each may live out its life to the fullest, discharge its duties, and fulfil its destiny.

Next let us observe how the desire for reputation and rest, perfectly natural, legitimate, and praiseworthy, kindles within the soul a hope of immortality. The connection between these two and immortality is indeed so obvious that it will be enough merely to observe how true to the facts of human life the desire for reputation and for rest is, and then the result follows at once: the same remark may indeed be made as to any of the primary elements in man's moral nature which we shall adduce, for all alike, the moment they are mentioned, seem to breathe the air and suggest the idea of immortality. The desire for fame is then the craving to be fairly judged and recognised according to the way in which we have used the "power" of which I have been speaking. It is an universal instinct of mankind, from which no civilised man has ever been exempt, and exemption from which would be treated as utterly immoral. No one who has tried to do his duty does not wish to be kindly remembered after death: man has a right to a just judgment, which in turn is not a thing to be escaped from, as a false theology teaches, but to be welcomed as an inestimable privilege from the Creator. For no one can really be content to be subject to the

Morality and Immortality. 55

unaided judgment, the rough, partial, hap-hazard decisions of men, even of those dearest to us. The praise of men, like their gratitude, oftener leaves us mourning. One of the most certain results of modern thought is that the so-called verdict of history is a mere pretence for hiding man's incapacity to decide upon the actual character of historical personages, and that history will more and more occupy herself with the delineation of great movements and the part that each man played in them. And what is true on a large scale is true on a small one: no man is ever known for what he really is. A poor consolation indeed for those who have endured neglect, obloquy, and, what is far worse than either, the being compelled by the inequalities of the world to live a life far below their power and their deservings. Real reputation is the reflection of the glory of God upon the lives of men, but when men feel that they are not really known for what they are, nor condemned for their real faults, nor honoured for their real merits, then with desperate despair they make their appeal to another life, and claim to stand before the eternal judgment-seat as men who are wrestling with the sharpest agony of death. On such a matter we may perhaps be willing to listen to the authority of one of the chief of those who have needed eternity to repair the mistakes of time:—

> "Fame is no plant that grows on mortal soil,
> Nor in the glistening foil
> Set off to the world, nor in broad rumour lies;
> But lives and spreads aloft by those pure eyes
> And perfect witness of all-judging Jove;
> As he pronounces lastly on each deed,
> Of so much fame in Heaven expect thy meed."

Next comes rest, which men, being what they are, must

also demand. The analogy of nature, the needs of the body, the usages of life, the instincts of their being, leave them no choice in the matter, so long at least as sleep, holidays, old age, amusements, and the like, remain upon earth. But it is important to observe what rest really means. Physical science explains to us the allegorical assertion that God rested from His work, by showing that He ceased from the travails and birth-pangs of creative work, from the slow crushing power of ice and water, from the upheaval of surfaces, the submerging of continents, the gradual curbing and restraining the youthful powers of nature till she became answerable to man's control, or at least afforded him a foothold in her midst. So does moral science proclaim that man needs rest, not from work, but from the conditions under which work is carried on here, from the chaos, so to speak, of life. He is placed here to perform onerous tasks under painful conditions, and he desires, as the real source of rest, that change to a higher form of existence which every modern discovery (evolution more than any other), tends to make familiar to him, and a right conception of which takes all selfishness out of rewards, because in the light of science it is seen to be a regular, upward, orderly progress. That religion has yet to learn from science what are the true primary elements of rest, reward, and judgment, may be true, but it affords no ground for disbelieving in the great facts which religion teaches, though much for attempting to teach her to teach them better.

The next great fact in man's existence which I shall adduce as proving the necessity of wishing for immortality, is the necessity under which he finds himself for loving;

and here it may be well to say a word or two upon the nature of love, for there is a kind of spurious sentimental view of it which I take leave to denounce as being (among other things) utterly unscientific. Love then is sometimes regarded as having its roots in simple self-sacrifice for the good of others, and Christianity is appealed to as giving weight to this opinion by those who are willing to accept a few "elegant extracts" from its moral teaching, while repudiating its historical truthfulness. Now the plain fact is, that whatever a plausible humanitarianism may say on the subject, the teachings of the Bible and of science agree in representing the essence of love to be rooted in the delight or benefit which the thing loved conveys to him who loves it. God, says the Bible, saw that the world was "good," that is, a source of delight to its Creator. Men love their fellows, says science, ultimately and originally from the same instinct that teaches animals (and for that matter the vegetable world also) to love those in whom they find comfort, pleasure, and support. Everywhere love is measured by and pre-supposes a self-conscious " I," so that in its deepest and most natural utterance men are commanded to love their neighbours *as* themselves.* And the whole effect of religion, as historically developed in the Bible, is, while keeping this natural self-love in mind, to raise men up to true, that is, to divine conceptions of what real pleasure, comfort, and support consist in, and to show how they are to be obtained. The life of Christ answers both questions by declaring that goodness is the only thing really worthy of love, and that this must be created

---

* And yet we could not apply this standard or formula to the love of God (see p. 10). I prefer to leave the discrepancy, if such there be, unsolved.

in others by self-sacrifice on our part, so that we may enjoy their goodness. He revealed the perfect working of the law of self-sacrifice, namely, to give up everything for the cause of human goodness, that humanity might become delightful to God and to itself. It avails very little to enter into bewildering discussions as to whether this idea of self-sacrifice is or is not as noble as the one which contemplates entire destruction and abnegation of self as a being conscious of the results of its own sacrifice, but it is surely of the greatest importance to discern which idea has its foundation in fact and law. And if the theory of evolution be true, then what Butler called "reasonable self-love" is found to be a natural instinct, shared with the animals, from which man can no more emancipate himself than he can give himself a new parentage, though of course this instinct requires to be made "reasonable" by the teachings of morality and religion throughout the progress of humanity. Therefore whatever a transcendental philosophy may say (such philosophy having no foundation in the realm of fact), men will continue to love that which is good to them, just because it is good to them, and religion will continue to teach them what goodness is, and how they are to create it in others by their own self-sacrifice.

I beg my readers to observe the force of this argument. It is one of the many instances in which the verdict of science is given in favour of religion, and, it must be added, of common sense. If Mr Darwin's account of the origin of morality in the social affections be true, then, by the law of man's being, love must have a conscious reference to self and cannot be mere self-abolition and annihilation. Exactly this the Bible recognises as true of the love of the

Creator, and recounts in history as true of the love of the Redeemer, who will "take his friends to himself, that where he is they may be there also." And exactly this the daily experience of common life testifies to as being true of the love which binds human souls together. The desire for immortality lies imbedded in the primary instincts of our nature. If to any human soul any other soul is dear or pleasant—in one word, good—then that soul cannot choose but crave for a continuance of such love after death. A man may of course rid himself of these desires, because he has an unbounded power of perverting his nature, resisting experience, and doing violence to facts. But wherever the course of human life is true to the law of nature as expounded by science and enforced by religion, there love will be an intimation of immortality. And so in fact we find it to be, though details that would require a volume must here be discussed in a few sentences.

Take, for instance, as a type of the love of equals in age, that of married life. Its essence is that it is progressive. It deepens with the deepening forces of life, and grows with the growth of years. All common labours, trials, joys, and cares, form so many links invisible but real that are binding souls together. The memory of the past and the anticipations of the future fuse two souls into one common life, one moral being, and yet they are haunted by the dim sense of approaching change, that breathes in the words,—

> "There's something flows to us in life,
> But more is taken quite away;
> Pray, Alice, pray, my darling wife,
> That we may die the self-same day."

And so the thought of final separation becomes impossible. That love should perish they resent as the worst of blasphemies. The inspired genius of St Paul, which shed light upon every aspect of the spiritual world, exactly as Shakespeare upon the world of man, or Newton upon the world of nature, saw this when he called Christ the "husband" of the Church, that is, of humanity. Take again the love of parents for children, as seen especially in the case of those who die young. They will not endure to part for ever with the object of so much hope, labour, and care. They know that there is no such thing as death, in the sense that anything perishes entirely, and that a dead body is but resolved into other forms, and so passes into new life. Modern materialists wax eloquent on the eternity of force or matter, and I for one can sympathise with them. But then I crave leave, again with St Paul, to carry this truth into the analogous domain of moral life also. A child may have a power hidden within its brain capable of moving the world, and it dies before it utters a word. There must be use for this power also in a world in which there is no waste; so love declares and triumphs over death. At death, physical power passes into new modes of existence; if so, then why should not spiritual power also—in both cases to carry out the dictates of what we see to be an universal law? To desire the immortality of a dead child does not indeed require any such analogy; men desire it because to do so is true to the instincts of nature and to the facts of their creation. It was some such instinct as this that, in spite of the national unconsciousness of immortality, touched the heart of David with a vague sense of a life to come, and suggested words that meant so much more than he could grasp, "I shall go to him, but he will not come back to me."

The same may be said of the love of children for parents; indeed, the parent is to the child the very idea and possessor of immortality, merely because it is the fountain of his life. We might parallel David's yearning for his child with Augustine's love for his mother. But enough has been said to indicate that, left to themselves and to nature, men do and will desire immortality, that they may continue to love and be loved in turn. To strengthen and purify this love in families, and then in wider circles of neighbourhood, country, Church, Christianity, and humanity itself, is the office of religion. It is here emphatically, that men are asking for morality at her hands, and are being put off with theology and ceremonies. If religion can succeed in making men moral in respect of such things as these, they will, if I may so speak, make themselves immortal. People who love cannot bear to die, and people who do not love, have by the nature of the case, no wish to live. As Arthur says,—

"Thou hast not made my life so sweet to me,
That I, the king, should greatly care to live."

If a man came to me in anxiety as to his own immortality, and desiring arguments to convince his reason, I should be inclined to ask him upon what terms he was living with his wife, his children, his parents, and his neighbours. And it is because religion, occupied as it is in teaching men of one school to "save" their souls, and of another to "make" them, has got no real voice or power in that which makes up so large a part of the normal life of ordinary men, that they are beginning to seek for instruction and morality elsewhere.

I proceed next to consider the effects of another great fact in human life upon man's desires for immortality; I mean the sense of sin, or in less theological words, the consciousness of evil. And, here once more I will endeavour to adduce nothing more than the simplest truths of everyday experience. The first consciousness of evil comes to men in the order of nature, when they realise that they have done irreparable wrong to other people. They have done mischief in the world, set a train of evil going which they have no power to stop, corrupted others, done them harm, and added their contribution to the great heap of human error, folly, and crime. And in so doing they have offended against a law of goodness and beneficence, which may be expressed in these terms: that if all men were good, then all men would be happy. Therefore, the first desire is to be brought into harmony with the law of goodness—in religious terms, to be reconciled to God. But then this desire for pardon, which has assumed such disproportionate, not to say monstrous, forms in modern theology, is soon followed by another; for mere pardon is nothing if the evil still continues; to save one's soul, a very poor thing if souls that one has helped to ruin remain in ruins. And so the next demand is for another state of things altogether, for a world in which there shall be, if not perfection, at least progress towards perfection, so that the results of evil shall die and fall away, or be seen to have wrought out the purposes of God. Thus, from the simple consciousness of evil, men spring upwards to the desire for immortality, for if there be no life after death with a transmuting harmonising power belonging to it, then the evil they have done remains perpetual, running throughout all generations of men, not to be washed away by any amount of repentance, or counteracted by any good actions in other directions: a thought which is simply unbearable, the agony of which is generally the first prelude to that literature of immortality which we call prayer. Or again, a man reaches the same desire for perfection in a life to come, when he regards not so much the evil that he has done as the evil that is in him. He sees in himself boundless capacities for good, as though he had all the makings of a perfect man in him, and yet he is constrained by an evil power over which he longs to gain a decisive victory. Professor Huxley's whimsical desire to be wound up like a clock every morning, in order that his moral being may perform its functions with mechanical regularity, has at least this about it, that it expresses, from the scientific point of view, a theory of moral duty, which corresponds pretty closely to the religious hope of heavenly perfection. And the same idea of perfection, man, when he looks abroad, finds everywhere present, only broken up in bits and scattered abroad among different men. If something could be taken from one man and added to another, if the self-devotion of Howard could be joined to the faculties of Julius Cæsar, if things could be got out of disorder and confusion, then that idea might be realised,—

> " That type of perfect in his mind
> In nature can he nowhere find ;
> He sows himself on every wind."

Another fact of human experience completes the picture, and it is one that has exercised a profound influence upon the greatest souls. Man, gifted with an instinctive desire for justice, finds that there is no such thing in this present world, except what his own feeble endeavours may achieve. The contrast between the elaborate care with which society, in the effort of self-preservation, seeks to mete out justice, and the indifference with which nature, or law, or chance, or fate (by whatever name we call it), mocks the vain attempt, is suggestive indeed, and has ever been felt as one of the greatest of the mysteries of life. The effects, for instance, of the destruction of Lisbon upon two such men as Goethe and Voltaire are a case in point. That men do not suffer because they specially deserve it, we know from the lips of Christ himself; and if there be another life we can acquiesce, although even so with difficulty, in that which it is hard to understand. Once more, however, I must say, that to my mind the doctrine of evolution, carried forward by analogy into the realms of spiritual life, suggests the explanation which later moralists and theologians will have to elaborate. A perpetual reaching forward into higher modes of life by means of catastrophe, death, sorrow, and suffering, fills men's souls with submission to the workings of a higher Will, while the hope of personal participation in the higher life, satisfies their cravings for justice to themselves and others. Thus, then, it comes to pass that those whose sense of sin compels them to long for pardon, perfection, and justice, will also continue to long for immortality, and will welcome the evidence which purports to establish it as a fact. And although the remark does not belong logically to the precise proposition I am endeavouring to make out, yet it would be doing injustice to the tremendous power which the argument has upon the human soul, if I did not observe in passing that the proof of the bare fact of immortality, derived from the Resurrection of Jesus Christ, is bound up with a life, a character, and a teaching, that claim to meet, and, as Christian people think, succeed in meeting every natural requirement of man for power, rest, and reputation, for love and reunion, for pardon, perfection, and justice.

Another class of arguments is derived from a totally different source from those we have been considering, and possesses even more value from the strictly scientific point of view. It may no doubt, to a certain extent, be contended that these facts of human nature and experience may be modified and altered to an extent almost inconceivable at present; and I readily admit that if a morality more suitable to man's wants, and more true to his nature, can be devised, he will cease to believe in his own immortality. But then, I also affirm that no trace of such morality has yet been propounded in theory, much less been wrought out in practice; and what is more to the point still, I maintain that so far scientific discovery goes to show that the facts which lead to a belief in immortality are rooted in the constitution of man. The next class of arguments, however, has to do with the external world, with our material surroundings—in a word, with the home in which we find ourselves placed. Now, from the impressions thence arising there is no escape, as there need be no mistake about their meaning. Man's home is prepared and provided for him, and just as differences in scenery or climate work ineradicable distinctions upon the minds and bodies of those who are subject to them, so is humanity at large subject to impressions from nature and from external conditions, which are simply unavoidable. The world is not ours to make or unmake; it forces itself in upon us through eye, ear, and brain, and is in truth a real Revelation, a word from that power which is not man, and is therefore, in the words of religion, God. Now, endeavouring once more to grasp an immense subject within a few convenient divisions, what are the things that man, both in fact and by right, asks of the world in which he lives? I answer, to know it, to use it, and to enjoy it, because these correspond to man as a scientific, an industrial, and an artistic being. Nor shall I be prevented from asserting that the same conceptions floated through the mind of the writer or writers of the book of Genesis, in the allegory which represents the first man as giving names to the beasts, tending the garden, and living in an earthly paradise.

First, then, man desires to know the earth on which he lives, and which seems to be ever inviting him to know her better. Nature lies open, as it were, to the embrace of the human mind, not tendering any information about herself, but yielding it to the pursuer after that truth which is nature's word for love. But it is when men contrast the possibility of unbounded knowledge with the reality of their actual information that the desire for another life is generated, and this in more ways than one. Many, for instance, are absolutely, not to say shamefully, ignorant of common scientific* truths, because nature (even when bountiful to them in other respects) has denied them the time, or the faculties, or the education, or the inclination for the pursuit of scientific knowledge. Speaking for myself, I may confess that the desire to be put to school, and, if necessary, to a sharp school too, to learn something more about the creation of God, stirs within me a longing for

---

* The word is here used, as it is occasionally in this volume, where necessary, in its narrower sense of "natural" science. Generally, of course, it is used simply to describe the process by which knowledge is gained from facts by reasoning.

immortality hardly inferior to the desire for pardon or rest. Those, again, whose lives are devoted to scientific studies can hardly refrain, if they give utterance to their true convictions, from hoping that they may share in the "eternal" knowledge; nor will they welcome as a higher morality the teaching that they ought to be content to believe that men will learn after they are dead, and that it is selfish and unnatural to seek for a participation in the harvest of that knowledge, of which in patience and faith they sowed the seeds. But there is yet another and a stronger argument still to be stated, and it is this: Nature proclaims distinctly that there are secrets quite beyond the range of human faculties to discover. The origin of life, the mystery of thought, the essential meaning of "law," are instances that will at once occur to every one. "In ultimate analysis," says Professor Huxley, "everything is incomprehensible, and the whole object of science is simply to reduce the fundamental incomprehensibilities to the smallest possible number." But however we may reduce them, the desire to know the residue will still remain as an intimation of immortality, just as the confession of the existence of the incomprehensible affords a basis for religious faith. The incomprehensible—that is God : to know it—that is life eternal. Elsewhere he says that "he does not know, and never hopes to know," the connection between the mental process of thought and the physical process of the brain. These words seem to me at once entirely scientific and entirely unscientific. They are the former, because they are evidently meant to take a candid and accurate estimate of the facts of the case; they are the latter, because any confession of hopeless ignorance upon problems that are presented to human intelligence, and come within experience, is an absolute contradiction to the spirit of science. If we read them with the addition of a simple religious phrase, as follows, "I never hope to know IN THIS LIFE," then they still remain true to the facts of the case, while leaving scope to that spirit of inquiry from which all life departs the moment limits are set to its aspirations. No man has any business to confess hopeless ignorance of anything whatever. In this saying, therefore, I think I detect science melting into religion, and bearing unconscious witness to man's desire for an immortality in which he shall no longer "know in part, but know even as he is known." Furthermore, the confession of ignorance lies at the root of the poetry of nature, and accounts for its Pantheistic or Polytheistic tendencies. Poetry takes up the tale exactly where science lays it down. When once we have discerned the existence of the Incomprehensible, then a voice is heard in the breathing of winds, the murmuring of waters, in all the teeming prodigality of life, in all the tremendous powers of destruction, the words of which, when interpreted by a religious mind, seem to recall a promise once given by the Master of nature and humanity Himself, "What I do, thou knowest not now, but thou shalt know hereafter."

Man's right to use the world is but another expression for that instinct of civilisation which found its first utterance in the words of the ancient writer, who represents God as bidding men go forth and replenish the earth, and subdue it. The key-note thus struck of the true harmony between God, man, and the world, was never wholly lost in the Jewish mind, and presents another bond of union between it and modern thought. The same spirit is breathed in many of the Psalms, notably in the noble and exalted language of the eighth—"Thou hast put all things in subjection under his feet"—language which, when contrasted with the actual facts of the case, suggested to the writer of the Epistle to the Hebrews the hope of a future immortality to be realised in Christ, "crowned with glory and honour." Every word of this seems to me to be a prophecy, in the true sense of the word (that is, a presentiment of an inspired mind), of the modern spirit of industrialism and civilisation. But when men possessed by this idea begin to reflect that under any circumstances many generations must pass before there is an approach to the fulfilment of their hopes, and that there is much reason for thinking that ultimately the world will be exhausted in man's service, its treasures used up, and itself relapsed into chaos; then it seems impossible for them not to desire a further life, in which this contradiction, having fulfilled its work in the great process of evolution, shall have disappeared.

Lastly, in respect of the enjoyment of nature, I must refer my readers to its legitimate exponents, poets and painters. The argument of Wordsworth's famous ode is capable of being expressed in logical forms, but assuredly would gain no weight from being thus treated. A solid fact, which would be none the more impressive from being dragged forth, lurks under Shelley's lines of one who does

> "Not heed nor see, what things they be
> But from these create he can,
> Forms more real than living man,
> Nurslings of immortality."

But if I might make the attempt in humble prose, I would

say that men who view nature with the poet's mind, or through the medium of his descriptions, do in sober fact get themselves involved, as it were, in the consciousness of God and of Immortality. The down-flutter of an autumn leaf, the patient field resting its winter's rest, the curve of a stream, the far-off echo of a solitary wave, a lonely tree— these, and a thousand other such things, cause the human soul to bow down before the altar of God, and swell with the thoughts of ages past and to come. The mystery of love, of labour, of purity, of judgment, and of power shines around, and the thought of God drifts into the mind through a thousand channels. And yet men cannot enjoy nature enough or understand her aright; she is seen to be doing something for them which must be finished before it can be either enjoyed or understood in all its perfection. A poem of Mr Browning's, "Two in the Campagna," illustrates this idea, and its closing words bring out the inevitable contrast between what man has and what he wants :—

> " Only I discern
> Infinite passion and the pain
> Of finite hearts that yearn."

So far, then, science, civilisation, and poetry add their contribution to man's desire for immortality. But it must be remembered that man does not merely live in a world which by its nature and laws suggests the possibility of another life to come, but rather amidst a universe of worlds which suggests the very place and mode of future existence, and makes it impossible for him to confine his aspirations to this " dull spot which men call earth." A modern writer denounces Napoleon's appeal to the stars— "Very true, gentlemen, but who made all these?"—as the most inconclusive reply ever made since the days when Berkeley was refuted with a grin. If by this is meant that the existence of other worlds can afford no demonstration for the existence of a Creator which is not already afforded by the world in which we live, and further, that such demonstration does not amount to evidence that science can deal with, then I agree with him, though the somewhat needless strength of the protest does but engender confusion in a discussion in which everything depends upon the parties in it clearly understanding what each other means to assert. And what is meant by arguments of this nature (however rhetorically they seem to assert more) is, that so long as the stars exist, no merely negative argument will avail to hinder men from wishing to believe in a personal Creator and an eternal life. It is striking, moreover, to observe how all progress in knowledge fortifies and gives assurance to this desire. Science puts forth a faltering hand towards the mystery of what may be man's future home, just as faith sends an anxious hope heavenward. We now know something, and hope to discover more about the stars; not merely that they obey the same laws of motion, but that their composition, so far as it is yet investigated, resembles that of the earth; and thus a more keen and vivid interest in them is excited which will assuredly modify the scientific mind by creating a link between this world and others, or, in religious words, between the finite and the unknown infinite, between earth and heaven. The same idea is also forced upon us by the limited use and enjoyment which we have of the starry universe, which, though far away from us, and, as it were, unconscious of us, does nevertheless come within the scope of our mental and moral being, and suggests to us an irrepressible hope for a share in the larger life which it seems at once to predict and to contain. In plain words, no man can see a thing of beauty, majesty, and grandeur, without desiring a further and fuller acquaintance with and enjoyment of it. We shall gain nothing by robbing men of the natural hope that somewhere and somehow in the midst of so vast a universe room may be found, in the order of development by the law of evolution, for him and his. Much, on the other hand, may be gained if the proper office of religion is forced upon those who teach it—that is, if science, adopting the natural hopes of men as facts of humanity, insists that religion shall strip immortality of all sentimental, foolish, unworthy, and sensuous accessories, and shall describe it in the brief Puritanic fashion of the Bible as a "new heaven and a new earth wherein dwelleth righteousness."

There remain two points of considerable importance to be discussed. First, if the desire for immortality be so rooted in the constitution of man as I have been endeavouring to show, how comes it that many minds, even of the highest order, and, at present, in increasing numbers, should be without it? and secondly, can it be shown to have any practical effect upon human morality that could not be obtained in any other way? The answer to these questions will lead us to consider the abuse and use of the doctrine.

One difficulty, indeed, which I have been astonished to find seriously felt, may be dismissed at once. It is urged that nations of antiquity did not possess the consciousness of immortality, and that many savages do not possess it now; but surely it is a reason for believing it to be true, that the truth about it has grown up gradually. We might just as reasonably be surprised that the arts of cultivation have not always been practised, or the use of steam understood. The knowledge of immortality was not put into each man's soul at the beginning (a most unscientific conception), but grew by virtue of the same laws as led men to discover musical harmony, family life, or natural causation: nor does the fact of a special objective revelation in the "fulness of time" in the least interfere with the true bearings of the analogy between the progress of religion and civilisation. And, like all other good things, this knowledge grows, whether in the consciousness of mankind or of individuals, in proportion to their energy, their industry, and their zeal for truth.

A different reason must, however, be found for the fact that good and great men have renounced the hope of immortality after it has been distinctly put before them. And yet here, too, the answer is not difficult to find. Recurring to the three typical instances mentioned in the last essay—Moses, Buddha, and Julius Cæsar—we discern at once the law underlying the unconsciousness or denial of a life to come. In each case it arose from the abuse of the tremendous spiritual force placed in the hands of religion by man's belief in a future state, for all history goes to show that if religious belief becomes corrupt or false, the truest and noblest souls are thrown into some form of opposition, which again reacts favourably upon religion herself. Thus the thought of judgment to come did not prevent the Egyptians from being sensual, cruel, and superstitious; rather it was employed to give a fictitious sanction to some of the worst tendencies of human nature.

Therefore the Jewish people were called under Moses to be the spiritual worshippers of one righteous God, and to build up a commonwealth owning no King but Jehovah; nor is it at all wonderful that, having a very practical and pressing work to do in this world, nothing was said to them about the next. The hope of the Messiah was to be to them a substitute for that of immortality, and the temporal fortunes of the kingdom took the place of judgment to come. In a word, the knowledge of immortality had been so debased by the Egyptians that it was withheld from the people through whom God was laying the foundation of a religion that was to make men good.

The examples of Buddha and of Cæsar illustrate from immensely different points of view the same law. Like Moses, Buddha was a reformer, and the preacher of a new religion; like him, he revolted from the depraved morality of his times, by which the demon of priestcraft was turning to its own purposes man's natural hope of a life to come. His work and teaching, need it be said, fill an important and necessary place in the history of religion, especially when we remember the surrounding tendencies, which centuries afterwards culminated in the gross and immoral conceptions of a Mahometan paradise. It is only by running into extremes that the balance of forces in religion and morals (there is something akin to this in nature also) can be sustained, until some truth emerges which harmonises apparent contradictions. Julius Cæsar once more represents the same law at a different stage of its history; that is, at a time when the greatest minds, cast in a secular, and not in a religious mould, can only show that the religion of the day is worthless to them by revolting from it altogether. It was surely for nothing but good—at any rate it was necessary by the law of continuous moral development—that Paganism should be seen to have lost its hold upon men like him. Here, again, we have the same state of things: a religion founded on emotions, fancies, legendary tales, and perverted for immoral purposes by the priestly spirit which then, as ever, assumed to keep the keys of the kingdom of heaven. And I make bold to say that Christianity, while claiming to reveal immortality as a simple fact, did nevertheless follow the example of the older religious movements in this, that it reduced the doctrine to the fewest and plainest moral conceptions, and called men's attention to the practical duties and work of life. The kingdom of heaven which Christ founded, and the keys of which the Apostles did in sober fact hold, was not that to which later (and, in their time, perhaps needful) notions have reduced it—a blissful state to be enjoyed hereafter by the chosen few—but was in its essence the establishment of God's rule, order, and righteousness upon earth, to be continued hereafter in other spheres of thought and action. It would be amusing, were it not inexpressibly saddening, to see how the whole stand-point of the Messiah has been unconsciously changed by those who have claimed to represent His teaching throughout Christian times; but it is a question which does not immediately concern us now. To sum up the whole argument, it is plain that the law of evolution applies to religious as well as to physical development, and accounts for the rise of different types, each of which has arisen out of surrounding circumstances, to meet pressing wants, to do a special work, to preserve one side or portion of the truth of humanity. And a Christian clergyman may be pardoned for adding the expression of his own personal belief that in religion, as in nature, there is a "survival of the fittest."

The application of the law to this present day is, I should hope, clear enough. There are men, in every way entitled to be heard, who disavow all necessity for a belief in immortality as a motive for duty or a part of humanity. And (a far worse sign) it is plain that, whereas many men *hold* this belief as a doctrine, it has the slightest possible *hold* upon them, and does not enter into their lives as an animating and consoling faith. Religion invents a hundred reasons to account for this, and to conceal her own fault. These, shallow and unreal as they are, are often no more than a mere statement of the fact in other words, or empty lamentations over the depravity of human nature, which are just as reasonable as the complaint of a doctor that his patients persist in dying. We hear, for instance, that the tendency of science is to make men materialists, and to crush spiritual life; that it is a revolutionary age in which people like to shock their friends by extravagant assertions; that disappointment and failure cause men to give in and despair of justice and righteousness to come; that the intellect is more thought of than the heart, and knowledge held of more account than duty. All which does not touch the root of the matter; indeed, it is a mere evasion to lay the blame upon human nature, or the circumstances of the times, or the spirit of the age, instead of holding those responsible to whom the care of Christianity is committed—that is, Christians themselves. By their own confession, or rather claim, the duty of bringing men to believe in immortality as revealed in Christ, devolves upon them; and if, for any want of moral right or intellectual truth, the duty is not fulfilled, the blame must rest upon them, and not upon the world or the age which they have failed to convert.

I have no desire, however, of entering upon the unwelcome task of drawing up the indictment against the religion of the day; enough to say that Christian teaching, practices, politics, morality, and society, in respect of such virtues as self-sacrifice, sympathy, union, love of truth, and the like, must bear the responsibility for what goes amiss in respect of the belief in immortality. This truth has precisely the same effects upon those who believe it, as the hope of inheriting a large estate has upon the heir when young. If he be selfish, weak, and indolent, it will do him harm; if otherwise, the knowledge of future responsibilities will make him doubly watchful and industrious. Therefore, the world at large looks to see what are the moral and intellectual effects of the doctrine of immortality in accordance with a certain wise saying, " By their fruits ye shall know them." The point is *not* that outside observers detect flagrant inconsistencies between men's lives and their beliefs, which, though a common, is, in the case at any rate of "thinkers," a most absurd excuse for infidelity; but it is that the very belief itself is perceived to have a bad and perverting effect upon the mind and morals of those who hold it; in plain words, men are beginning to suspect that the hope of immortality is ceasing to make people good. And that this is the case to a large and growing extent, who that knows anything of current opinions upon the secret of happiness, the principles of

God's judgment, the nature of eternity, can venture to doubt? But then, the same law which teaches that reaction follows upon a corruption of religion, and in turn creates a reformation, explains also within what limits the reformation will work. Evolution means progress as well as destruction, and when certain truths have once clearly emerged, and been satisfactorily established, they, however perverted they may have become, will survive as the basis of the new teaching. Thus, it is extremely significant to observe that when Luther confronted the old evils in the most aggravated form, he was not obliged to cut men off altogether from the consciousness of immortality, but only to reform, and in a measure rationalise it. It has been once for all, so we believe, brought to light by the Resurrection, and has become an abiding possession of the human race; therefore, although man's weakness and folly, or the inevitable corruptions of time, may still drive souls into revolt, yet religion will always be able to reform herself upon this basis, and will never cease, so long as she exists, to believe in immortality as defined, explained, and demonstrated by Jesus Christ.

We are now to consider the moral use of the belief in immortality in answer to the challenge whether it exercises any special effects upon human conduct which can be obtained in no other way. It is at once tempting and easy to answer that the great mass of weak and ignorant men require some such motive as this to enable them to struggle upwards into a higher moral life; but it must be confessed that this answer would carry no weight with those to whom these arguments are addressed. A belief in immortality, it would be urged, may have its relative and temporary uses until the world at large becomes philosophical; but that does not prove it to be true in the most real sense, and to the highest minds. Still, it must be remembered that this consideration has of all others the most legitimate and powerful influence with minds that are already disposed to embrace religious truth, and all that is required is that Christian advocates should perceive to what uses it may be logically and fairly put. For ourselves, and for our present purpose, we must look elsewhere. And examining the moral tendencies of an age in which the hope of immortality is waxing faint, we find that there is a growth of evil exactly in those directions which a more vivid consciousness of a life to come would tend to check; these are (amongst others) materialism, revolution, and despair, having a rough correspondence to the old division of flesh, world, and spirit.

It is needless to say that nothing can be attempted more than the briefest mention of the facts that mark the growth of these tendencies. Concerning the first it is enough to indicate what every newspaper confesses and deplores. Over-eating and drinking (the former attributed to the highest intellectual circles); barbaric splendour in dress and equipment; the gradual invasion of the professional classes by the spirit of money-making (I know nothing more sad than to see how men.coin their brains into money, and call it success); the resistance to diminished hours of work by the employing classes; sensuousness in art, poetry, and religion, the latter becoming more and more a thing of materialistic mysteries and ceremonial show, all these are some of the admitted signs of the times which wise people view with regret and alarm. Something of this sort surely lies at the root of Professor Huxley's protest that he is not a materialist. Now surely it is as capable of demonstration as anything of this nature can be, that the consciousness of a spirit—that is, of continuous personal existence after bodily dissolution—is a specific remedy for this disorder. Given a man anxious to raise himself above the dead level of his sensuous surroundings, feeling himself tempted and provoked to mere bodily enjoyment, despising himself for being what he is, and yet not capable of any great moral and mental effort, and it is clear that no remedy could be devised so powerfully and precisely adapted to give him the requisite help and support as a distinct persuasion that he himself was an immortal being, distinct from and higher than his present body, from which his personality must be one day separated, when the work of evolving a higher type of life was accomplished. People, it is to be feared, will continue to "eat and drink," if they are persuaded that "to-morrow they will die."

The spirit of revolution is not very easy to define in words, but the expression is, perhaps, the best that could be chosen to describe that over-impatient zeal which, by a refinement of selfishness, causes men to do more harm than good in their attempts to make things better. Men find themselves in a world of injustice, inequality, suffering, and disorder, too often thinly cloaked under the name of law, and deriving a decent sanction from religion. And yet, though animated by an almost fanatical love of humanity, and ready to make any sacrifices in its behalf, they become in practice guilty of gross immorality and selfishness; they give way to violent passions of hatred and revenge; they adopt desperate schemes, sometimes foolish and sometimes wicked, of change and revolution; practically they come to regard the happiness of men as coincident with the reign of their own unchecked supremacy; and they die readily for an ideal humanity which they love, if only they may curse the actual human beings whom they hate. It is this mixture of good and evil in the better spirits of the Commune that divided the heart of feeling men with these mingled emotions of censure and sympathy best expressed in the single word pity; but thinking men may well set themselves to work to discover the cause why persons so possessed by the desire to do good to mankind should be capable of doing so much harm. And yet, after all, the reason lies upon the surface. Revolution is not the cause of the decay of the belief in immortality, but exactly the reverse is the case. Let us put ourselves in the position of one who thinks that this life is his only one, who is, at any rate, sure that it is the only one he cares for. He sees its blessings and advantages unequally distributed, withheld from himself, his friends, or his class. Shall he then be cheated out of the one existence he can call his own? Better that everything should be pulled down now, at once, without delay, in the hope that the good may come to him; surely some change, radical and immediate, in the laws of government and property, or in the rulers of the State, will give him the enjoyment he desires. Now, to such a cry of agony, with which it must be a callous soul that can find no point of sympathy, the one only sufficient answer is that this life is not the only one, but a progress towards another and a better one. If science, as expounded by Mr Darwin, gives a true account of the origin of man's social instincts,

F

then the desire to share in the welfare of our race is imbedded in our constitution, and is not to be satisfied by the shadowy hope of a fleeting reputation after death, or by a mere self-approval, or by the thought that men may be better and happier when we are gone. False religion, with its perpetual depreciation of the world and humanity, inculcates a tame acquiescence in hardship and wrong, and so drives men into that negation of religion which cannot acquiesce in anything. True religion, on the contrary, by setting forth a future world to be evolved out of men's moral and spiritual exertions and experiences here, creates that spirit of divine patience, self-sacrifice, and above all, self-control, which can die at least as bravely as the other, and leave with its parting breath, and in its abiding moral influences, a blessing, and not a curse behind it.

And as the belief in immortality confronts the revolutionary spirit with the power of patience, so does it breathe hope into the spirit of despair. What turns some natures to madness causes others to retire heart-broken from all conflicts and labours that have humanity for their object, and produces the feeling that in Pagan times found its last and most mournful expression in self-destruction. Suicide, then too often the last and applauded action of noble minds, has become in Christian days the meanest and most despised resource of the weak and feeble, and this contrast measures the extent of the practical good that religion has done for morality in setting forth a life to come. Napoleon's final reason for not committing suicide after his abdication is a curious illustration of this—"Moreover," he said, "I am not altogether destitute of religious sentiment." If humanity,

Morality and Immortality. 83

and each man that comprises it, is to be developed through many stages, then the work of each stage becomes inexpressibly important, and to abandon it is to abandon the future as well. But if all ends here, and failure here means failure absolute and perpetual, then I know not what should prevent a man who has clearly realised what failure is from saying with Brutus at Philippi, " Certainly we must fly, but with our hands, and not with our feet."

It is necessary to make one more remark, or rather to repeat one already made, before I close. The case for immortality may have seemed so strong as to suggest the possibility of dispensing with positive evidence, as though the Resurrection could not make it much more certain than it is. Now this is a state of mind with which it is incumbent upon science to wage incessant warfare. Wherever the positive evidence is nil, that is, where no instance of the conclusion desired can be adduced, then the more vehement, universal, and what is called " natural," the desire is, the more certain is it that men are the victims of their own delusions, the more likely they are to allow themselves to form erroneous conceptions of life and work, the more imperatively it becomes the duty of positive thought to warn them against the evil results of believing what they wish to believe. If a thing be true, there must have been some instance sufficient to establish it as a fact throughout the course of ages; failing this, immortality sinks to the level of the elixir of life or the philosopher's stone, a thing much desired, but having no existence in the solid ground of fact, and a fruitful source of misleading errors and misdirected labours. Or at best, it might be admitted to be possibly true, if it were debarred from exercising any vital influence upon human conduct. I am, of course, well aware that the same remark in an altered form may be applied to the evidence afforded by Christianity, and the assertion that men believe the Resurrection only because they wish to believe it, is one that may be fairly made and must be honestly met. But then there is no reason why it should not be met; we are here upon the solid ground of events and evidence; we can discover for ourselves who are the witnesses, what they say, and whether they are dressing up a tale to satisfy their own desires for a future life. To believe a fact for which there is not a scintilla of positive evidence, because we desire it, is one thing; to believe the evidence for a fact, because we desire it, is another and very different thing. The former must be scientifically wrong; the latter may or may not be right: and time is the only ultimate arbiter in the contest.

I have now brought to a close this rapid, and I fear I must add, perfunctory survey of the conditions and circumstances of human life as they bear upon man's desire for immortality. I have taken the best pains I could to draw my conclusions from indubitable facts of human experience and consciousness by a process of reasoning which would satisfy the demands of the logic of science. What I think I have proved is this: that it is in accordance with man's natural instincts and with the necessities of morality, that he should desire a life to come; and that this being so, he will welcome, in spite of its indispensable supernatural element, the evidence of historical fact, which purports to prove it, and so attempts to rescue humanity from a maimed, unnatural, and lifeless condition. Much that has been said may appear trite enough, but it has been placed, I hope, under a new light, and been read under the influences of those mental conceptions and that theory of the universe which the doctrine of evolution has made familiar to the minds of men. In such cases details are everything, and to work out the details may afford labour and satisfaction to the science of religion for years to come. But this will be impossible so long as religion and science remain apart in a defiant and disdainful attitude, more anxious to spy out defects than to combine the truths special to each in one harmonious perfection. Any attempt, therefore, to apply the methods of science to the phenomena of religion, and thus to bridge the gulf between the two will be, I feel certain, candidly judged, if seen to have been candidly made.

CHRISTIANITY AND IMMORTALITY.

IT may be desirable to explain at the outset what is the precise object of this essay, inasmuch as the title may be thought to cover much wider ground than I am at all disposed to enter upon. The relations of the Christian belief in the Resurrection of Christ to the doctrine of immortality, have been already pointed out, and do not need to be further discussed. That the Resurrection, if true, amounts to a scientific proof of immortality, that the witnesses for it are honest, and the testimony sufficient to prove any non-miraculous event, are statements which, even if they be challenged, I do not think it necessary to substantiate by additional arguments. Life after all is but short, and may be wasted in endless discussions upon matters perfectly obvious to all who are not blinded by invincible prejudice. The man who says, " I do not believe the history because it is avowedly supernatural," is, need it be remarked, an intellectually honest man, and deserves the most respectful attention. But the man who says, " I have no prepossessions against the supernatural, but I disbelieve the history upon exactly the same grounds as I should any ordinary statement ; " who tries, in short, to reach Hume's conclusion without the resolute common sense that marked his method, must be dismissed as impracticable. There is, it must really be remembered, an enormous *a priori* probability attached to every straightforward statement made by, apparently, honest men, which holds good in all cases where it is not balanced by some antecedent improbability, such as the existence of a supernatural element in the narrative. There is, indeed, a conceivable case in which a man might claim to be heard. If there be any one who believes that miracles have occurred more or less frequently, but that the Resurrection of Jesus Christ is not proved to be one of them, then the very absurdity of his position entitles him to be considered an honest thinker. But I deny that the term applies to any (if such there be) who do not, as a matter of fact, believe that miracles have occurred, and yet pretend to reject the Resurrection upon the ground that it is not proved by evidence sufficient to substantiate ordinary historical events. Some little impatience with the men who are constantly throwing up barriers against the progress of reason to right conclusions, or who try to direct her march into bye-ways formed by their own intellectual idiosyncrasies, is surely not altogether unjustifiable.

But the task I have in hand is a much more serious and, to say the truth, a much more unwelcome one. I have let it be understood with tolerable plainness that, in my judgment, modern religious teaching is answerable for the errors, whether of disbelief or of superstition, which have gathered about the doctrine of man's immortality. Modern Christianity does not make the doctrine acceptable or useful to men, because it does not possess the mind of Christ, and does not teach the nineteenth century the things which He taught the first. A kind of moral weakness and littleness is creeping more and more over the minds of religious people; and religious doctrines, once full of life and power, have become mere dogmatic negations of some error as unreal as themselves. Somehow or other the salt has lost its savour in the judgment of those to whom intellectual truth and practical morality are things of the first importance. I say this with the same kind of feelings that might inspire a French soldier to speak of the moral and professional corruptions that plunged the French army into the depths of disaster. My life is bound up with the religion, to the faults of which it is impossible to shut our eyes. I am not insensible to the good works, the doing of which has come down to us as a tradition from the great Evangelical or Catholic revivals. I am keenly alive no less to the exalted history of the past than to the equally noble responsibilities and duties of the future; but in spite of all this, or rather because of it, the truth requires to be proclaimed aloud, that modern Christianity, as generally received, does not represent the teaching of Christ, and is not fit to be charged with the task of teaching the world a suitable and satisfactory morality. That this is true with respect to the doctrine of the immortality of the soul I now proceed to show.

The popular conception of the religion taught by Jesus Christ—a conception that underlies the doctrines and practices of all Christian churches—is to the following effect:—He came to reveal the facts of a future life, which, when revealed, are found to consist of an endless life of happiness or misery, our destinies therein being decided by the relation which we hold towards Him. In this conception we must distinguish two erroneous notions: the first, that His teaching mainly concerned the next life; the second, that it consisted in the proclamation of heaven and hell as the ultimate destiny of mankind. Of these, the first, though not so striking, contains a more subtle power of evil than the second, and will require careful examination.

I must, however, first say a word in answer to the objection that these conceptions have ceased vitally to affect the religion of the world, or can be said fairly to represent it. I am convinced that no greater mistake can be made. It may, indeed, be admitted that the belief in endless torments is ceasing to exercise a real influence upon men's minds, but even this admission must not be made too much of. In the Roman Church, and in many Protestant sects, it is still a predominant feature of religious teaching, while in none has it been formally withdrawn as an article of faith. It is, perhaps, thought that it may die out in silence; but, apart from the moral cowardice this involves, all history seems to show that, when once a doctrine has laid firm hold of the popular mind, nothing short of active denunciation and determined opposition can destroy it. And then, too, it must be remembered that the system of theology of which it forms a cardinal point, still remains and flourishes. All the power of the priesthood, and all the logical value of the Calvinistic scheme of salvation, are really involved in ultimate ruin with the rejection of this doctrine. And again, though hell as a place of endless torment may be vanishing from men's minds, yet the idea of heaven as a place of endless happiness is almost as potent as ever

This seems to me the worst feature of all. Whatever may be said of the evils wrought by the fear of endless punishment, those wrought by the hope of endless happiness are certainly greater. The former is, at least, due to man's sense of the greatness of sin; the latter is the result of his selfish desires for enjoyment. The fear of hell has kept many a rough, wayward spirit in something like conformity to decent behaviour, and it has unquestionably been the turning-point in thousands of lives, and the beginning of better things to men beyond the reach of any argument save fear. But the common idea of heaven can claim no such moral achievements, while it has enfeebled the character of myriads of human beings, and has ministered in the name of religion to human selfishness and love of ease. And if this assertion seems a strong one (as in truth I mean it to be), let any one who doubts whether it can be justified bethink himself of the hymns which have become more and more popular in these latter days. Sentimental longings for paradise, excessive, though easily understood amid the moral wretchedness of the middle ages, are now among the most marked features of modern praise. Sensuous descriptions of mere outward details, passionate longings for happiness and idleness, are put into the mouths of grave British citizens, whose one great virtue is to do their duty like men, and who hate idleness as the source of all evil. How far we may believe that the minds of men are really drawn off from the realities of life, or how far they are merely softened and diverted for the moment, depends upon the amount of practical weight we are willing to admit that religion now possesses. All I am concerned to observe is, that there are tendencies which seem to be powerful, and are certainly popular, that are demoralising in the extreme.

And lastly, as an additional proof that, however details may have been modified or abandoned, the general conception of the future life under the forms of heaven and hell is still a living part of the consciousness of man, I would point out how in times of earnest feeling it exercises a subtle influence upon the strongest minds. Two of the most eminent of living Englishmen, desirous of expressing themselves strongly in antagonism to popular notions, have done so by declaring their intention under certain circumstances of "going to hell." It is odd, on the other hand, to read of a man like Descartes affirming that he was as desirous to go to heaven as any one. The very idea of the two, hell especially, has been engrafted in the minds of men by grotesque poetry and legends. All this is indeed compatible with the truth, which I do not for a moment deny, that there is a gradual loosening of the hold these beliefs once had upon the minds of men. What was once a tremendously-earnest conflict between the preacher and his hearer, in which neither of the two ever doubted that the stakes were the endless destiny of an immortal soul, has now shrunk into a kind of amicable contest, in which the latter easily stops every attempt made by the former to reach his heart by means of the fear of hell. Respectable men no longer leave church with the same profound conviction that without conversion their damnation is assured, and so that the only practical question is, how long it can safely be postponed. But then this is just the state of things in which doctrines, the errors of which might well be pardoned in consideration of their effectual moral power, have become nothing but pernicious. To confine all men's ideas of a future life to the one notion of decisive judgment, was certainly a mistake in the face of Christ's teaching, and of simple elementary moral truths. But to keep the idea of judgment before men's minds and force it upon their thoughts, had at least a useful deterrent effect. But now that this is practically vanishing, there remains but one duty for all who love the truth as Christ taught it, and to whom human morality is unspeakably precious. Once more we are face to face with a popular religion that abuses the tremendous fact of man's immortality to unworthy purposes. The second Reformation must treat heaven and hell as the first treated purgatory and indulgences: it must preserve the moral idea while abolishing the literal fact, and must supersede the old forms of thought by new conceptions, gathered from the experience and the discoveries of the ages, but founded upon a closer adherence to the actual teaching of Christ.

In examining what the main characteristics of that teaching were it is of great importance to observe in what relations it stood to the common religious teaching of His time. To begin then, it is not in the least true to say that Christ was the first to stamp the idea of immortality upon the minds of men under the forms of heaven and hell. He found, indeed, those ideas already existing, and He used them for His own purposes; but He took from them their future and remote, in order to give them a present and immediate, force and aspect. The Pharisees believed that the souls of good men would be for ever blessed (there is some doubt as to their ideas about the resurrection of the body), and that hell, or gehenna, would be the inevitable portion of the wicked. These beliefs had grown up exactly on the soil that might have been expected to produce them. They were the fruit of that, taken as a whole, dark and melancholy period of Jewish history which intervenes between the return from captivity and the coming of the Messiah. As in the middle ages, so in these, which are the veritable middle ages of Jewish history, men had taken refuge from the intolerable miseries of life in the hope of paradise, and, powerless themselves to avenge the wrongs they endured, had fastened on the idea of endless and horrible torture in the world to come. In proportion as the ancient hopes of Israel became in the bad sense of the word merely secular, so, by a strange but easily explicable contrast, did the minds of men conceive the idea of immortality; for, after all, a Messiah who should at some time restore their temporal greatness, could never satisfy the, yearnings of individual souls for eternity. Something, too must be ascribed to the influences of Paganism, to which they were ever after the Captivity increasingly subject; and thus it came to pass that the fierce wrath of the Jew against the enemies of his people or the apostates from his religion took, as it were, visible form in the purely Pagan idea which turned the valley of Hinnom into the symbol of the place of endless torment, and even placed the gates of hell within its limits. Add to this, that the virtues which were to win heaven were compliance with ceremonial observances invented or maintained by an arrogant priesthood, who grew rich and powerful by trading on the superstitions of mankind, and we have a picture of a religious teaching concerning immortality, on the one hand clear and definite, on the other corrupting and demoralising, resembling, in short, all the worst epochs of spiritual degradation with which history makes us acquainted.

How, then, did our Lord treat the religious ideas about immortality with which He was confronted? Mainly, in two ways. First, He seized upon the current notions, and used the truths which they contained, to enforce a present heaven, an immediate judgment, a hell that was yawning to engulf the whole Jewish people. Secondly, He substituted by act and word the fewest and simplest moral conceptions of a future state, in place of outward, local, and detailed descriptions of it. Or, speaking more generally, He revived the old true Jewish belief in Messiah as the representative of God's government upon earth, and brought heaven down to men as the first and urgent preliminary to raising men one by one to heaven. He planted in the minds of His followers the necessity of a spiritual resurrection now, as being of far more consequence than that of bodily resurrection hereafter, and He recalled them from the contemplation of remote rewards and punishments to the tremendous realities that were already closing in around them. To make good this assertion it is, however, necessary to examine, with all needful brevity, the teaching of Christ concerning the Kingdom of Heaven, Hell, and Judgment, and then to note how few, how guarded, and how practical were His words upon the subject of the life to come.

There are statements, which, though really new, are nevertheless confounded with truths that people have always held, or at any rate believe that they have always held. Such, for instance, is the statement that by the Kingdom of

Heaven Christ meant almost, if not quite, exclusively the establishment of God's rule and order upon earth. Upon hearing this, people immediately bethink themselves that this is merely another way of saying that the Kingdom of Heaven means the Christian Church. But the error lies not so much in denying any true interpretation of these words, as in substituting a secondary and comparatively unimportant interpretation for the primary and true one. Practically, the thought of heaven as part of the future life has swallowed up the thought of heaven as the rule of God upon earth. Popular theology is like a bad picture, in which all the foreground is blurred and confused, while the mountains in the background stand out in hard and unnatural distinctness. People think of Christ first as revealing a future heaven, and then, quite in a secondary sense, as establishing a community that should lead men into it. But the fact is that the foundation of the Kingdom of Heaven upon earth, for its own sake, and for the present good of man independently of his future destiny, was the one great object of all His teaching; and the more we examine that teaching for ourselves, the more clearly we shall appreciate the truth of this assertion, and discern how entirely His soul was wrapped up in the work of the immediate present. As painted by the Master's hand, the picture is altogether clear and well defined in the foreground, while behind it the landscape fades away with a dim suggestiveness, infinitely more subtle and impressive than the coarse, naturalistic details with which later human teaching has obscured the outlines faintly drawn by the divine hand, and just relieved from darkness by a few far-glancing rays darted forth from the divine inspiration.

The above remarks are necessary, if we would avoid the appearance of making a series of observations concerning Christ's teaching so obviously true, not to say commonplace, that every one will be inclined to believe he has always known them. The history opens with the announcement by John the Baptist, repeated by Christ, and put into the mouth of His messengers, that the Kingdom of Heaven was at hand—that it was shortly to be set up amongst them. The Sermon on the Mount, the first recorded instance of His public teaching, begins by declaring that the poor in spirit and in fact were the persons to whom it was specially preached; and a great reward in heaven, that is, in the new kingdom, was promised to those who were persecuted for His sake. How many thousands of sermons have been preached to account for the self-invented difficulty that God meant endless happiness to be the portion of the poor rather than of the rich! How many delusive hopes have been fostered in the minds of poor people by the thought that after a life of suffering here they would be rewarded by a life of enjoyment hereafter! The key-note, however, thus emphatically struck in the first teaching, was never forsaken or altered. "The Kingdom of Heaven is among you;" "Thou art not far from the Kingdom of God;" "There be some of them that stand here that shall not taste of death till they see the Kingdom of God come with power"—words which have exhausted the ingenuity of sophistry to explain them away. And, again, we hear of Capernaum exalted into heaven, but to be cast down into hell at the speedy approach of that day of judgment in which it should be more tolerable for the cities of heathendom than of Israel. Or, once more, in one single passage, the Jewish gehenna is distinctly named, and the disciples are told that anything in the world, however dear, which causes them to stumble at the Kingdom of Heaven then preached, or, still worse, which causes them to make others stumble, must be resolutely cut away, lest they come to the doom described in prophetical language as the place of the valley of Hinnom, where the worm never ceases to fatten on the dead bodies from within, or the fire to consume them from without. These, then, are the notes of time expressly laid down by the Teacher himself. But the doctrine of the Kingdom of Heaven is expressly and specifically contained in a series of parables, many of which begin with the well-known words, "The Kingdom of Heaven is like." Read in the light of modern theology, these all have reference to the last day and to a future life; read in the light shed upon them by the above-mentioned marks of time, they speak of immediate judgment and of a present life, and can only be applied to the former by indirect and very often incorrect references.

The first group of parables, in St Matt. xiii., which explains the mysteries of the Kingdom of Heaven, is plainly an account of the laws which govern the foundation and the progress of the Church on earth. In two of them, however, the notion of judgment is added; and I call attention to the parable of the Tares as containing the germ of all future misunderstanding of Christ's teaching. The field, He says, is the world ($\kappa\acute{o}\sigma\mu os$). Now, when, in the next verse, the unsuspecting English reader finds it said that the harvest is the "end of the world," and in the verse after this, reference is made to the "end of *this* world," he little thinks that the first word translated "world" is quite a different word from that in the two latter instances, though if he considered the matter for a moment even he might wonder how the harvest can possibly be the end of the field and not rather the end of the crop upon it. That this last is our Lord's meaning, as in truth it is the only one compatible with common sense, is abundantly clear from the word used, αἰών, which means age or dispensation, and answers, therefore, to the crop which was then growing upon the field of the world. The good seed is the children of Christ's Kingdom; the bad seed is perverted Judaism; the harvest is its coming complete downfall, to which surely may be added a glance at that break-up of all civil, social, and political order, when the genius of Paganism passed away at the destruction of the Roman Empire of the West. It is not necessary, once more let me remark, to deny that in a derived and mediate sense the moral truths expressed in the parable may be applied to all times and places, though even then a strict interpretation would require us to limit the application to the existing world. But what it is of the greatest importance to understand, is that the actual vision that was before the mind of Christ was the destruction of Judaism, and perhaps of Paganism, together with the foundation of the Church; and that, were there never to be another judgment upon earth, the parable would still be adequately fulfilled. And that this was the fulfilment of which He was thinking, we shall find abundant proof if we turn to a similar passage in the thirteenth chapter of St Luke, in which the establishment of the Kingdom of God is predicted. In this the Gentiles are represented as coming in from all quarters, while the Jews are thrust out with weeping and gnashing of teeth, the whole at once suggesting and culminating in the lamentation over Jerusalem, "their house which is left unto them desolate." And all this prediction of coming temporal judgment seems to be, if not certainly in the words of Christ, at least in the mind of the Evangelist, connected with His answer to the question, " Lord, are there few that shall be saved?"

Before we pass on to consider the final prophecy in which the idea thus started is worked out in some of the grandest utterances that ever fell even from the lips of Him who spake as never man spake, I must call attention to one parable upon the interpretation of which I am willing to stake the whole of my argument. It is the parable of the Labourers in the vineyard (20th chapter of St Matthew), one of the simplest and most practical of stories. If ever there was a parable easy to interpret, this ought to be the one. It stands between the lesson, twice declared, which the Lord meant to be derived from it—" The first shall be last, and the last first." The circumstances which gave rise to it— namely, the sorrowful going away of the rich young ruler, and Peter's question, "What shall we have therefore?"—are clearly stated. Yet, in spite of all this, misled by false conceptions of the Kingdom of Heaven, the commentators find it almost unintelligible. Assuming that the day's wage is endless happiness or heavenly reward in a life to come, they are met by the insuperable difficulty as to how murmurers can enjoy it or be fit for it, still less how the first can be last and the last first. And thus they are driven to all kinds of shifts, such as the unphilosophical notion of degrees of happiness. Now, all that is required is to regard our Lord as giving a plain, moral description of what would take place at the establishment of His Kingdom upon earth. The departure of the ruler suggests the reflection that it is hard for a rich man to enter into that Kingdom. This, again, suggests Peter's natural but dangerous question, to which the answer is given that in the Regeneration, in the coming new birth of humanity, they should share the labours and the glory of their Master, as in truth they have done, and that in place of those which they gave up they should have new spiritual relationships and possessions upon earth, together (elsewhere it is added, as though to admit no possible mistake) with persecutions. How abundantly this promise was fulfilled we may conclude from the life of St Paul, who had children and brethren in every city, and to whom the whole world was, as it were, a home. But then He goes on to warn them not to let the mere desire for a reward debase their spiritual character, for in that case the men who, like the twelve, had been called first, might become last in moral goodness. And he illustrated this tendency by a simple story of every-day life containing just the one moral that religion dislikes to face, namely, that a life of outward service and real Christian work may, if not watched, end in an envious, selfish, murmuring disposition, concerning which he says nothing and implies nothing as to its ultimate destination; but merely points out that it has missed the real blessedness of work, and has lost for all moral purposes its true reward, while strenuously seeking to obtain it.

We now come to the group of prophecies and parables which form the close of His teaching. And here we notice an important note of time occurring at a critical moment of the history. On His way to Jerusalem for the last time He delivered the parable of the Pounds, to counteract a delusion on the part of His disciples that the Kingdom of

God should immediately appear. Up to this moment, then, this had been the natural result of His teaching and of the wide success with which it had been attended. Now, therefore, it becomes necessary to make it clear to them that this coming is to be a work of time and labour, and that they are to be employed in it during His absence according to the measure of their several capacities. The mental view is gradually enlarging, the horizon is receding farther into the distance, while yet the main interest is attached to the immediate present. Then He enters Jerusalem, and begins that last contest with the Pharisees which ended in His death. After a parable or two in which He puts before them the Kingdom of Heaven for their immediate reception, and warns them of the consequences of refusal, He delivers that tremendous forecast of coming doom which must either be a shameless forgery or else stamps Him as one who knew more than it is given to mere men to know. And just at this point it is that commentators, old and new, English and German, have launched out into their wildest excesses of interpretation. By some it has been asserted that the account in St Luke refers to the destruction of Jerusalem, that in St Matthew to the end of the world, in utter forgetfulness that this is simply to play into the hands of the mythic school of interpreters.* By almost all (for what I myself know, it may be by all without exception) it is understood that the chief thing which occupied His mind was the destruction of the world, the fall of Jerusalem being a comparatively unimportant type of the great and distant

---

* In using the word "commentators," it did not occur to me that it might be taken to include Mr Maurice. Need it be said that it is to him I owe the true doctrine of the Kingdom of Heaven?

reality. Now I say that this is absolutely false. The true canons of interpretation are these: first, that every word must be applied first and fully (due allowance being made for metaphorical language mostly gathered from the prophets) to the fate which the Jews were then bringing upon themselves, and, I also think, to the general break-up of the foundations of society by the destruction of the old "world," which He apprehended as inevitable; second, that any reference to future judgments can only be understood as being based upon general moral principles herein laid down, and is quite independent of outward details or of special times, such as a supposed end of the world. The prophecy is, in short, a description of all judgment indirectly, but directly only of the judgment of Jerusalem. Nothing can be more precise than the notes of time by which He appears to have endeavoured to guard their minds from exactly those errors into which men have since fallen. He begins with the declaration that not one stone of the Temple shall be left upon another. He speaks of the persecutions and false rumours that should assail the disciples. He bids them flee from Jerusalem, compassed about with armies. He tells them that they shall see the Son of man coming in the clouds of heaven, and gathering in His elect from the four quarters; and lest this metaphorical language, descriptive of the growth of the Church, should be misunderstood, He adds that then they shall know that it is near, even at the doors. Then He emphatically announces that this generation shall not pass before ALL these things be fulfilled: and if any man wishes to see what human sophistry, stimulated by a false tradition, can accomplish, let him read the attempts that have been made to explain away these words. It is an instructive but mournful spectacle.

After this, follow three prophetic parables, the Ten Virgins, the Talents, and the Sheep and the Goats, all turning upon the same point, but with one notable exception. The first describes his rejection or acceptance by the Jews as individuals. The second explains His relations to His own servants, that is, to all Christians, and prescribes their duties till His coming; though here, again, that coming once more seems to recede into the distance, nor need we deny a possibly direct reference to a future world, the more so as a doctrine of rewards is laid down quite at variance with that of mere endless happiness, and suggestive of work, responsibility, and development. But in the third, the Master does, as it seems to me, in His closing words, practically abandon His standpoint in the present, and contemplate Himself as related to all mankind. I say this, not because the details of the parable would not equally well fall in with the other interpretation, but because the test by which He will try men at the eternal judgment is declared emphatically, not to be that of personal relationship to Himself, but of simple human kindness on the part of those who never heard His name. Humanity, itself, may take heart and rejoice, the strongest opponents of Christianity may cease to strive, when they remember that in His final words, when He was claiming to be the judge of mankind, He asserted that righteousness would be recognised as the work of human nature in kindness, love, and help, and that every man who lived and laboured for his fellow-men would be found to have lived and laboured for Christ.

It was thus, then, that Christ called men's attention

away from dreams of the future life to the present realities of their social, moral, and political condition; but it must be pointed out that, in assigning to these the first place in His teaching, we are not limiting the scope of the parables, but very much enlarging it. They become morally true of all human life, delineations of man in all his many capacities and relationships, all being ultimately referred to God. Heaven and hell, pardon and judgment, become very present and pressing realities, and religion is seen in the teaching of Christ to be throwing all her weight into the task of giving divine sanctions to the duties of the present world. The same applies to His teaching about the Resurrection, and, as linked with it, judgment to come. The Pharisees believed in some sort of physical resurrection and future judgment. Our Lord, in the very beautiful discourse contained in St John, ch. v., proclaimed that, as the Father raised the dead and quickened them, so the Son quickens whom He will, and that to Him all judgment has been committed. This He further explained by saying that all who believed in Him had already everlasting life; and to show beyond all doubt that He was thinking of the present life, He added, "The hour is coming, and now is, when the dead shall hear the voice of the Son of God, and they that hear shall live." And as though this were not enough, He used, a little further on, words which seem naturally to refer to the last final Resurrection as believed in by the Pharisees, to describe the present spiritual Resurrection and rapidly approaching judgment—"The time is coming in which they that are in the graves shall hear His voice and shall come forth: they that have done good unto the Resurrection of life, and they that have done evil unto the Resurrection of condemnation." Once more, when Martha adopts the current Jewish notion concerning her brother, "I know that he shall rise again in the Resurrection at the last day," she receives the rebuking answer intended to show that the raising of Lazarus was typical of the immediate raising of humanity, "I am the Resurrection and the Life." So that we have here the fourth Gospel from its very different point of view bearing witness to the truth I am upholding, and we see from it as from the others that the Lord declared His desire to raise Judaism as it were from the dead, and foretold certain condemnation to all who would not hear His voice. And it is words like these that give to the actual Resurrection of Christ that moral power which St Paul afterwards saw so clearly and proclaimed so earnestly. To him it was the Resurrection of humanity, and of every human being that believed in Christ, from sin and darkness. The teaching of the apostles, indeed, bears evident traces of the difficulty they experienced in seeing clearly what was meant by Christ's coming in judgment, while their opinions seemed to have varied just as might be expected in the case of men who were living in the midst of the perplexities and agitations which that judgment caused, and whose very position prevented them from separating the outward and temporary circumstances from the abiding moral principles contained in His prophecy. However this may be, the fact, that the Resurrection was bound up first and chiefly with the rise of humanity from its past degradation, exercises a most important influence upon the value of the evidence by which the account of it is supported. For if it could be shown that the belief in the Resurrection of Jesus Christ was connected in the minds of the earliest Christian teachers with old Jewish opinions, or that it grew up in their minds almost unconsciously from the natural desire to give force and certainty to the longing for immortality, then the value of the evidence would be very seriously impaired. But when we see that it was attached to an entirely different set of moral conceptions, that it was welcomed rather as calling men to a life of practical goodness here, than as holding out to them the certainty of a life of endless happiness hereafter, we are obliged to admit that, except for the inevitable difficulty of believing in anything supernatural, the history has everything to recommend it to favourable reception by candid minds.

It may, however, be urged that we run some danger of cutting off the teaching and life of Christ from all reference to immortality whatsoever; but to this it may again be answered that, to adjust things into their proper places, it is often necessary to wrench them vigorously in the direction directly opposite to that in which they have been distorted. And I do not only maintain that the real application of the parables is to future life in this world, its judgments, rewards, and penalties, but I am also convinced that the sayings, in which the next world is expressly mentioned, bear witness, when examined, to Christ's desire not to fix men's attention upon the life to come to the prejudice of that which now is. Three of those exceptions, that prove the rule, occur to me now; the first, His own voluntary teaching; the last two, forced upon Him by circumstances. In the parable of Dives and Lazarus He uses common Jewish expressions to point out the danger of wealth and luxury, but He does so in such a manner as to make any pressing of the details in their literal meaning a mere absurdity. The wildest imagination could hardly conceive this parable as meant to be a serious description of the actual future world. His answer to the Sadducees about the Resurrection was forced upon Him, and He contents Himself simply with clearing the doctrine from material and unworthy notions, asserting it as a fact. and proving the assertion from the words of God to Moses. The third instance is His promise to the dying thief, "To-day shalt thou be with Me in Paradise," where once more the necessity of consoling the penitent man obliges Him to give a promise of the world to come in words which the man himself and they that stood by could understand. Sad, indeed, is it to think what a superstructure of barren speculation has been raised by the prying spirit of human dogmatism upon these simple words, and how the language of metaphor, used simply for the purpose of being intelligible to those whom it chiefly concerned, has been perverted into a literal statement of actual fact. But though I am sure that sayings of this kind are not to be taken for more than as affording a general indication of the existence of a life to come, yet it still remains to be pointed out that Christ did actually meet the cravings of the human soul for immortality. And this He did, not by making it the one main object of all His teaching, but by a single pregnant saying and by a single suggestive act.

Now let us ask at what time should we expect that Christ presented the idea of immortality plainly and decisively to the minds of His disciples. Any knowledge, however slight, of human nature and its necessities would teach us that the appropriate and, so to speak, moral occasion for this would be when the agony of approaching separation made it necessary to find consolation both for Himself and them, and when a new spirit was breathed into the men upon whose love and faithfulness depended the future destinies of the Kingdom of Heaven. At the beginning, therefore, of His final discourse to the disciples we find a plain and direct reference to what we call Heaven, but which He carefully described under those simple personal and domestic terms which have made this saying especially dear to Christian minds:* "In My Father's house are many mansions; if it were not so, I would have told you : I go to prepare a place for you. And if I go and prepare a place for you, I will come again and receive you unto Myself, that where I am there ye may be also." Compare this sentence, in which the whole of Christ's direct teaching about immortality is contained, with the vast superstructure of the so-called Christian doctrine of the future state, and the striking contrast between the two will become apparent. How few, and yet how pregnant with all the thoughts that human nature requires for support and consolation, are the words of the Master! How many and how fatal to human morality are the words of those who speak in His name! The meaning and moral force, indeed, of what He taught in this saying it is not necessary to point out here; it is sufficient to call attention to it as Christ's authentic description of the life to come. It embraces all the beautiful or morally-useful associations which are attached to a house that shelters us, to the home where our Father dwells, to resting-places, to variety of interests

---

* Even this passage has been thought to apply first to the Kingdom of God upon earth. But the words chosen are certainly such as to suggest strongly the idea of its future continuance in another world.

("many"), to suitability of occupations ("prepared places"), to eternal communion with Christ himself. But more than this, though straitly questioned, He will not reveal: once more He turns their thoughts to the heavenly life upon earth, bidding them follow Him as the "Way," and to know the God whose house they were to inhabit hereafter by knowing His Son now and here. Instead of dreams of the imagination, curious questionings of the intellect, selfish desires of the heart, dogmatic utterances of miscalled authority, He confined His teaching concerning the future world to that which can be safely gathered from the moral analogies of the present. And if Christians had taught immortality as Christ taught it, they would not have been compelled to witness the revolt of man's heart or mind from the assurance of the life to come.

Still it may be said that a single sentence, standing almost alone, upon so vast a subject, affords but little ground whereon to build the fabric of man's belief in immortality, so far as it is revealed in the teaching of Christ. But a moral power, greater than can be conveyed in words, is contained in the act of His to which I have alluded. I mean, of course, the Ascension; for it is this that gives, as it were, external shape to what He said, and certainty to what He promised. But, to bring this out more clearly, we must trace the connection between religion and science in working out the moral development of man.

When the Jewish poets looked up into the heavens they found themselves alone with God, the universe, and their own souls. Not only would they abstain from worshipping the heavens, but they would, as it were, look them in the face and consider them. And it seemed to them that they were the home of God, who had set His glory above them. Still, however, in the thought of the Jews, as of the Gentiles, in religion as in philosophy, the earth was the centre of the universe, and for its sake the heavens existed: it was that for which God had framed and designed everything else. So that the heavens, while testifying of God to the Jew, did not testify of immortality. He saw only that all men perish and come to an end. But with the change of our belief as to the true relations of heaven and earth, the idea of immortality first becomes practically and morally possible. And this change we owe, first to the Ascension of Christ, to the simple fact that He had been seen to go up from earth heavenwards, which thus became the goal of man's hopes, the real centre of God's universe. But then man's ignorance of the real facts as to the physical relations between the earth and the heavens, prevented him for centuries from entering into the meaning of Christ's action, and gave occasion for the revival, or rather the continuance, of the old Pagan conceptions of heaven and hell. Copernicus was the best commentator on the Ascension, and the Ascension was a prophetic intimation of his discovery. A true religious idea was given as the necessary step to a true scientific one; but the scientific idea, in turn, exploded all the errors which religion had built upon the original truth, that the earth is not the centre of the universe. In short, the ultimate end of this discovery is to banish the hope of selfish happiness, and substitute the idea of infinite variety, occupation, and progress, which the heavens, read in the light of modern science, now preach to us. They convey the same kind of impression as the earth itself must have conveyed to the minds of those who believed it to be boundless space; and we look up to the sky with much the same sort of feelings as men gazed across the Atlantic before Columbus crossed it. As the earth grows less the heavens grow more and more. Our scientific discoveries do not measure things as they are there; our wisdom about man suggests much, but explains nothing as to the inhabitants of the worlds above.

Now it is just at the time when the "earthly" sciences are making it difficult to conceive the idea of a spirit, separated from its natural bodily organisation, that the science of the heavens adds her emphatic testimony to the teaching of Christ, and to His action, more powerful than words, in ascending heavenwards. There is a place, or rather there are places, where men may live after death—so says science. There is a Man who has gone there—so says religion. The law of progress will not consent to be bound down within earthly limits; when it has accomplished everything upon earth it sighs for new worlds to conquer. So that the truest conception of immortality is precisely that with which we are becoming more and more familiar; that which on the physical side we may call evolution, on the moral side, education. To take the commonest instance, the soul of a thoughtful man, looking into futurity, resembles the soul of a thoughtful child just standing on the verge of this world's life. There are dreams of work, of honours, of friendships, and of success. Both are leaving school and beginning the larger life into which they will carry the character already formed, the preparation already made. The man is as sure that there is a world of work and of life beyond this as the boy who hears and sees traces of the various callings and occupations of the world in which grown men act and move. Here, after the discipline of life is over, will be his future abiding and working place. Here, in one of the unnumbered worlds of God, may he carry onwards and upwards the life of an immortal being.

From the two propositions which I have thus endeavoured to substantiate—first, that Christ's direct teaching concerned almost exclusively the present world; second, that His teaching about the world to come represents it simply as the development of our moral qualities and spiritual life under higher conditions—there follow two conclusions, to which I invite the serious attention of all who desire to see truths harmonised with each other instead of being set in endless contradiction. The first is, that the objections urged by modern thought against Christian morality do not apply to the teaching of Christ himself; the second is, that this teaching, so far from being opposed to the spirit of modern science, is in exact accordance with it. We are familiar with the objections to which I refer. Religious men, it is said, are diverted from the duties of this world, from realising the sacredness of humanity, from seeing the necessity of immediate reforms and improvements, from sympathy with national and social life, owing to the too-present and absorbing contemplation of the life to come. No one, I suppose, really believes that this is practically the case to any considerable extent, at any rate at the present time; but it is contended that this escape is due simply to the fact that human nature is strong enough to triumph in the long run over the perversions of religious truth. But the objection, as an objection against Christianity, vanishes, if once it can be shown that the mind of Christ was full of the present evils and pressing wants that afflicted His countrymen; that His moral teaching was meant above all things to throw light upon human life and human nature under their present conditions; that to do our duty here, to look for judgment now, to set up righteousness and justice in the world we live in, to be citizens, patriots, masters, and servants in that larger and deeper sense which He saw and proclaimed, is the true Kingdom of Heaven which He died to establish. All this shines forth in the parables the moment they are removed from the false, unnatural glare which the almost exclusive notion of a Heaven to come has cast upon them. But I confess that even this reconciliation, important as it is, does not satisfy my ambition. I believe that the truth I am here insisting upon is the missing link needed to bind together the morality of Paganism and Christianity. Whether Christian morality is or is not perfect, whether there is in it, not only something wanting, but even a certain one-sided, perverting influence, has been, and still is, the subject of a long and unsatisfactory controversy. On the one hand it is seen that there are certain moral truths which Christianity does not teach, and certain factors in human nature of which it seems to take no account; on the other hand, to lay this at the door of Jesus Christ, or even of St Paul, appears manifestly unreasonable. The object of the life of Christ was to add to humanity those last and highest ideas which complete man's conceptions of duty and of character, not to go over ground already traversed. In a single word, His object and mission were purely religious. He is the Head of humanity, but not the whole of it; He does not supersede what is true in other teachers, but gives motive power and divine perfection to what they have already taught. There is nothing exclusive about Him, when we understand His mission aright, any more than there is about the call of the Jewish nation, when once we have realised that they were not the only nation pleasing to God, or exclusively occupied in accomplishing His will. The objection, however, that Christ's teaching is not only negative on some points (which in truth it could hardly fail to be, if it were to be human at all), but that it is absolutely one-sided, requires a different answer, and cannot be said to be unreasonable when we remember the absolutely pernicious effects which have, according to the testimony of history, flowed from that which has authoritatively claimed to represent it. The problem is this:—There are certain faulty results arising from Christian morality, and yet it is not fair to charge them upon Christ's teaching unless it contained something positively untrue, or upon His character unless He plainly did something wrong. If so, then, where do they come from? Now the answer is, that perversions creep into the moral teaching of any man when the end which he himself has in view is altered, and the facts to which his teaching was adapted are wrongly stated. View, for instance, the character and teaching of Christ through the atmosphere created by the ever-present consciousness of a future endless heaven to be obtained, and a future endless hell to be avoided, and then every evil effect which can, with any truth, be traced to Christian influences is accounted for at once. Softness, unreality, carelessness of intellectual truth, obstructiveness to the march of new ideas, unconscious selfishness, neglect of worldly virtues (so called), sectarianism in its best sense (that is, anxiety by any means for the salvation of souls in the only way believed to be true), can all be traced, not to Christ, but to Christianity, to the framework in which His teaching has been set. His morality is distorted when it is made to fit a different conception of life from what He intended. I do not venture to hope that the difficulty is altogether solved by this consideration, though I certainly think that the right clue to the solution has been suggested. Let us get rid of the notion that the future world was the chief and direct object of what He taught, and then His teaching will stand out as the crown and completion of all practical present morality, and will be seen to comprehend all other teaching by adding just the element of divine self-sacrifice which was required to give power, light, and life.

And secondly, I affirm that the teaching of Christ, rightly interpreted, is in harmony with the predominant idea which science is engaged in attaching to morality at this present time. The Kingdom of Heaven is civilisation viewed religiously, owning God as its Creator and Judge, and looking for still nobler developments in other spheres. Men's moral capacities fit them for their place in the great hereafter, and judgment consists in assigning to every man the place for which he is fit, just as the true reward of a child at school is not the prizes which he gains but the place in the world for which he has prepared himself. And if this be so, I challenge any reasonable man to deny that this view of Christian immortality is conducive to human morality in this present life. It finds man out exactly as science wishes him to be found out, that is, as a being growing upwards to higher modes of life which are conditioned by his present conduct. It brings before him a responsibility to his fellows, which death, so far from terminating, only intensifies. It makes judgment a very searching and personal matter, and allies it with the perfect justice and eternal purposes of God. It gives special sacredness and power to common things, and makes the ideas of the duty of citizens and neighbours to be larger and more fruitful of good. It holds before men that hope of self-culture and improvement which apart from God and immortality is so unspeakably selfish, non-human, and futile. And lastly it is in accordance with what common sense teaches men to think as concerning their own immortality. Left to themselves they do not, even when religious, think much of the future world, and they are right not to do so. As with Christ, so with all who are most true to the best instincts of their nature—present duties, hopes, and responsibilities fill the mind with thoughts enough to occupy their attention and maintain their interest in sufficient and worthy objects. But with all this the future life is felt as well, and that all the more powerfully for good because its impressions are vague and transient. It cheers, but only at specially dark moments; it blesses, but only at times of exceeding sadness; it explains, but only when disappointment is unwontedly heavy; it is the firm ground which men touch when the floods come over the soul, and whence they rise to work and hope once more; lastly, it forms the background of the picture of human life to which men rarely look, though they are never without the consciousness of its existence.

To conclude. Let science set herself to reform man's belief in his own immortality, instead of engaging in the unnatural and hopeless task of destroying it.

RELIGION AND FACT.

THE object of this essay is to examine the relations between religious beliefs and the doctrine held strenuously and enforced vigorously by the whole tenor of modern thought, that fact can only be proved by fact, and that religion has no claims upon the allegiance of men except so far as it can be shown to rest upon this basis.

Now the proposition that fact can only be proved by fact forces us to ask two questions—" What do we mean by fact?" and "What is the proof which fact alone can give?" By fact I understand that which has been presented to the mind through the medium of the organs of sensation.* This definition does, indeed, require to be somewhat elaborated in order to meet the various details which seem at first sight not to fall within its scope. For instance, there are things, such as the fact of a man being angry or sorry, which cannot in the strictest sense of the words be proved through the senses, but the existence of which we nevertheless believe in only because we are assured by some outward marks or words which experience invariably associates with them. Or, again, there are facts which have come within

---

*The facts of our own internal self-consciousness are not here included as not coming within the scope of this essay. I doubt whether they are really distinct from other so-called objective facts, the consciousness of self alone excepted.

the perception of other persons, and which we accept as true upon their evidence. In this case once more the basis of knowledge is the presentation of facts through the senses to the mind, only that the perception by the original witness is transferred by the act of belief to ourselves, and becomes as it were our own. Of course, this act of belief opens another door to the possibility of our being mistaken; still, so long as we do believe, the fact is as much a fact as though we had witnessed it ourselves, and we act upon it subject to this increased possibility of error. There are also what may be called composite facts—that is to say, something abstracted by the intellect from an immense number of events or individual things, and summed up in one word. The Reformation, for instance, may be called a fact because it is a word used to describe the course or tendency or meaning of a long series of events, but in this case, as in all others, the ultimate basis upon which all knowledge rests is that some one was made aware of individual facts by the organs of sense.

Then, next, we inquire, What do facts thus explained prove? As I write these words I become conscious of a certain number of bits of straw lying in the roadway in front of my window. What does that fact prove? I answer, it proves itself—that is, that there is straw lying as I have described; and secondly, it proves its own possibility—that is, that straw may lie and may have lain where I see it. In other words, each separate fact as presented to consciousness can, taken by itself, only prove its own existence, together with the possibility of similar facts to itself. Taken in combination with other facts, of course each may prove an innumerable quantity of laws or truths or generalisations.

My pieces of straw, for instance, when combined with the fact that the collector has just left the parochial demand for rates, may suggest unpleasant truths as to the advantages of that local self-government under which it is our privilege as Englishmen to exist. Or, they may illustrate the operation of the law of gravitation. But in all cases I repeat that when it is said that fact proves fact, we mean that each separate fact begins by proving itself, and then is ready to be taken into combination with other facts and prove whatever the laws of reasoning, as summed up under the heads of Induction and Deduction, will enable or allow it to prove. And let me observe that, by submitting religion to a test of this description, we are not in the least degrading it, but doing it the best service that we can. For if there be anything in the world to which the term divine may be properly affixed, or which may be truly said to be the operation of God, it is facts. My pieces of straw may be insignificant in themselves, but they are at least a real something and may be used to explain or illustrate a thousand truths—mathematical, scientific, artistic, moral, and religious. Or, what is even more, they may ask us a hundred questions which we cannot solve, and some few of which, lying as they do beyond the limits of the knowable, bring us face to face with God. A fact is, indeed, that which, because it comes to me from without and from a power other than myself, is to me as the works or voice of God. Once existing, it has become part of the eternal order of things, and transcends the limits of time, which may cause it to cease to exist, but cannot take away the fact that it has existed. There is, therefore, an infinite seriousness about that which is, or that which has been done, or that which has happened, which constrains the mind in the direction of religion, obliges it to confess a Power that is the Master and Author of facts, and even induces it to pay a reverent worship, though it may be only of the "silent sort," at the altar of the unknown God.

I do not put forward this explanation as altogether adequate, still less as original. I merely desire to have some statement of the meaning of the dictum, "fact alone proves fact," which may enable us to examine the doctrines of religion by its light, and which also satisfies the just requirements of positive thought. But it is difficult to imagine a more rigorous definition than the one just given, and certainly if anybody can invent one I shall be glad to know it. To pay homage to facts, and to accept nothing as true but what may legitimately be derived from them by the strictest processes of scientific reasoning, is imperative upon all who wish to treat religious subjects in a way that will secure a hearing in the first instance, and command assent in the second. Let us now proceed to consider how far and in what sense that which is called natural religion is based upon facts.

Natural religion is that effort by which the mind of man, by dint of dwelling upon himself and his circumstances, endeavours to attain to conceptions of God. And in common with all ultimate human thought it arrives at this conclusion —that there is something unknowable in the origin and constitution of things which it calls by the name of God. However much men may disagree, and however far they may advance beyond this, yet, practically, this definition seems to represent the point from which they all start. It is moreover, as it stands, merely a negative idea, the positive fact consisting simply in this, that something is presented to the mind which the mind in turn refuses to entertain as intelligible. Nor must we allow ourselves to depreciate the importance of this idea, though merely negative. By itself it amounts to nothing, yet it is essential to all positive conceptions of the Deity. If there were nothing that men could not understand—if, indeed, there were nothing that they could not hope at some distant time to understand, then they would be in no need of the idea of God, they would be gods unto themselves. The existence of the unknowable is, therefore, the one indisputable fact which natural religion contributes to the knowledge of God.

But when we are asked to admit further that natural religion is able to furnish us with adequate positive conceptions of God, or even proofs of His existence, then I own that I am entirely unconvinced. Most certainly, if the sense given above to the dictum "fact alone proves fact" be correct, then I deny absolutely that any proof can be given by natural religion that deserves for one moment the description of scientific. The existence of God is never presented to the mind by objective facts of an ordinary character. He never, if I may so speak, proves Himself in nature. No doubt the mind, arguing from what it sees around, may form conceptions of God, and no doubt, also, these conceptions may possibly be true, and may certainly exercise a most beneficial effect for the time being. But scientific proof there is none, and unfortunately this is just the proof that the mind of man, having drunk deep of the joy that comes of absolute demonstration, is becoming more and more resolved to demand. This has, indeed, been disputed in an article in the newspaper—the *Spectator*—which contains perhaps, the best theological thinking of the day. The argument was briefly this. Every specific organ is correlated, as the eye with light, with some external arrangement, without which it could not have existed. Hence the desire or hunger after God implies the existence of food to satisfy it; or the faculty of conscience bears witness to some really external Judge, who is with us and knows us. Now, to this it is obvious to reply that it rests not upon direct evidence, but upon analogy—at best a somewhat precarious foundation. We know that hunger is correlated with food, or the eye with light, because we have direct immediate knowledge of both food and light; whereas, in the other instance, a supposed necessity, derived from what we know to be true elsewhere, is the only basis of our belief. Again, it is only in a metaphorical sense that we can speak of the desire of God as a function, or of conscience as a faculty. What is the source of actual hunger, or what is the organ called the eye, we know quite well; they are separate conditions or parts of the human frame adapted for specific purposes. But the others are mere descriptions of the power of thought applied to certain objects of thought, which may or may not have a real existence. The fear of ghosts does not imply that ghosts have any existence; the intense desire for turning baser metals into gold does not assure us that it was ever accomplished. And, lastly, as a mere matter of history, the belief in God is always connected with and derived from some supernatural revelation. From the dawn of thought men have, whether rightly or wrongly makes no matter to the argument, believed in outward manifestations of the Deity, and have transmitted this belief to their posterity.

From this condition of things, it seems to me at once idle and, indeed, impossible to try and emancipate ourselves. The idea of revealed religion, of some outward proof or manifestation of God, is prior to the idea of natural religion. Men begin by giving an objective reality and positive character to that unknowable element in themselves and in the world which is almost the first fact presented to them, which is presented, indeed, in greatly exaggerated forms. This attempt to go back to a state of so-called nature, and to discover what man apart from his history does or would believe concerning religion, is only part of a wide-spread error. Mr Maine, to take one instance, has made us familiar with its working in the domain of law. " Rousseau's belief," he says, " was that a perfect social order could be evolved from the unassisted consideration of the social state, or social order, wholly irrespective of the actual condition of the world and wholly unlike it. It is not worth our while to analyse with any particularity that philosophy of politics, art, education, ethics, and social relation which was constructed on the basis of a state of nature. It still possesses singular fascination for the looser thinkers of every country, and is no doubt the parent, more or less remote, of almost all the prepossessions which impede the historical method of inquiry." To this list I venture to add religion, and to affirm that all men's positive convictions concerning the nature of God, as a Being who governed and judged them, were derived from a revelation of Himself, real or supposed, under objective forms. Hence the true method in religion, as in the other branches of knowledge enumerated by Mr Maine, is the historical, and our business is to examine both the nature of the various

Revelations and the proofs by which they are supported. And if on the one hand the consciousness of the fact of the unknowable has been the fruitful source of the most grovelling superstitions, so on the other hand must it be remembered that it creates a legitimate expectation that facts will be forthcoming to explain it in accordance with all known analogy. There is, therefore, no *à priori* improbability for a Revelation, but the reverse.

Now, this Revelation is of course founded upon facts that have occurred, or have been supposed to occur, within the experience of men. He who accepts the Revelation believes that the unknowable has, so to speak, translated itself into facts in order to meet the moral and intellectual necessities of mankind. This belief will be acquired, as I have elsewhere maintained, not by means of intellectual arguments, but by virtue of moral predispositions. These predispositions again it is the business of Christians to create, as well by their lives and teachings as by a careful and candid examination of the facts which Revelation presents to them. Candour is, indeed, the one conspicuously-absent feature in the writings of Christian apologists: the very assumption that they have already exhausted the meaning of the facts, and are precluded by some dogmatic authority from re-examining them in the light of modern thought, exposes them to the contempt (very often unmerited) of scientific thinkers. If we wish to recommend Revelation to the minds of men, the best course we can adopt in these days will be to consider and develop the true meaning and real moral value of the events upon which it claims to rest. This may be done in many ways. Thus the unwillingness to believe anything avowedly supernatural may be balanced by calling attention to the fact that, if this be so, then religion as a positive conception and a moral power becomes impossible. It is always best that the true alternative should be plainly presented in the interests of truth itself. If men can escape from their dislike of the supernatural into the region of an unnatural and unhistorical Deism, they will on the one hand never do justice to the strength of their religious instincts, and on the other never have the courage of their opinions by proclaiming non-Theism as the only rational attitude of the human mind towards the unknowable. Logical indecision in matters of opinion is adverse to the progress of truth alike in the judgment of science and religion.

But this indecision must not be confounded with another disposition of mind towards Revelation which is sometimes alleged as a fault against Christian believers, but which examination of facts enables us to defend as rational and becoming. If there be even the trace of a suspicion lurking in the mind that the Revelation is not true, then both the belief in it and the practice founded upon that belief become hypothetical; and science, we are told, abhors hypotheses. I doubt very much indeed whether science does anything of the kind, and I am sure that in certain departments of thought and action hypothetical belief may be our wisest course for the present. This attitude of mind may be explained as the feeling which enables a man to say, "I believe in Revelation now, but looking at the tendency of thought around me I cannot be certain that I should believe in it a hundred years hence; at any rate, in the form in which I do now." Granting the existence of the unknowable, then, an hypothesis which explains it in a manner sufficient for the (present) moral necessities of man certainly falls within the express approval of no less a name than that of Locke himself. "Not that we may not," he says, "to explain any phenomena of nature, make use of any probable hypothesis whatsoever. But we should not take them up too hastily, till we have very well examined particulars, and made several experiments in that thing which we would explain by our hypothesis, and see whether it will agree to them all; whether our principles will carry us quite through, and not be as inconsistent with one phenomenon of nature as they seem to accommodate and explain another, and at least that we take care that the name of principles deceive us not, nor impose on us by making us receive that for an unquestionable truth which is really at best but a very doubtful conjecture."

Locke is here thinking and speaking of "natural" science, but it needs no excuse in these days to claim to apply his method to all phenomena whatsoever; to the mind of man as seen whether in the history of the race or the character of the individual. We are not only justified in acting as though revelation was true, but in examining the facts upon which it rests as though they actually took place. It may be that when thus tested the hypothesis may fail to recommend itself either morally or intellectually to the mind that has provisionally adopted it. If, for instance, the effect is merely to create mysteries for the mind to accept, instead of throwing light upon difficulties with which it has hitherto struggled in vain, then the Revelation stands condemned as insufficient for the very purposes for which it was hypothetically accepted. And yet it is difficult to deny that this has been the result of theology taken as a whole, and so the necessity of a further and closer and more rational examination of the facts becomes at once apparent. Most assuredly the rejection of the facts of Revelation is not as a rule accompanied by any thorough appreciation of their meaning and use; but then whose fault is this? The Christianity that has to recommend itself to modern thought, weighted with the incubus of—to take the worst case out of many bad ones—the doctrines of the Church of Rome, may well be ashamed to cast the blame upon any one save those who profess to be its champions and exponents.

This, again, suggests another branch of the great inquiry into facts—namely, the consideration of the relations between Christianity and other religions professing to be historical, that is, to rest upon events in which God revealed Himself by supernatural methods. And here we should be called upon to realise what Christianity is in respect of time and extent. When the comparatively late appearance of Christianity in the world is insisted upon, it is really necessary to remember that it claims to be coeval with the dawn, if not of thought, at least of history. A notion seems to prevail that men can obtain for themselves a certain amount of natural religion, which God then steps in to supplement and explain by Revelation. I can only say that if this be true, then I for one should be compelled to abandon the belief in Revelation as at once unscientific in itself, and as unnecessary for the civilisation and development of man. The religion that claims at this time to be the only religion adapted for civilised man claims also a continuous descent from days in which men were preserved by outward methods in the belief of the true God, and in which one man was specially chosen to propagate this belief by means of a posterity governed by the direct interposition of God himself. It will be observed that the stress of this argument is not in the least affected by the question as to whether these providential and miraculous events took place, upon which I offer no opinion whatever. It is enough for my present purpose to point out that men have not, as an historical fact, elaborated their religion for themselves by any process of reasoning or inquiry, and that every iota of the Christian religion is at this present moment based upon a long series of supernatural events, which trace their origin back to the time of the call of Abraham, and even beyond that. Whether these events are true, whether some are true and some not, in what the miraculous element consists—all these, and many more, are questions of the gravest import; but it admits of no question at all that the men who have built up the Christian religion from the time when Abraham left his father's home, down to the half million or so of last Sunday's preachers, have laid its foundations upon the revelation of Himself in history, which they believe that God has given.

This, men will exclaim, is a hard saying. I admit, indeed, that I have purposely made the assertion as broad and sweeping as I could, in order to challenge attention to a fact or state of things, the true importance of which is surely very far from being appreciated as it deserves to be. But I go on to guard myself against obvious attacks, not by modifying this assertion, but by explaining it. And first it may be said that I am drawing a broad line of distinction between Christianity and other religions just at the time when the whole object of scientific research is to trace affinities and resemblances. To which may be added the still more serious charge of throwing unmerited contempt upon the latter with a view of obtaining equally unmerited reputation for the former. That this charge is painfully true of much Christian advocacy I do not deny, and we must be content to share the blame which attaches to the community that permits, encourages, and rewards such a line of argument. But for myself I disavow it with the utmost energy. To begin with, other religions resemble the Christian in nothing more than in this, that they too have felt the necessity of believing that the unknown God has made himself known by special revelation. Their doctrines and their morality, no less than ours, are traced upwards to the deeds or words of divine or divinely-inspired beings, who at some time or other, or at more times than one, in the history of their religion, have been commissioned by outward signs to speak in the name of God. And it ought to be at once our duty and our pleasure to acknowledge the vast amount of moral good which has thus been contributed to the sum of human virtue and happiness. But then it will be asked in what do they differ from Christianity, or in what do its special claims upon our homage consist?

Now, this is just one of those questions that can be answered by nothing short of that examination of facts for which I plead. But the general principle which will be established as the foundation of the distinction between the two, lies upon the surface, and admits of being succinctly stated. The morality of other religions is relative and temporary; that of Christianity is absolute and permanent. Or, to put it in another form, the teaching and the actions attributed to God are in the latter case identical with our highest moral conceptions of power and goodness, whereas in the former they are not; the morality of the Old Testament being of course viewed as imperfect in itself, but necessary in the religious education of man. Whether or no this distinction can be ultimately proved to exist remains for the present doubtful; but there is a consideration connected with the extent of Christianity which gives an enormous *à priori* probability that it can. I am alluding to the distinction between progressive and non-progressive nations, concerning which I will once more quote the words of Mr Maine, because the history of law comes, on the whole, nearest to that of religion, and the same facts are available for the study of both alike. He observes that nothing is more remarkable than the extreme fewness of those progressive societies with which alone the student of the history of law is concerned. "In spite of overwhelming evidence, it is most difficult for a citizen of Western Europe to bring thoroughly home to himself the truth that the civilisation which surrounds him is a rare exception in the history of the world. The tone of thought common among us, all our hopes, fears, and speculations, would be materially affected if we had before us the relation of the progressive races to the totality of human life. It is indisputable that much the greatest part of mankind has never shown a particle of desire that its civil institutions should be improved since the moment when external completeness was first given to them by their embodiment in some permanent record. The difference, however, between the stationary and progressive societies is one of the great secrets which inquiry has yet to penetrate."

Let us now carefully observe what the facts have been in respect of the religion of these two classes of societies up to the present time. They may be summed up as follows:— First, Christianity is at this moment the religion of all progressive races. Not only has it shared this progress, but at more than one memorable crisis in their history it has been the mainspring of human energy and endeavour. Second, the other religions of progressive societies have decayed in almost exact ratio to their improvement in nearly every department of thought and action. All the wisdom and virtue of ancient Greece and Rome failed alike to retain a belief in the old religion, or to elaborate a new one which should take its place. Third, the immense proportion of stationary societies have not been Christian. In religion, as in science, art, or law, they have neither made nor desired any advance beyond a certain point. There is something in Christianity with which they have no sympathy, and so they have rejected it—a very different statement, be it observed, from the one usually made, that the rejection of Christianity is the cause of their want of progress. Fourth, the reception of Christianity by non-progressive races is due to special causes. The Slavonic nations, for instance, if they or any of them are to be numbered among the stationary races, may be pronounced to have the seeds and elements of a future civilisation; whereas the Christianity of people like the negroes is at most an external covering, its real spiritual influence, wherever it exists being due to the perpetual and overpowering contact of superior races. At any rate, this much is certainly true:

that the Christian religion shares for good or for evil the fate of all the elements of progress in whatever nations of the world it exists, and so appears *à priori* to have a real and natural affinity with them. It is consistent with the tiny ray of light that shines amidst the darkness of Abyssinia, and it manages, though it must be admitted, with steps at times somewhat faltering and laggard, to keep its place in the march of human progress amidst the blaze of civilisation and knowledge of Western Europe and North America.

Now, it is difficult to account for facts such as these except upon the supposition of some essential difference between Christianity and other religions. Why is it that, in the case of stationary races, the cause of their want of progress is attributed by the best thinkers in no small degree to religious influences? Why is it, on the other hand, that from the days of Abraham onward religion has been the exciting cause of some of the greatest revolutions through which the progressive races have advanced on the pathway of civilisation? Contrast, for instance, Christianity in this respect with two of the most splendid and beneficial systems of religion that the world has known. Hellenic Paganism may be called—though I greatly distrust these symmetrical definitions, and only adopt this one as being in common use—the religion of beauty, the worship of God under artistic forms. Like all religions, it professed to have its origin in events and actions; like all religions, except one, there came to it a time when these were unable to abide the test of criticism and of moral philosophy. And yet while the old beliefs perished and no new ones took their place, it must never be forgotten that the original source and ground of all religion remained exactly as it had ever been; or, rather, it became intensified, and gained in reality and power. The men who shattered into pieces the legends of Greek mythology did not get rid of the unknowable. On the contrary, then as now, the more they discovered, the further they penetrated, the more firmly they grasped the limits of that which man can know,—so much the more clearly did the unknowable rise before them, the more mysterious and awe-inspiring became the secrets of God, of life, and thought and goodness. Like explorers in a new country, they caught glimpses of strange things, which filled them with curiosity and wonder, and yet one by one, whether with the plaintive acquiescence of Aristotle or the pathetic earnestness of Plato, they came back to say that there were no means available to man for penetrating into that unknown land of silence and of God. And so the old mystery remained, while the old explanations, having done their work, died away. It was no rhetorical adroitness, but the simple instinct of truth itself, that caused St Paul to sum up the religion of Pagan antiquity in the words of the inscription he noticed at Athens, "There is a God, but we do not know Him."

The second instance to which I am alluding is the religion of Buddha, though this might more properly be called a philosophy of goodness illustrated in actual life. And it is an instance in some respects specially adapted for purposes of comparison, because it has exerted an influence almost as wide, as lasting, as searching, and as beneficial as Christianity itself. I entirely repudiate any wish to institute comparisons between the two merely for the purpose of praising Christianity at the expense of Buddhism. But the plain instincts of historical criticism compel us to ask for a reason for the simple fact that, whereas Paganism ceased to be the religion of progressive, Buddhism has remained the religion of stationary, races. Why is it that both alike are so plainly distinguished from Christianity? The more we insist upon the likeness which they bear to it the more incumbent upon us does it become to find some explanation for this fact. We are accustomed to be told that all religions have a relative and transitory value, and that the world stands in need of what is good in all. The affinities of Christianity with, say, the Stoical philosophy, or Rabbinical morality, or Buddhism itself, are clearly pointed out, and much insisted upon. I accept all this, and ask still more urgently why Christianity is what it is now, the religion of the civilised or progressive nations of the world. There are, indeed, things with which we can compare it, but not religions. Greek art and philosophy, Roman law, Germanic family life (together with positive science) are spiritually imperishable; they have been adopted by modern civilisation, and become its component and vivifying elements. To account for this we say that they are all based upon some absolute truth or other; some rightness of method; some conformability to fact, to nature, and to law. But then that form of the old Hebrew religion which we call Christianity has fared exactly as they have, and it seems strange to refuse to attribute the same fact to the same causes. At any rate, it enables the Christian believer to assert that his religion owes its success to this alone: that the events upon which it is founded were real occurrences in the history of the world, and form a true and adequate revelation of the character, the relations, and the intentions of God towards mankind. And thus the burden of proving the contrary is thrown upon those who deny this assertion.

A very common and popular objection to this view of things fills me, I own, with simple astonishment. Believers in the historical truthfulness of the Christian records are derided for their love of the supernatural, and it is asserted that to rely upon miraculous events is dishonouring to religion, and to the humanity that is supposed to stand in need of them. I readily admit, of course, that in coming to a conclusion as to the value of the evidence, men may be deceived by their wish that their own opinions may be proved to be true. This is a temptation which we share with all investigators in every branch of learning, and truth is for the most part advanced by men who urge upon public attention one side of the case or one aspect of the facts. The severely judicial temper is rare in all departments of thought, and, owing at once to the nature of the evidence and the magnitude of personal interests involved, it is especially rare in religion. But the further assertion that a belief in the miraculous is *à priori* foolish, or that a miraculous element dishonours religion, is to me quite unintelligible, when the subject is regarded in a scientific point of view. Our business is not to decide what seems to us the best kind of religion, or in what way we should like to think that it was originated in the heart of man: it has simply to ask, as a mere matter of fact, whether miracles have or have not occurred. There are some to whom the possibility of the miraculous appears most necessary and beneficial; there are others to whom it appears in the exactly opposite light. But whatever may be our prepossessions, and however strongly they may sway our minds, we are not to be told that *à priori* considerations of this kind settle the matter. Let us know what happened, and then we shall know what is the true source and real meaning of religion. The history of what is supernatural claims our attention like anything else that purports to be true, and requires investigation at our hands. In some sort it comes to us as a fact already, because it rests upon a large amount of evidence; because it has influenced myriads of human beings; because lastly, if true, it carries with it the most important results to our own lives and conduct. Whether it be believed to be true or not, let us accept the conclusion that seems most reasonable, provided always that we accept with it all the tremendous results that flow of necessity either from a rejection of the supernatural or from a belief in it. The *à priori* convictions of any one man may be to him a very good reason for taking one side or the other upon a still disputed issue, but they are merely impertinent when they assume to decide the question by the summary process of abstract definitions as to what is right, or best, or worthy of God, or suitable to man. Surely the time has come when propositions of this nature may be banished from religion as they have been from science, and men may be content to discover what God ought to do by the humble and patient method of inquiring what He has done. Let them take sides as seems to them good, but not, therefore, confound their subjective beliefs with absolute truths, or make their private ideas the measure of the actions and character of God.

The account, then, that I would give of the origin of

religion is briefly this: Man, from the very first, is conscious of the existence of something he cannot understand, and, down to the very last, this consciousness not only continues but increases. Its modern expression may be seen in the philosophy of Mr Mill, who says "that on the inmost nature of the thinking principle, as well as on the inmost nature of matter, we are, and with our present faculties must always remain, entirely in the dark." Next, this unknowable gives rise to an immediate belief in the existence of God. Then God is believed to have revealed Himself in facts or events, and thus, what was formerly a negative assumption becomes a positive belief. Lastly, a religion of morality and practice is founded upon the character and dealings of God as revealed in His real or supposed actions, and having gained this clue, it becomes possible to explain nature, history, and man himself from the religious no less than from the physical point of view. It is necessary, however, to add at this point a word of explanation. Although man, it may be urged, can by his unassisted strength form no adequate conception of God, yet he can form, and as a matter of experience always has formed, a conception of a Being in some way resembling himself. This is of course true. Man cannot transcend the limits of his own experience, and God, however made known, will always be imagined as a tendency towards some human perfection, whether of outward majesty or supreme power or moral excellence. But I cannot see that the foregoing argument is in any way affected by this truth, all important as it is. It is equally reasonable *à priori* to say, "men must think of God as in some way like themselves, therefore the highest effort of their imagination was to create a perfect character in Jesus Christ;" or to say, "men must think of God as in some way like themselves, therefore God revealed Himself as perfect man." The question to be decided is, which of the two alternatives actually took place; whether, that is, the facts of Christ's life are fictitious, and His character an ideal, shaped in the imagination of His too-devoted followers. Natural religion, we are all agreed, may, and does, invent facts upon which to repose. It may, therefore, have invented the character and actions of Christ as it invented those of Jupiter or Odin. But the moment it has been shown that this is actually the true account of the matter, then, just as in the case of Greek myths, natural religion ceases to have any true knowledge of God. We may part from the Christian conception of His character with even tenfold more reluctance than Plato felt in abandoning the beauties of Greek legend and art, but inexorable science would point out that we have no positive ground for our conception whatever, and God would once more become the unknown God, before whose altar the only acceptable worship that could be offered would be homage of the "silent sort," though practically, who can doubt that it would be at least for generations, if not centuries, to come superstition and fear?

It is necessary that this position should be made perfectly clear. In maintaining that religion, to be effective and permanent, must be based upon objective facts in which God reveals Himself, I am as far as possible from asserting that Revelation depends upon the merely marvellous element which it contains, or that it is merely relative to our faculties, and not an absolute display of

God as He is in His essential moral attributes. I look to history, and I find it there stated that God has made Himself known to man by actions which, if true, convince us that He is; that He is good in our sense of that word; that He is interested in our welfare as our Father, and has displayed that interest by one act of surpassing love and tender mercy. Therefore, my first object must necessarily be to come to some sort of conclusion as to whether this account is true. In what way is this to be accomplished?

This question brings us one step further on the road towards the conclusion at which I have been all along aiming, because it forces us to ask what are the positive objections to receiving the history of supernatural events as true. By the word positive, I mean objections which are based, not upon *à priori* opinions as to what we think ought to be true, but upon scientific examination of the facts presented to us. We find in history certain events, and certain results connected with these events, which have to be accounted for. This may be done either by believing that God was their Author in a supernatural way, or else by asserting that they fall under the general class of supposed miracles which the human mind has in all ages and races been prone to invent. The force of this last argument is, of course, exceedingly great, especially at times like this, when the discovery of general laws governing alike things, events, and even thoughts, is the one great ambition of the human intellect to accomplish. To this, however, it has been answered, with great effect, that the supernatural element in the Christian history is a totally different thing from the same element in other religions, and is not to be accounted for by the same causes. The controversy is, it need not be said, an old one; but it is also exceedingly unsatisfactory and undecisive. Both parties, as usual, succeed in making good their own position. The same forces that have elsewhere produced false miracles are to be seen at work in nearly every page of the Bible. On the other hand, there are other forces also, at least as distinctly visible, which take the Bible quite out of the category of ordinary histories containing miraculous accounts. These are they to which we have already alluded as making Christianity the religion of civilised races. Its moral tone, its sober, measured style, its exact accordance with all the highest thoughts that men can have of God, its duration and extent, above all, its systematic growth and purpose are elements that it is difficult to account for on the hypothesis that its heroes and historians were half-deceived, half-deceivers, more entirely right in their moral ideas, and more entirely wrong in their mental beliefs, than any human beings that ever existed. The result, then, of this controversy, in spite of the ability with which it has been conducted is, on the whole, *nil;* it leaves the matter pretty much where it found it.

But the aspect of the controversy is entirely changed the moment that men condescend to examine the history itself, without any foregone conclusion as to the abstract possibility of the miraculous occurrences. So long as men approach the subject with an avowed conviction that nothing in the world shall convince them that the miraculous can happen, so long their opponents will have a position at least as strong as the arguments to which it is opposed. So long, again, as Christian advocates assume the literal accuracy of every event they find recorded in the Bible, so long will they find themselves committed to all kinds of damaging conclusions. The real scientific interest begins, and with it the real difficulty of the whole question, when we ask ourselves what precisely are the events which, though miraculous, we believe to be true. If men lay aside the attitude of mere opposition, and assume that of candid inquirers, they may put a whole series of questions to which Christianity has, at any rate in England, not attempted to give satisfactory or definite answers. I can imagine these men, still better I can imagine the public mind, which they do but represent, saying as follows:— "Granting, then, that the miracles are possible, we find a great number recorded in the Bible, some of them descending to the lowest level of mere marvels, some of them ascending far above the utmost dreams of the human mind. Which of these are true, or are all true? And why are some to be received and others not? What canons do you lay down by which to determine the true and the false? And what is the precise meaning of those which you retain, and what information do they give us about God? Can you, moreover, give us an account of the mode of operation, or adjust it to modern conceptions of law and modern theories of the mind and of substance? How are miracles affected by the laws of evidence? In one word, can you give us a new theory of the miraculous, a science of the supernatural, a history of the actions of God?"

I do not suppose that any reasonable man will deny that this is a fair account of the attitude assumed, by what may be called the popular mind, towards religion at this present time. Men are by no means disposed to give up Christianity, and their common sense refuses to dismiss the supernatural from history, merely because it appears to militate against a present tendency of human thought, which may possibly prove to have been only relatively true, temporarily useful, and charged, like all its predecessors, with a full cargo of man's prejudices and littleness. But on the other hand, they cannot but see that judgment is going by default. What they want is knowledge based upon an inquiry into facts; what they get on both sides is theory derived from personal predilection or preconception, and making a more ingenious than candid use of the facts it has to deal with. Perhaps, indeed, the time is not yet fully come; certainly the man competent to answer this craving for knowledge has not appeared. He must be a man of reverent disposition, thoroughly imbued with the spirit of positive thought, acquainted with the histories of religions, swift to see analogies, patient to investigate, apt to generalise, above all, careless of the hard names with which he will certainly be at first assailed. But assuredly this does not prevent men, however humble alike in capacity and aim, from making those preliminary attempts which are the necessary precursors of final success. Every detected mistake stops one avenue of error; every confessed failure suggests another and a better way; every imperfect argument calls attention to the missing link; every refutation of accepted but erroneous beliefs clears the ground for some better explanation. It is in this spirit that I propose to investigate some aspects of the miraculous element contained in the Bible, and to attempt some sort of answer to the question everywhere addressed to us; "What are the facts upon which the Christian religion rests, and why are we to believe them?"

But any hesitation which I might feel at attempting such a task with powers so inadequate, is more than removed when I survey the actual state of Christian opinion, and notice the way in which the Christianity of the past, with the full approbation of the Christianity of the present, has dealt with the grave and serious question, "What are the facts to which revealed religion makes her appeal?" The sight fills me with astonishment and indignation, and then *facit indignatio verba.* This is what has happened. The Bible contains a great number of alleged supernatural events, some of them approaching to the grotesque, as, for instance, the speaking of Balaam's ass; others so "caught up" into the divine that the merely marvellous element disappears in the moral grandeur of the action, as, for instance, the Resurrection of Jesus Christ, or the Conversion of St Paul. All these have been accepted as equally true, and the attempt to draw distinctions between one and the other has been denounced as fatal to all. But then, as many of these events derived no support from the rules of historical evidence, or from their moral significance, it was perceived that some external anthority was needed. Whereupon the doctrine was laid down, or was assumed, or grew up, I know not how, that the Bible could not possibly contain any statement not exactly and literally true; so that—I beg the attention of even the most cursory reader to this—every statement in the Bible, whether of opinion, or argument, or calculation, or of mere remark upon subjects of passing interest, was elevated into the region of fact, and became the unquestioned basis of theological science. Then a step further was taken. It was seen that the human intellect could, by process of ordinary logic, derive certain abstract truths from the words of Scripture assumed to be absolutely true; hence metaphysical abstractions concerning God took their place among undoubted facts, and dogma became essential to the Christian faith. But dogma implies an authority, just as an infallible book requires an interpreter; and, therefore, a Pope, or the Universal Church, or, more modestly among Protestants, articles which should be binding upon the members of each church, grew into being, and all that huge and heterogeneous and contradictory multitude of canons, decrees, creeds, institutes, articles, homilies, trust-deeds, under which religion groans in vain, was added to the already portentous mass of supposed facts. And lastly, with that daring logic which fascinates the noblest spirits and wins a passing tribute of admiration from the sternest opponents, the Roman Church saw instinctively that this mass was but dead and dissoluble matter unless the spirit of a living guide was breathed into it, and so, as the ultimate outcome of Christian development, we have an infallible Pope. And then we wonder that religion is discredited in an age of positive thought, and fall to and abuse the Rationalist or the Sceptic as the author of that dark cloud of suspicion and doubt which is descending upon the world, so that all hearts begin to "gather blackness."

Let us review the position. On the one hand we have a demand for positive facts, and a challenge addressed to religion to say distinctly what are the facts upon which she relies. On the other, I gladly admit that Christianity has always more or less clearly perceived that this challenge was a fair one, and has alleged facts in support of her claims. It is this alone which, among all her aberrations from the truth, spite of all her halting paces and timid concessions, has enabled her to retain a place in civilisation and to exercise her enormous spiritual influence for good upon the heart of men. Furthermore, there are a few events, in the number of those which she accepts, of such overwhelming moral significance that these alone would be sufficient for every religious purpose, especially in days when scientific thought, just in proportion as it detracts from the power of believing in miracles, adds to the power of miracles when believed. But to these she has added, as articles of faith, as follows :—First, a number of stories of no moral importance and no historical value. Second, thousands upon thousands of statements of writers believed to be inspired and incapable of error upon, at any rate, religious subjects. Third, all the metaphysical abstractions which human ingenuity could frame from these data and persuade the Church to accept. Fourth, the articles binding upon separate churches. Fifth, the utterances of the Pope binding upon a large and not decreasing number of Christian people. And, encumbered with all this vast array of mostly non-combatant followers, she has to confront the spirit of an age which delights to reduce every branch of knowledge to the fewest possible principles, and which will assuredly say of religion that miracles, like essences, *non sunt multiplicanda.*

To all which I confidently reply that, as there is no knowledge save that which comes from undoubted facts, so there is no authority save that which proves the facts to my mind and approves them in my heart. When St Paul went forth to preach the gospel of man's redemption, he went as one who had been brought face to face with the most tremendous events in human history. He needed no other commission than his knowledge of what had happened; he claimed no other authority than to recommend what he knew to the consciences of men; the very idea of dogma had no place in the mind of one who remembered his Master's word, "We speak that we do know, and testify that we have seen"—who himself could say, "I delivered unto you that which I also received"—whose brother Apostle could say, "that which was from the beginning, which we have heard, which we have seen with our eyes, which we have looked upon, and our hands have handled, of the Word of Life (for the life was manifested, and we have seen it and bear witness, and show unto you that eternal life which was with the Father and was manifested unto us); that which we have seen and heard declare we unto you, that ye also may have fellowship with us." In other words, the preachers of Christ acted as every human being who has contributed anything to man's improvement or happiness has been obliged to act by the unchanging law of nature. That is, they bore witness to the truth they knew, in the full assurance that truth would be its own authority. Let me illustrate this by instances taken from the famous men of one nation only—our own.

Shakespeare looked into the height and depth of human nature, and saw well-nigh all the actual workings of human passion and thought. He came back to tell us what he had seen, and we believe him, not because he said it, but because his words interpret all our own experience, reduce to law a mere chaos of objects more or less clearly perceived, throw light upon dark places, explain ourselves to ourselves, harmonise with what we know of beauty and pleasure; in a word, make facts known to us. Newton caught sight of a law that fills all space, and also explains the movements of all phenomena: we believe him because, once more, though by a different method, we can assure ourselves that demonstrable fact lies at the foundation of all he said. Edmund Burke looked into the facts that bind polities together, and we have paid him the greatest honour that man can receive by accepting his thoughts as the informing and guiding spirit of the English Constitution, not because he—a party politician—uttered them, but because our experience has stamped them as true and useful for our national life and order. We might go on to speak of Watt or Adam Smith, each in different spheres of thought, catching a vision of facts and translating them into instruments and rules, which our experience verifies and adopts. But I mention one illustrious name worthy to be ranked among famous Englishmen who have revealed truth to mankind. Mr Mill has discerned the true source and conditions of knowledge, of logic as the science of knowing, and more and more we begin to see that the basis of a lasting union between philosophy and science has been laid by him and others like him in our own days. Is there, then, no hope that a similar work may not be accomplished between science and religion, viewed, that is, as a revelation of facts? Is the shadow that darkens the face of Revelation a mere temporary obscuration of the splendour of the mid-day sun, or is that sun hastening to its grave amidst the clouds that are gathering in the western sky? I know not; but this I do know, that they who are endeavouring to face the facts of the case without fear and without bias, will be able to submit to the result, whatever it may be, with dignity and patience. They will have, indeed, if so it must be, to accustom themselves to the gray twilights of a world in which God has never revealed Himself by any act that could be specially called His, or attributed to His will in any strictly personal sense. They may, if they like, continue to call Him Father, but not a Father who has given His only and beloved Son for the sake of His other children, and they may meditate on immortality, but hardly pretend to believe in it. They will part from the ancient faith with reluctance and regret, but still they will part from it, if they needs must, and begin with silent heart yet resolute to repair once more that ruined altar of the unknown God, which a noble but mistaken spirit broke in pieces at Athens with a few wonder-working words, based, as he thought, upon what God had done. I think, indeed, that even the opponents of Revelation as a record of supernatural events will, in that the day of their victory, not grudge their captives the pleasure of recalling the beautiful legends of the olden days when men believed in a God who had suffered with them and conquered for them in the person of Jesus Christ. Nay, it may even be that they will ask us to sing one of the songs of Zion in that "strange land" of silence unbroken by the voice of the living God. The words of one such song come across my mind as prophetic now of what men will feel then, and with them I conclude :—

> " There was a time when meadow, grove, and stream,
> The earth, and every common sight
>   To me did seem
> Apparell'd in celestial light,
> The glory and the freshness of a dream.

It is not now as it hath been of yore;
Turn wheresoe'er I may,
By night or day,
The things which I have seen I now can see no more.

" The rainbow comes and goes,
And lovely is the rose;
The moon doth with delight
Look round her when the heavens are bare;
Waters on a starry night
Are beautiful and fair;
The sunshine is a glorious birth,
But yet I know, where'er I go,
That there hath pass'd away a glory from the earth."

THE MIRACLES OF GOD.

THE attempt to treat the subject of religion by what may be called the Positive method, subjects those who make it to several inevitable difficulties, and is of necessity accompanied by conditions which render it distasteful to many religious minds. Especially we seem to miss those tendencies of human thought and devotion which give birth to and animate large and idealistic phrases, such as "Christ dwelling in man;" "the universal Fatherhood of God;" "the revelation of God to the conscience;" "the communion of the soul with its Maker;" "the inspiration of man by God's spirit." I am very sensible of this, the more so as it is by phrases such as these that religious life is kept alive: they contain elements of poetry, metaphysics, romance, and sentiment which are not only essential to religion, but which are in some sort its highest and most genuine intellectual efforts. But on the other hand, we may be permitted to remark that science also has its aspect of poetry and awe; and that, if sentiment and idealism are to be of any use whatever, they must repose upon a substratum of facts. I think it of so much importance that this truth should be clearly apprehended that I will go on to make my meaning clear by means of an illustration.

At the close of his account of the story of the golden

calf, and of the intercession of Moses with God which followed it, Professor Ewald writes as follows: "A glorious picture, perfect in its kind, and full of eternal truth, if only it be not treated as dry historical fact." Now there are minds so constituted—I confess mine to be one of them—to which this saying appears to be nothing short of high treason against the majesty of truth. To many persons the word eternal represents that which has never happened; is, indeed, incapable of happening; is, so to speak, above happening. To science it means all that has happened, together with all the results, hopes, fears, and intimations that have been, or may be, founded upon it. In the first case it amounts to no more than the productions of human imagination and ingenuity; things that men think of as being probable, beautiful, useful, and which would somehow or other suffer degradation if they abandoned the region of thought, and were regarded simply as facts that had occurred. To which science has but one invariable reply: "Probable—when proved; beautiful—if true; useful—so far as actually existing."

No one, I hope, will be foolish enough to object that this cuts at the root of dramatic and epic poetry. Nothing whatever of the sort. These have their abiding beauty and interest because they are pictures of the human soul, and true to the experiences of human life. But then they profess to be nothing more than this, or if the phrase be liked better, to be nothing else than this, whereas the history of the golden calf professes to detail the relations that have subsisted between God and man in history. And everything is true if it is and does that which it professes to be and to do. "Macbeth" is entirely true as a picture of human passion and character; it would become absolutely false if it pretended to recount the history of Scotland. And the word eternal, if by that we mean independence of time, seems to me to be much more accurately applied to truths of the latter than of the former description, to those of history rather than of poetry. For truths of poetry are essentially limited by temporal considerations. Deeper and truer views of human character may be presented to us; or again, those of Shakespeare may vary with the varying minds to which they are addressed, or they may have little value for particular persons or epochs. Whereas an historical fact (there is here happily no question of miracles) remains true eternally; no idiosyncrasy of character, no defect of critical powers, no development of intelligence, no national or local peculiarity can take anything from it or add anything to it. It lies beyond the limit of suspicious phrases, such as "this is true to me," or "this finds me out," or "this expresses my sense of the beautiful." Nor does it need to be pointed out that in the realm of religion, which professes to be a revelation of the dealings of God with man, this eternity of fact is all-important. It makes an immense difference whether Moses did actually, at a great crisis of his people's fate, address to God this intercession, or whether some Jewish poet centuries later painted it as dramatically true and poetically beautiful. In religion, which is the science of life in its relations Godward, we want facts first, and imagination, with all its treasures of worship, idealism, sentiment, and mysticism, afterwards.

Nor can I have the smallest doubt as to what will be the result of the conflict between the two modes of thought, if conflict there is to be. It is not merely that science is powerful enough to carry its own conception of truth into every region of thought, or that the mind of man under its influence is slowly awakening to the tremendous seriousness and absolute necessity of facts, or that this tendency, being as it is the one original contribution of this century to the history of human thought, cannot cease to operate till it has modified religious no less than so-called secular truth. But I take my stand upon the one decisive consideration, that science does not take from religion any power of imagination or idealism which it possessed before, does not interfere with the operation of these two faculties, does not censure or depreciate their productions. The play of the human mind about facts and events would still be as free as ever, provided only it did not pass itself off as being historically true. So far as regards poetry and art, no contradiction could arise: they do not pretend to be true in any sense of which historical criticism could take account. But in religion let it be granted that science busied itself ever so minutely with the facts, that could not destroy the ideal or poetical truths which have been built upon them. I mean this: If the story of the golden calf were reduced to the level of legend, religion as a science of facts would so far cease to exist. But if it were proved to be historical, not one atom of the beauty and power of the narrative would be lost. Why that which purports to be history, and often is of immense historical value, should lose its "eternal truth," if it could be shown to have actually happened, passes my comprehension. I entirely fail to understand how that which is poetical and true in the mind of an unknown Jewish writer becomes "dry" if actually

The Miracles of God. 155

spoken by Moses in the agony of his intercession. And to pass to wider spheres, it is surely equally true that every beautiful or fruitful Christian phrase or idea, such as those I quoted at the outset, can receive no injury from the most careful and prosaic examination of facts. For if they are independent of historical events, as some people like to think, and were derived from the thoughts and emotions of great men, then clearly the reduction of the Old and New Testament alike to the region of fables would not injure them. If, once more, they are really derived from events *falsely* supposed to have taken place, then they are neither beautiful nor fruitful themselves, and must perish, as they deserve to do, at the touch of science. But if, as I believe, they are founded upon real historical events, then the result of scientific investigation will only be to add that touch of positive truth to these large and noble phrases which will enable them to survive even the sceptical tendencies of the nineteenth century.

The question then to be decided is, whether we have in the Bible an account of what God has done by special intervention in the case of one chosen people, or whether we have an account of what that people imagined He had done. And I contend that this question can only be approached—I do not say decided—by the application to it of scientific method in a manner totally different from what has hitherto obtained. This last may be designated, for convenience of classification, the *à priori* method, and I shall proceed, at the risk of seeming to recapitulate what I have said before, to give two or three illustrations of its application and results. I do so in order to distinguish it clearly from the object I have before me in this present essay, and also to show how unsatisfactory the results have been in the way of deciding the question now before us. The course of discussion has been this. Objections have been raised to the possibility or credibility of miracles as such; these have been answered with more or less success as they have appeared; finally, the contest has ended in a drawn battle, neither party being able to convince the other, although, of course, many valuable results have been indirectly arrived at. No less than four such discussions may be mentioned as having taken place.

First, it has been said that there is no trustworthy historical evidence. So far, indeed, as regards the New Testament I have assumed, and shall continue to do so, that, apart from the miraculous element, the evidence is perfectly satisfactory—is, indeed, overwhelming. But the case of the Old Testament is obviously very different. On the one hand we have a continuous history showing one main purpose running throughout its whole course; displaying a noble and progressive morality; joined with exquisite gifts of poetry, eloquence, and prophecy; wonderfully accurate in local details and colouring; strikingly faithful to human nature and character; based upon a conception of the being and attributes of God, which, however its origin be explained, falls little short of the miraculous; finally, written by men impressed with a profound belief in the supernatural interposition of God, and attributing to Him actions entirely worthy of His grandeur and goodness. On the other hand, there is little or no external authority; there are internal difficulties of the most serious character which it is not necessary to particularise in detail; there are stories of, to say the least, the most legendary appearance; there are, above all, suspicious similarities to the temper of mind which has produced the supernatural in other nations. Professor Ewald has made one attempt by omitting, not only miracles, but also details to bridge the gulf, and we have as the result what is no doubt an invaluable account of the general course and spiritual meaning of the history. It is too soon to predict with any certainty the fate of this attempt, but no critic will deny that it is at times arbitrary in the extreme, that it fails to explain many of the phenomena, and that it bears a perilous resemblance to Niebuhr's attempt to re-write the history of ancient Rome.* Nor is it easy to overcome the feeling that his almost unbroken silence on the subject of miracles is like the play of Hamlet with the part of Hamlet omitted. Yet upon one occasion, strangely enough in dealing with the miracles of Elisha, that silence is broken in a passage too significant not to be quoted at length :—

"The province of religion is always the province of miracles also, because it is that of pure and strong faith in the presence of heavenly forces, actively as well as passively; where, therefore, true religion makes the most powerful efforts, there will be a corresponding display of miracles which will either actually take place through the activity of the believing spirit, or will be, at any rate, experienced by the believing heart : while to be vividly penetrated, though only from a distance, with the might of such forces, is in itself a gain. Thus far the age of Elijah and Elisha, when the true religion was obliged to maintain itself with the utmost force against its internal enemies, was as rich in miracles as the days of Moses and Joshua, or the conclusion of the

---

* It may be well to give an instance in passing of what I mean. Professor Ewald describes the character and conduct of Saul with almost as much minuteness as, for instance, Mr Grote delineates Alcibiades. Yet in a note on page 51, volume iii. (English Translation), he says, "The account of the first narrator is probably derived from a drama." What would be said if we should write a history of Henry VIII. founded upon Shakespeare's drama? One feels inclined to exclaim, Oh for an hour of the late Sir G. C. Lewis!

Judges had been; only these miracles do not now, as in the time of Moses and Joshua, affect the whole nation, nor, as in the era of the last Judges, are they directed against a foreign people, but they proceed from a few individual prophets who are compelled, as instruments of the ancient religion, to exert all the greater power, as in the nation itself the true faith threatens to disappear. No such stories can be anything more than scattered traces of a spirit itself miraculous, and of the impressions immediately produced by it; but that there is some spirit of power in religion, to the agency of which they all point, is only the more certain."—(English Translation, vol. iv., page 83.)

No one can say that this is a satisfactory account of the miraculous element. It concedes too much to meet the approval of science and it falls short of the demands of religion. And thus we come round to the old position that those who stumble at the miraculous will reject the evidence, and those who do not, will accept it. One result does, however, emerge from this discussion, which might almost be termed a canon of criticism. It is that the strength of the evidence for miracles is, on the whole, that of the strongest part of the chain, and not, as might be supposed, of the weakest. Once admit that any one miracle, such as a Resurrection, has actually taken place, and the *à priori* objection to any other miracle is removed. But again, the spirit which accepts even a true miracle is so far liable to accept and to record without due caution and inquiry the stories of false ones. I am inclined to fancy that we have in this "canon" a key which may be found to unlock several difficulties.

Secondly, the miracles in the Bible have been objected to on grounds derived from a comparison with the miraculous inventions of other nations. I have alluded to this already, and need not repeat the reasons for my conviction that here again the battle is a drawn one.

The Miracles of God. 159

A third objection, derived from an antecedently supposed impossibility of breaking the laws of nature, may be dismissed with precisely the same remark. Professor Mozley's book is entirely devoted to the task of meeting this and similar *à priori* objections: the idea of examining the miracles themselves, of classifying and arranging them, in a word, of submitting them to an inductive process, never seems to have crossed the mind of the Bampton Lecturer, whose book, nevertheless, purports to be "On Miracles." In the fourth Lecture he distinctly affirms that the proof of miracles depends upon the assumption of a moral and personal God, a concession which, so far at any rate as we are concerned, renders the whole position untenable. If there be such a God as we can, by our unassisted efforts, form an adequate conception of; if that God created the world by an effort of His will and an exercise of His power, then every reasonable man will not deny the possibility that He may, if He pleases, interfere, not, indeed, to suspend the laws of nature, but to produce special results by the agency of His will acting through and upon them. (If I take up a stone, I do not alter the laws of nature, but I do alter the condition of things.) But then this assumption of a creating and sustaining God, possessed of will and purpose, is just that which positive thought refuses to make, and so once more the battle is a drawn one. "Your belief in God," it is answered, "is derived ultimately from the supernatural events with which He has been associated from the dawn of reflection, and therefore the existence of God cannot, as you assert, be admitted to prove the credibility of miracles, while the miracles are by your own confession incapable of proving the existence of God."

And so we go round and round the weary circle of *à priori* argumentation.

The fourth and last objection, however, requires a little careful consideration, because to a certain extent it deals with miracles as they are, and distinguishes between the various events to which the name has been indiscriminately applied. Certain of these, then, it is said, cannot possibly be true, because they are inconsistent with our highest notions of morality, and, therefore, must on no account be ascribed to God. Either they are not true or God did not do them.

Perhaps the real force of this objection will be best observed by taking as an example, not a mere passing story of no great interest or value, but one of moral significance and real importance. Such an example is presented by the account of the rebellion of Korah during the wanderings in the wilderness. Can it be true that God caused the earth to open and swallow up whole families of misguided men and innocent women and children? Our first instinct is to deny it altogether; our second is to ask with some uneasiness whether even thus we get rid of the difficulty. The narrative is, like the Bible stories in general, if regarded apart from the supernatural element, perfectly rational, straightforward, and consistent, probable alike in the actions it records, the motives to which it attributes them, and the human nature which is thus delineated. Then we go on to ask, as Mr Maurice has done, by what tests we are to distinguish actions of this sort from the destruction of Lisbon, whether it may not be regarded as the explanation of similar catastrophes, a revelation of the eternal law of God against selfishness, sin, and rebellion, which have sacrificed and continue to sacrifice their myriads of victims with Jesus of Nazareth at their head? But if this be not thought satisfactory (it is not to me), why may not a sober utilitarian philosophy come to our aid and suggest that morality is, after all, not an undeviating law of conduct intuitionally apprehended, but the power of dealing rightly with facts as they arise? We are, therefore, unable in some cases to decide whether any course of conduct was right, not because our moral nature is different from God's, but because we do not adequately know the facts. And if this merely negative position be thought unsatisfactory, we may go on to say boldly that granting for one moment the possibility of the interposition of God by supernatural means, then this destruction was warranted by plain considerations of utility. For the rebellion must have led to civil war, in which, not merely the national life of the people would have run great risk of perishing, but more lives would have been lost, more innocent people would have suffered, and (to use the one triumphant nineteenth-century test of what is right), more property would have been destroyed, than by its sudden and miraculous overthrow. And, therefore, it is just as truly moral as the destruction of the Egyptian army in the Red Sea, which, again, is hardly to be distinguished from that of the French army in the Russian campaign of 1812.

So true, then, is it that these *à priori* considerations lead us nowhere at the last. Once more, I must again and again affirm, does it become apparent that neither Rationalists nor believers have any effective arguments at their disposal wherewith to confute each other by summary intellectual processes. If so, then the true work of the intellect is to create a moral predisposition by presenting, enforcing, explaining the facts which it thus enables to speak for themselves and recommend themselves to the consciousness of mankind. If arguments for and against the miraculous come to nothing, why not examine the miracles themselves? If science and religion are to be made friends together, it will be accomplished by applying the methods of the former to the study of the latter. Miracles, like other events, may be classified, grouped, arranged, submitted to the intellectual microscope, made to give up their meaning, whatever it may be. Such an examination is strictly scientific, whether the miracles are assumed to be true or admitted to be productions of the Jewish mind; in the former case they belong to the region of actual facts, in the latter to that of ideas. Hitherto, very little indeed has been attempted in this direction. It is as though men had been content to argue about the nature of the unknown interior of the Australian continent, instead of sending exploring parties to see for themselves. To be sure there is great danger that the first adventurers may perish, especially if they make the attempt with inadequate powers and insufficient equipment. Yet even then the desire of ascertaining their fate and doing honour to their remains will lead to future expeditions and further discoveries. It is with some such feelings as these that I survey the wilderness of stories that make up the supernatural element in Jewish history, before proceeding to plunge into it. And, that I shall come to an untimely intellectual end in the midst of it, I am more than afraid.

Now on glancing at this confused mass of events, can the eye discern any principle of classification and arrange-

The Miracles of God. 163

ment? The first thing we ask about actions is, Who did them? and then all at once we are brought face to face with the surprising confusion of thought which attributes them all alike to God. In reality we find that they divide into three classes: those done by God alone; those done by God and man together; those done by man alone. I take these three in order.

The miracles done by God alone are those which come to man simply as a recipient, without any expectation on his part or any co-operation of his own will. These are by far the most important, comprising as they do the first call of God to the spirit of man, as evinced in the appearance to Moses in the burning bush, the call of Samuel, the Annunciation, the Resurrection, and the conversion of St Paul. And let us at once observe that they demand an intellectual conception entirely different from those which we apply, rightly or wrongly, to other miracles. They are not signs, nor marvels, nor proofs of revelation, nor arguments for design, but in the simplest sense actions of God. Let us emancipate ourselves once for all from the necessity of regarding them from the point of view suggested by the doctrine of final causes. Why should we apply to the personal actions of God some theory of causation which we never apply to our own? While we are surveying the large field of general design, or ultimate purpose, or imaginary necessity, we are simply missing the whole value of the events themselves which the Bible represents, merely as actions done to meet each pressing need as it arose, whose one only continuous motive is this, that they proceed from a heart that never ceases to love mankind, and a wisdom that never fails to watch over man's growth towards perfection. To the writers of the Bible, at any rate of the Old Testament, they were, as has been often remarked, not supernatural at all. God was in the midst of them, and might at any moment act or speak as He pleased. They drew no distinction between natural and supernatural; any trivial law that occurred to Moses was attributed to God, "Who spake unto Moses," as much as the most tremendous events of their history. This consideration makes it exceedingly difficult for us to draw the line now, and may, indeed, render theories of the miraculous and tests of the supernatural for ever impossible. But, on the other hand, it removes the whole subject from the influence of artificial modern notions of proof and design, and places it in the region of actions done by a just and merciful Being. So that if the theological intellect has done its best to dry up and wither the history of God's dealings with mankind, the imagination may still have power to reanimate it, and make it intelligible to the human heart and conscience.

And when we go on to inquire what was the effect of these actions, we find that it resembles that of actions done by man to man. Not primarily to startle or to convince, but simply to communicate with him and gain a mastery over his spirit by revealing to him facts and truths—such was the purpose of God, as it is the purpose of every being who adresses himself to another being capable of receiving spiritual impressions from him. This, indeed, is the specific peculiarity of this class of miracles, in which the work of men is merely receptive, and God, for the first time in the life of each of His servants, reveals Himself to them, claims them as His own, assigns to them their duty, and elevates them henceforward into what Ewald calls the miraculous spirit. For when once men are convinced by external evidence, sufficient for themselves, that God is in special communication with them, then two results immediately take place. They acquire a command over nature because a power greater than nature is known to be overruling all things for their good, and they acquire a mental certainty that the thoughts which come and go are not the mere chance workings of their own minds, but the inspiration of God, subject, of course, to the one invariable test that they are right and just in themselves. In short, the very first result of miracles of this discription is to eliminate the idea of chance or fate from the operations alike of nature and of the human mind, and to substitute faith in that which is orderly, regular, systematic, and designed by a benevolent will for our happiness and improvement. All faith* is, indeed, ultimately the apprehension of the laws underlying physical and moral phenomena. The human

---

* The use of the word "faith" is so various and puzzling that it may be well to recapitulate here the meanings which it bears, and their relations to each other.

1. Faith is assent to any proposition whatever—a belief that it is true.

2. Faith is assent to propositions which come to us upon the evidence of others, and therefore implies, (*a*) some trust in the witnesses, (*b*) some moral or immoral tendency in ourselves which makes the testimony satisfactory to us.

3. Faith is assent to the propositions that are the most general conclusions of human experience, and are therefore fundamental. These are such as the following: That experience is to be trusted; that law is universal; that there is a tendency in things to goodness; that there is a right and wrong. Moreover these have an appearance of being intuitional, because they are born in individuals as the inheritance which they receive from the accumulated experience of ancestors. But there is no essential distinction between faith in these elementary propositions and faith in the latest scientific discovery. And in all cases faith means assent. Lastly, the strength of the assent—much more its moral influence—does not depend solely upon the conclusiveness of the evidence, but upon this as related to the moral or intellectual condition of the person assenting.

mind, whether religious or scientific, postulates the existence of something regular behind appearances, which is good just because it is regular, and the knowledge of which is useful merely because it enables us to live our lives and frame our conduct accordingly. I am not, of course, denying that this apprehension may and does rest upon very different degrees and kinds of evidence in the respective regions of religion and science; but what I contend is, that in both alike men crave to believe in the existence of something fixed and stable upon which they can absolutely rely. When they have attained to this belief, no matter whether it be in a law of nature or in the presence of God, then the absolute conviction which results is the final triumph of faith, and produces the same kind of effects upon their character. Thus the certainty of men like Moses and Elijah, their prophetic control over nature, the moral decisiveness of their actions, create a real bond of sympathy between them and the scientific mind, while a religious mind will not fail to remember that these great qualities were consistent with the deepest inward struggles and torments. To sum up, then, I place in the first rank of importance and reality this class of miracles, because they are simply communications from God to men that explain their future lives and actions, by giving them that moral power which is best described as faith apprehending the unchanging will of God.

But then what was the nature of the outward fact by which the call of God was made? Was it in the first place an objective reality? Now the time may come when the whole conception of the relations between subject and object will be modified by positive thought; but waiving all considerations of this sort, I answer the question by asking how we can possibly tell. What method of investigation can we follow that would tend in the least degree to throw light upon a difficulty of this description? Personally, my sympathy is on the side of those who receive the history of these calls in their literal simplicity, because every attempt to explain them does but evince that curiously purblind spirit in which men, dazzled by the lights of the nineteenth century after Christ, approach the history of nearly as many centuries before Him. But no explanation whatever ought to be demanded as an article of faith or rejected as a product of heresy. Men really argue the question as though Moses went next day in the spirit of Faraday to see whether he had been the victim of an optical delusion, or as though he recognised to himself that it was henceforth his bounden duty to deliver his nation, while smiling within his heart at the superstitious dread which had, nevertheless, suggested or confirmed his purpose. The rational student of miraculous history will, I feel sure, decline to pronounce dogmatically upon such a question. These events may have been produced by the efforts of an excited imagination; but then, also, they may not; and some of them are plainly not susceptible of such treatment, and must, therefore, if objective reality be denied, be relegated into the number of simple legends and fables. What he will feel is that there is something ultimately inexplicable in the simplest operation of nature, or the most ordinary action of man, and the exact nature of these miraculous appearances will take its place in the region of ultimate incomprehensibilities: the more so as by virtue of being believed to be supernatural, they are at once taken out of the ordinary distinction between subject and object. But what he will maintain resolutely, positively, and dogmatically about them, will be as follows. First, that the men to whom these appearances came received them as simple actual facts declaring to them the will and mind of God. If it were admitted that even a trace of a suspicion ever crossed their minds, that their belief was only the result of their own imaginations, then St Paul, for instance, would be reduced to the level of the grossest deceivers by whom mankind has been afflicted. Secondly, that, therefore, to the men themselves they were really objective, that is, they had all the moral effects and natural consequences of actions done to and towards us by some power, will, or person lying outside ourselves. This may be proved by the simple test of what they did. Moses did not draw near to the bush, but hid his face and took off his shoes. Joshua did the same. Samuel ran twice to Eli and insisted that the voice he heard had come from him. Elijah went out and wrapped his face in his mantle. Zacharias came out of the temple dumb, and insisted upon calling his child John. Mary went with haste to see Elizabeth, and "her soul magnified the Lord." The Baptist knew the Messiah by the descent of the Holy Ghost in the shape of a dove, and told the people so in plain words. The Apostles declared that Christ was raised from the dead, and went into Galilee to meet Him there. St Paul went into Damascus blind, there to wait till it should be told him what he was to do. Nothing, therefore, is gained morally if, in our eagerness to attribute every event to man's unassisted imagination, we refuse to believe in any actual sensible interposition of God. The men themselves gave the plainest proofs that they did believe in such interposition, and could it be shown to-morrow that the burning bush was a natural meteoric appearance, our view of the character, the beliefs, and the actions of Moses would not be in the least modified—unless, which is absurd, it could be also shown that he himself suspected as much. Thirdly, that those who believe in a living God are justified in speaking of these events as, in a special sense, actions of His, done out of His wisdom and benevolence towards His creatures. The only alternative, except rejecting them altogether, is to attribute them to mere chance events, a meteor, a dream, or a storm—which fell upon minds rendered susceptible by previous inward struggles and reflection. No man of science, possessed of the reverential spirit which springs from the homage paid to facts, would, I feel persuaded, speak of events like these, or, indeed, of anything in the world as chance or accident, though he may be quite unable to connect the outward event and the inward mental effect by any law of causation. He might decline, though I do not see why he should, to follow the religious man in his assertion that, explain their nature as you will, events which wrought such prodigious consequences upon men like St Paul, and through him upon the world, are best attributed to the overruling will of a personal God; but science goes all lengths with religion in abhorring the idea of chance or accident—science, because it seeks to reduce everything to the operation of law; religion, because it believes in a moral government of the world. Some day or other these two, law and will, will meet together, to the infinite confusion of all who have tried to separate them, as though the One God were a different Being in His dealings in man and in nature Meanwhile, until some one discovers a better explanation than the philosophy of Atheism, which falls back as the last resort upon the doctrine of a fortuitous concurrence of incidents, we may continue to adopt the old Hebrew faith which found its simple expression in the words, "God did it."

The conclusion, then, to which we are led in respect of the objective character of these miraculous appearances is, that that which in other cases impostors invent or fanatics imagine was entirely accepted by some of the greatest and best of men; that it formed the groundwork of a profound belief in a personal God, who was with them; that it was soberly related to other people without the least suspicion that they were mistaken; and that their future conduct was shaped by the convictions impressed upon them by what they thought they had seen and heard. In this statement we have, as it seems to me, all that is required as a foundation for a revealed religion, while there is nothing in it to which objection can be made, provided that the narrative be accepted as historically, though not of necessity literally, true.

Another element common to all miracles of this class is that the appearance was always regarded as that of a person—was, in short, spiritual and not physical. It might be an angel, or a vision, or a voice, or a human form, but it was never a mere startling occurrence in the physical world. At first sight the burning bush might seem to be an exception to the rule, but the true Hebrew conception is preserved for us in St Stephen's speech, in which it is stated that an angel of the Lord appeared to Moses, and that when he drew near, a voice came unto him. No doubt, to a certain extent the converse of this is true also. I mean that the idea of angels or spiritual intelligences is bound up with the mystery of natural processes, so that they might even be called powers of nature. But it is interesting to observe how in the growth of the Jewish mind the idea and the appearance of angels became detached from any connection whatever with natural occurrences, till in the time of the New Testament, angels were regarded simply as intelligent messengers from God, bearing close resemblance to men. We may, therefore, lay down the important rule as applicable to all miracles of this class, and to nearly all Scriptural miracles whatsoever, that no natural prodigy, no physical disturbance, ever takes place apart from the co-operation of a personal will (human or divine) revealed in it, and giving it a moral significance. The few exceptions to this rule, such as the speaking of Baalam's ass and Jonah's whale, are precisely those which the most rigid orthodoxy is beginning to feel the necessity of explaining away at any cost.

We go on next to regard this class of miracles from the point of view of the recipient, to inquire, that is, whether there are any facts common to all of them which throw any light upon the disposition of mind of those to whom they occurred. Several things strike us at once.

First, we notice an unbroken silence as to what they were thinking about at the time when, as they believed, God addressed them. It may be that a certain moral predisposition was required, but this is not what the persons chiefly concerned attached any importance to. To them it seemed more true to believe that the Spirit of God comes where and when He listeth. It may well be that the heart of Moses was brooding over his people's wrongs; that the child Samuel was burning with indignation at priestly corruptions; that St Paul was shaken through and through by the unyielding constancy of Christian sufferers under the persecutions he was inflicting. But from first to last there is not a word to tell us that this was so, or that they thought of themselves as contributing in the smallest degree to their own call or conversion. "It pleased God," was the unfailing account given by St Paul. "The Lord God of our fathers has appeared to us," was the simple explanation of Moses.

If, however, in obedience to the demands of modern religious thought, we seek to discover in what this moral predisposition consisted, most certainly it does not lie upon the surface. Nothing can be at first sight more varied than the circumstances and characters of the men who were called by God, at the time of their calling. Moses after failure, followed by many years' retirement in the wilderness; Samuel as a child growing into the knowledge of good and evil; Elijah no one knows how or when; St Paul in the full tide of hatred and oppression; our Lord himself simply at the age of legal and actual manhood—what law runs throughout these and other widely different cases? Only, I think, the presence in them of perfect sincerity and truthfulness. But then consider what this amounts to. It means a perfect readiness to accept facts, and to act with absolute fidelity to the convictions which they inspire. These men were perfectly incapable of explaining away what they saw and heard and felt to be true. That this incapacity was in some sort connected with the temper of

The Miracles of God. 173

mind that did not require a scientific explanation may be true, but then that does not prevent this temper of mind from having its definite use and playing its destined part in the history of man. To it we owe the first outburst of poetry, religion, and art—three things that science may very powerfully modify, but could never have created. This moral sincerity, this incapacity of playing false with our convictions, is what we call on the intellectual side, genius, which may be defined in all its manifold varieties of operation as the capacity to receive and act upon communications from the Eternal. The burning bush would have had one meaning for Moses, another for Raphael, a third for Newton; but prophet, artist, and philosopher would all agree in this, that whatever truth it conveyed to them they would implicitly receive and faithfully declare. We can thus in some measure understand that the truth of the free grace of God was revealed to St Paul, or the name Jehovah to Moses, by reason of the same law of God's working as that by which the movement of the earth was revealed to Galileo. And, on the other hand, a fatal moral incapacity for seeing things as they are lies at the root of the Philistinism, Pharisaism, and spirit of obstructiveness which have watered the earth with the tears and the blood of the heroes and saints of God. In one single sentence our Lord, speaking as the representative of the servants and preachers of truth (of every kind), has summed up the unceasing conflict between these two spiritual powers— "Verily, verily, I say unto thee, *We* speak that we do know, and testify that we have seen; and ye receive not our witness (St John iii. 11).

A third remark which we discern as being applicable to

all these appearances is that they bear a close and natural relation to the future lives and labours of those to whom God made Himself known; and, further, that they are progressive in accordance with the onward march of the people in religious knowledge and spiritual life. With Moses we find that the idea meant to be conveyed was God's absolute power over the operations of nature, which henceforward should obey the prophet in working out the deliverance of His people. To Joshua the lesson was taught by the appearance of an armed messenger of God that Jehovah was no less able, and resolved to subdue the wrath and might of man before the face of His people Israel. Samuel was instructed by a voice that the special domain of God was the spirit, to which God would hereafter address Himself, and so he became the first founder of the prophetic order. But the succession of prophets immediately following him were men who by the power of human genius made Israel into a great and prosperous kingdom; in them—for instance, in David and Solomon—the voice of God spoke by what we should call, to use the most comprehensive available word, ability. Therefore the second founder of the prophetic order, Elijah, felt the inspiration of God as a still small voice under circumstances which taught him, and through him the prophets of the later monarchy, that, not in outward greatness nor in political success, but in inward spiritual fidelity to God, lay the true secret of Israel's grandeur and the real purpose of his calling. The call of Isaiah is represented as a purely spiritual vision, an unlocking of the mind of man to discern spiritual realities under forms which do not purport to have any material external existence; furthermore, the accomplishment of the divine purpose, no matter how weak or fallen Israel might become, is still more clearly recognised. The unnamed prophet of the Captivity speaks without any express call at all; suffering and experience had done their work, and the prophetic spirit could at length discern the mind of God in the march of events, such as the rise of Cyrus and the approaching fall of Babylon. More than 500 years later the same is true, in a still more significant manner, of the Baptist, of whom it is simply said that the spirit of God came upon him. It is also remarkable that it is expressly stated that John did no miracle, just as what may be called the miraculous spirit is entirely absent from the writings and thoughts of the second Isaiah. These two facts are, it cannot be doubted, closely connected. Not having had an outward call (that is, to define it again, a call which, whether objective or not, was for all moral and intellectual purposes real and objective to those who received it), they were not possessed of the miraculous spirit, and neither in their own minds nor in the minds of their followers were connected with the power of doing supernatural works. I shall, however, have to refer to this point again, when we come to consider the laws which seem to underlie the periodical and intermittent outpourings or outcomings of the miraculous power.

It is necessary now to call attention for a moment to this class of miracles as they appear in the New Testament. Remembering that they were defined to be the original call of God to men without previous knowledge or personal co-operation on their part (except by a passive susceptibility arising from absolute sincerity of disposition), we shall find that there were two persons, and two sets of persons, to whom God thus spake. First, there were those who were connected more or less directly with the birth of Christ. Practically, however, the Annunciation represents all these. Secondly, there was our Lord himself, to whom the call came at His Baptism. Thirdly, there were the Apostles, who were called by a series of appearances after the Resurrection, culminating in and represented by the descent of the Spirit at Pentecost. Fourthly, there was the conversion of St Paul. In each case we see at once that the object to be gained was the kindling of the spirit of man by a revelation of the being, the favour, and the purposes of God; in each case we also see that the miraculous appearance was specially adapted to the life and work of the persons therein called. The only case that requires a brief word of explanation is that of our Lord himself. The circumstances of His call are just what might be expected of One whom we believe to owe His existence directly to God, without any intervention of man. To be owned as the Son of God, in a way that symbolised the indwelling in Him of the Godhead "bodily," kindled in His heart and mind that miraculous spirit which depended upon His unbroken confidence in the Fatherhood of God. Henceforward it was His Father's works that He claimed to be doing, His Father's words that He felt sure He was speaking, because the "Father hath borne witness of Me," whereas "ye (the Jews) have neither heard His voice at any time, nor seen His shape." It is important to observe this, because if there had been no external calling in the case of Christ, then He would have been exempt from the general law which governs the experiences of all God's specially chosen servants in the Bible history.

So far from being unworthy of our conception of Christ, the picture presented to us at His baptism is in harmony both with the general dealings of God and the character of His Son. He comes seeking to fulfil all righteousness, meditating upon the deliverance of humanity from sin, growing into the consciousness of His divine origin and Messiahship. Henceforward undoubting certainty, perfect faith, absolute command over Himself, nature, and circumstances, mark the words and deeds of Jesus Christ. In this, as in all other points, He was as we are, and subject to the conditions of our human life, and yet He was still the Son of God.

I conclude this essay with calling attention once more to the special importance of the class of miracles we have been reviewing.

There is a temptation, to which I had nearly yielded, of attaching to them a purely evidential value. Nothing at first sight seems more natural. Here is a long series of miraculous calls stretching over a great extent of time, all conforming to some distinct moral principle, faithful to one type, developing one uniform purpose of God— namely, to communicate with and gain a mastery over the spirit of the great men by whom the world was to be taught religion. That such could have been the mere inventions of the Jewish mind, from Moses to St Paul, is more astounding than miracles themselves; it is a flagrant exception to everything we know to be true of the workings and the power of the human mind. But a moment's consideration suggests what the answer would be. A candid opponent would say, "I admit with you the impossibility that such ideas could have been invented, or rather one main idea persistently carried out through the changing circumstances and characters of fifteen hundred years, therefore I see in this record an argument for supposing that all these stories were due to a great outburst of Jewish thought at some period in their history yet to be defined, but which is undoubtedly connected with the spirit of the age that produced the book of Deuteronomy. This same spirit did, as a mere matter of historical fact, take hold of the Jewish people many centuries afterwards, inspiring them with new hopes and a higher morality. Hence it also produced another array of facts in the New Testament conformable to the main idea of Judaism, but conditioned by the growing and progressive spirit of its best and highest minds." Once more I must affirm that there is no answer to be given to an argument of this sort, just as there is no absolute proof that it is true, except such as is drawn from an *à priori* determination to reject the supernatural. The internal and external evidence for—say the Book of Exodus—is, apart from the supernatural element, consistent at present either with the conclusion that it is on the whole historical, with certain legendary admixtures, or that it is on the whole legendary, with gleams of history here and there shining through it. If, then, this book, or rather the Bible, of which it forms a part, can most worthily set forth the attributes of God, can create the highest morality in man, and produce the best and most useful characters, the events which it relates will carry their own conviction to the minds of men; if otherwise, they will reject them as a useful superstition that has played its part in the past history of the human race, and must now give way to what will then appear to be more worthy conceptions of truth And if I should seem to assert this principle with wearisome pertinacity, I must plead in excuse that I offer it as my one humble contribution to the settlement of religious controversies by arousing religious people to the necessity of a higher spiritual life, an increased moral excellence, a more vigorous and united action, a larger and more tolerant and more comprehensive charity. The jury— that is, the mass of educated opinion—is at present greatly perplexed on this point; advocates on both sides are beginning to admit that they have little expectation of being able to adduce fresh evidence of any material or decisive importance. Yet time, which cannot alter facts, may very decidedly alter the tone of mind to which those facts are submitted, and change the light in which they are regarded, so that the jury, now locked up for a night of doubt, darkness, and disputation, may at the dawn of morning after all be prepared with a tolerably unanimous verdict.

The true value, then, of this class of miracles is to be found in the religious influence which they bring to bear on human hearts and minds. If once accepted as true, we are assured by them that the unknown God has communicated with man and revealed His character and His will to His chosen servants. And yet it must in candour be confessed that these are just the miracles many of which have been most exposed to suspicion and rejection. Take, for instance, no less a person than the late Dean Milman. In the history of the Jews he defends strongly the reality of a supernatural interference at the Red Sea; but in the history of Christianity he appears to regard the appearance of angelic messengers to Mary and Zacharias as explicable by subjective impressions. Now I believe that the present tendency of religious thought is beginning to run in the opposite direction. Do what we will, we cannot get rid of the objective, for that miracle, which is the crown of all God's actions—I mean the Incarnation—is, even more than the Resurrection, either absolute fact or gross fiction. The latter may have been, as Renan supposes, a pious delusion of honest people founded upon events falsely but not dishonestly believed to have been witnessed; but the Incarnation, if untrue, must have been a pure legend, more or less deliberately invented. But if we believe, as Christian people do believe, in so distinct and unmistakable and tremendous a fact as the miraculous Incarnation of Christ, then I should really be glad to be told what possible gain there can be to the cause of rational religion if we attempt to explain away the messengers who announced it. How else could such announcement be made? and yet made in some way it must be, if God is to deal with us as spiritual beings, through whose wills He means to carry out His designs. The simplicity, propriety, and intrinsic naturalness of the whole narrative, are more than apparent. Here, again, I confess myself quite unable to enter into the state of mind of those who accept the Resurrection, doubt about the Incarnation, and "rationalise" the Annunciation. These all hang together, and form a consistent story to be rejected or received as a whole; in short, the attempt to discriminate between these New Testament miracles, in which God is the one original actor, and the nature of which lies, therefore, beyond the reach of human investigation, seems as unsatisfactory in a religious as it is pitiable in a scientific point of view. Either they all occurred as related, or they did not occur at all.*

But it must be observed that I limit this remark to the special class of miracles we have been considering. The more, as it seems to me that we can rationalise or explain by natural causes other miracles, such as, for instance, the crossing of the Red Sea, or the more we succeed in doing away with the supernatural element in them by further discoveries in the regions of mind and matter, the better it will be for the cause of religious truth. This will have to be enlarged upon hereafter, but what we want is non-interference with the supremacy and regularity of natural law on the one hand; on the other, some distinct revelation of God to the soul through the usual organs of apprehension. I hope that what has been said in this essay as to the purpose, the nature, and the "objectivity" (how far necessary to be accepted) of these revelations will remove from some minds certain difficulties they may have felt, and may demonstrate the exceeding importance of the revelations themselves. What men want, I must again repeat, is not signs, wonders, or convulsions of nature, but a voice from a living God, making itself heard by methods sufficient to satisfy a rational and sober mind of its reality. Such a voice may be heard only now and then, and may in its special outward manifestation be confined to a few chosen spirits, from whom it descends to us in the usual

---

* Every miracle done by God alone MIGHT belong to one of two classes :—
1. Really objective, but capable of natural explanation, *e.g.*, the conversion of St Paul.
2. Subjective—that is, the effect of the imagination, *e.g.* (as above), the Resurrection. The Incarnation alone can be neither.

channels of spiritual influence. But to *them* it reveals, in unmistakable language, not only the abiding character, but also the present designs of Almighty God, and (it may be, but this secondarily) produces in them that undefined control over nature which we call miraculous. We seem thus to have taken one step towards placing ourselves at the centre of the labyrinth of the miraculous, from whence we may hope to adjust its various windings in their true place of reality and usefulness. And yet every step only shows the more clearly what doubtful, hesitating, tentative work it needs must be, and how much easier it is either to swallow everything or reject everything according to our previous mental bias or education. It is not, however, thus that a belief in God has been maintained in searching and trying times; nor has mere blind defence or equally blind attack any real or fruitful interest for those to whom inquiry is one of the chief delights, and truth one of the main objects of their lives.

THE MIRACLES OF MAN.

I HAVE already discussed that class of miracles in which God for the first, or at any rate at a decisive time, approaches the spirit of man.* I turn, therefore, next to consider the miracles in the performance of which the will of man co-operates, or even predominates, our object being to gain some insight into the methods of miraculous working as it appears in history, and especially to obtain some clue as to its extent and credibility. In a subject that covers so large an extent of ground, and contains so many incidents, it is obvious that we must be content with taking one or two chief events and persons to illustrate the whole. Nor will this be found in practice at all difficult to accomplish.

The power of working miracles may be described generally as the control over nature obtained by those who believe that God has communicated to them some special revelation of His being, His character, and His purpose. To such men it becomes apparent that nature, history, and the soul of man, belong to God, who is supreme alike in the world of matter and of mind. But although this is the

* The distinction is difficult to carry out in all cases, and yet is all-important to my argument. Thus the stories of Balaam and Jonah belong to the first class, because the miracles (as reported) were actions of God, communications to men apart from, and independent of, any actions or knowledge of their own. On the other hand, the census-plague, and the safety of the crew at Malta, were in themselves perfectly natural events, and were only miraculous, so far as they were foretold and interpreted by the "miraculous spirit" of Gad and St Paul respectively. The first class contains all the miracles that are necessary to establish the fact that God has entered into special communication with man; and if the chief events in it are accepted, all other miracles can be explained in a natural and reasonable way.

general idea underlying the power of the miraculous, in the actual history we discern a very remarkable and orderly development. Beginning with Moses, this power is simply that of a discoverer, for Moses is represented as doing nothing by himself, but as foretelling what God would do in and through those forces of nature which formed the worship of the ancient Egyptians and dominated over their minds. Ending with Christ the power has become what we may call inventive, for Christ is represented as overruling by His own energy and will the same forces of nature for the welfare and salvation of man. Now, whether we accept the history as a statement of facts or as a record of ideas, it is not to be denied that it presents a remarkable resemblance to the development of scientific thought. First discovery, then invention. First the attempt to learn the laws and qualities of material objects, and then the attempt to mould them into forms suitable to the welfare of mankind. The age of Newton and astronomy precedes the age of Watt and the steam-engine. That all nature is subject to the will of a righteous God, and may therefore be directed by human agency to save men from misery and death, such is the thought of religion. That all nature is guided and established by undeviating law, and may therefore be adapted by human wisdom and contrivance for man's comfort and happiness, such is the thought of science. So that, view it in what light we please, the idea of the Bible is prophetic of the growth of civilisation. Moses knows what the course of nature will be; Christ knows how to use its powers to work out His own designs for man's good. Everywhere we have presented to us the idea of a progressive, harmonious, and moral development of man's control over nature.

Another point of affinity between the belief in miracles and the tendency of science may at this juncture be usefully alluded to. This belief rests upon the fact that there is a power external to nature (as we know it) which can adapt, modify, and accelerate the processes and properties of material objects. It does not matter for our present purpose whether the power in question is or is not personal and beneficent; it is sufficient that it exists as something external to our world and system of things. Now the testimony of science, if I understand it rightly, goes to show that the existence of such a power is both possible and probable. That it is possible I gather from the opinions of Mr Mill, who asserts that as our knowledge is confined to experience we can have no certainty but that the laws of nature, and mind and matter themselves, may be in other spheres of existence dissimilar from what they are here. I think that in view of the late discoveries starwards, it will have to be admitted that there is a very strong presumption to the contrary, and one that is likely to increase in strength the more we know concerning the nature of the heavenly bodies. But however this may be, it is clear that the strictest philosophy of experience admits that for all we can tell there may be powers external to and different from those with which we are acquainted here on earth. If this be so, then if they were brought into contact with our sphere, the effect produced would be miraculous, and thus room is provided for the exercise of powers supernatural to us, but not so in themselves. Nor is it any answer to say that as a matter of experience no such contact has taken place. That is to beg the whole question, and to beg it in a way contrary to what science demands, judging at least by one of her latest utterances. Sir W. Thomson having got to account for the origin of life, attributes it—as an hypothesis—to the fall of an aërolite from another planet. That is to say, he attributes it to what religion calls a miracle, and a very portentous, not to say absurd, miracle it is. For we inquire at once, What about the aërolite? where did that come from? It must have come ultimately from the void of the unknown, from that in which religion discerns a (to us) supernatural power, and which it will perversely persist, acting under the inspiration of great souls, in calling by the name of a Personal God, and even daring to address as a "Father in Heaven." And thus much having been granted, it is enabled to go on and explain that it is possible for men to work miracles, if they can appropriate or discern the external power by means of a revelation from God addressed to their spirits. Furthermore, when science undertakes to explain the creation of the original aërolite, or the first germ, or the first molecule, or the primal force (by whatever name it elects to call the origin of things), then religion will be in a position to explain by natural agencies that which she is now compelled to call miraculous, only because science is compelled to recognise it as unknown.

The existence of the miraculous is then reduced to a question of evidence, and considering, as I have before observed, what are the astonishing peculiarities of the Jewish people, and what the Bible is which professes to account for them, the presumption in favour of such existence becomes exceedingly strong. But then we are compelled to admit that as the legendary or the fictitious has crept everywhere into history, and especially into the sources of history, so we may expect that it will have gathered with especial force about the lives of great men to whom the power of working miracles has been attributed. The legendary spirit may work in two ways: it may invest facts with a peculiar atmosphere of its own, through which historical events loom in curious and disproportioned shapes; or it may invent facts as expressions of ideas which the marvellous excites in the minds of men. Our object, then, in dealing with the miracles of the Bible, is to attribute to their real origin the accounts as they stand, and to discover, if we can, in what the supernatural element (if there be one) consists. In doing so, we will abide by the following rules, which are, as it seems to me, sufficient to satisfy candid religious minds.

1st. The absolute good faith and veracity of the historians are to be preserved, for this, if for no other reason, that there is not the slightest ground to convict them of falsehood.

2d. No question is here raised as to the genuineness or authenticity of the books. That belongs to another branch of inquiry with which I am not at present concerned. *Adhuc sub judice lis est.*

3d. No miracle is to be rejected merely because it is improbable, incredible, or appears immoral to us. I again express my dislike of that method of criticism which makes the subjective impressions of one generation the test of the reality of occurrences that happened thousands of years ago. On the other hand, anything extravagant may fairly set us upon a closer examination of the facts or of the evidence, and cannot fail but exercise some influence upon our ultimate decision. But if the things recorded are, as many of them are, inconsistent in their naked simplicity with the possibilities of human life and human nature, then we are bound to find some explanation of them. There are narratives which do not merely seem impossible to us, but which are impossible to humanity itself. It is, of course, difficult to draw the line in the abstract, though by no means difficult to decide upon separate cases. The conduct of Pharaoh, for instance, is inexplicable if the narrative is to be taken in its literal simplicity. It is perhaps as well to add that we are here upon well-debated ground, upon which I shall therefore linger as short a time as possible.

The first question to be asked in surveying the history of miracles is this, Are there any that have no claim to be facts at all, simply because they are stories written for a moral and religious purpose? There are not perhaps many such, but as an illustration of this kind of story let us take the history of Jonah. The marks by which it may be distinguished from real events are these:—1st. It does not occur in a regular historical book purporting to give an account of the Jewish people. If it did, then to set it down as fiction would seriously impair the value of the whole book. 2d. All the incidents have that dramatic exaggerated appearance which belongs to the realm of fiction, and shows indubitable signs of being due to the imagination. Every dramatist is compelled more or less to force the natural order of events which flow too slowly for the necessities of his plot. "Plot" is indeed the word that exactly expresses the impression made on the reader by the history of Jonah. 3d. The events are adapted to produce certain moral lessons, and to teach certain spiritual truths. This is an evident sign of artificial production, and not of natural growth. 4th. The account of the swallowing

The Miracles of Man. 189

of the prophet by a fish would not be an insuperable difficulty to me if it were the only one, and if it were as well authenticated as other miracles. But the account of the preaching at Nineveh and its results is incredible *per se*. The limit of time, "within forty days," is like nothing else in the Bible, and pledges God to the performance of something so prodigious as to be impossible. How can we suppose that a great city like Nineveh should repent at the preaching of an entire stranger from a despised race? How can outward and ceremonial manifestations of repentance avert the wrath of God? What is the meaning of such a repentance as this?—did the Ninevites change their religion, or their social life, or their national policy? The moment we examine the story it falls to pieces if it is regarded as literal fact, though it is possible that Jonah, who is certainly a real personage, may have had relations with Nineveh, which formed the basis of the book. 5th. The moral lessons taught us—and very invaluable lessons they are—belong to that class which gains nothing by being derived from actual facts, but which might just as well be the results of the meditations of an inspired mind. Any pious Jew might well have written such a story as this with a view to the edification of his people, such parables being common to Eastern literature. No doubt it expresses in a general way what was probably the tone of Jewish thought towards Nineveh at one period of their history; but what was the main idea of the book (if there was any) I must leave to ingenious critics to discover if they can; every commentator has his own opinion, and is sure that it is the right one. Only let us be sure that the writer never meant his beautiful allegory to be regarded as sober historical fact.

I do not think, however, that this principle will help us in many cases. The miracles of the Captivity in Daniel, and the historical portions of the Book of Job, may perhaps be thus explained; but as a general rule, the Jewish mind was far too much occupied with the seriousness of facts to give room for the play of invention.

A second class of miracles which are not to be accepted as literal facts are those in which the narrative itself does not affirm that there was any personal contemporary evidence, but rather by the nature of the case excludes it. Surely we might be spared endless wranglings as to the historical value of the account of the Fall or the Deluge, if we did but remember so very obvious a truth. If indeed the writers claimed in so many words to have had an express revelation of the facts, or if any competent authority ascribed it to them, then it would be our duty either to accept their statements or condemn them as deceivers. But from this miserable alternative we are preserved by the artless wisdom of the Bible itself. What we have is a story of Adam or Noah told by men to whom the distinction between the actual and the ideal, so obvious to us, was non-existent. The existence of the world was a fact that had to be accounted for in a religious sense by men who were building up a true conception of God in the heart of the Jewish people. And it was accounted for by men who neither had nor claimed to have scientific information, but who had a clear and true insight into the eternal moral relations between God and man, and who threw their thoughts into that which we have chosen, naturally enough no doubt, to regard as matter of fact history. But then this test, which most people would not now hesitate to apply to the

The Miracles of Man.

account of the Creation, applies to several other miracles as well. What ear-witness took down the dialogue between Balaam and his ass? Are we to suppose that Balaam told the story against himself? Or who saw the destruction of the two companies by fire at the word of Elijah? Or who, be it spoken reverently, saw the Lord Jesus placed upon the pinnacle of the Temple by the Devil? In all these cases the matter of fact explanation is furthest from the truth upon the face of the narrative itself.

A third class consists of those which, if they are to be regarded as actual events, must have been notorious enough, and are too closely interwoven with the web of the history to be separated from it. An instance is the plague that followed the census of David. But then this is incredible in itself, for the simple reason that human life and natural existence could not be carried on under such conditions. The Jews were at that time, to a considerable extent, a cultivated and reasoning people, with settled institutions, political experience, and commercial aptitudes. They had amongst them musicians, poets, architects, and thinkers, so that we are obliged to imagine a state of society similar to those which, in our experience, produce these intellectual results. Furthermore, the performance of miracles had been practically unknown among them for some considerable time. Previous numberings of the people had taken place at the express command of God Himself, and the indistinct atmosphere in which the story is wrapped up is shown by the fact that one account ascribes the temptation to God, another to Satan. Lastly, it is a refinement of cruelty to force the unhappy King to choose one out of three extreme calamities. And yet the account is part of the history of

David's reign, and cannot be rejected as fabulous without throwing discredit upon the whole. Our problem is therefore this, Are there any means by which we can preserve the fact of these two events (I mean Balaam's journey and the census-plague, taken as examples of others), and preserve also the *bona fides* of the men who recounted them. I believe that it is quite easy to do so.

The key to all this and many another puzzle is simple enough, and works easily enough when once discovered and put in use. We have to remember that the modes of thought and speech in the Bible were Semitic not Aryan, ancient not modern, religious not scientific. As an instance of the way in which the stand-points of men may vary, I may mention that Keshub Chunder Sen regards inquiry into the historical truthfulness of the life of Christ as part of an "odious muscular Christianity which is fatal to its spiritual meaning." Now, like all other historians whose works have been worth preserving, the writers of the Old Testament sought for facts, but then the facts they sought for were primarily the works of God, and the operation of His will and wisdom. If we would understand what they mean us to understand, we must begin by accustoming ourselves to the language of men to whom God was all in all, just as Greek art is unintelligible without a conception of Greek mythology. Probably ten years residence among Arabian tribes would contribute no less to the better understanding of the Bible than much poring over modern tomes. Moreover, the point of view materially affected the arrangement and colouring of the facts. They were brief where we should be prolix, and *vice versâ*. They dwelt upon the objective where to us the subjective side would be of most vital interest. They spoke of God where we should speak of nature, and discerned His will where we see only the operation of law. And so we come to a safe test of the reality and meaning of these ancient narratives. Can they be told in modern prose so as to give a natural explanation of every fact? Let us try the story of Balaam in this way.

"The travellers set out at early morning on the 7th day of the third month. It was remarked by those about him that Balaam's face wore an expression of unusual sadness, and it is said that he intimated to more than one of those who had assembled to bid him farewell that he was starting on no prosperous errand. The journey was unusually toilsome and difficult, and his spirits were visibly affected by it. At one moment, indeed, his presence of mind gave way altogether. His favourite ass, which had borne him for several years without a mistake, turned suddenly restive, crushed her rider against the wall, and at last fell under him to the ground. The prophet, ordinarily a goodtempered and kindly man, gave way to violent irritation and beat the animal severely. Then, falling into a fit of melancholy, he exclaimed with tears that the very ass was declaring against his journey, and called God to witness that he would proceed no farther. It seemed to him as though the angel of the Lord was standing sword in hand to bar his path. After a while he became calmer, and was persuaded to continue his journey. No further incident marked their way, but the prophet repeatedly declared that come what would he would speak no word against the God of Israel. 'His very ass,' he bitterly remarked, 'was wiser than her master.' They arrived after (so many) days' travelling, and his attendants noticed that when he saw the preparations made to receive him Balaam's spirits began once more to rise, and he exclaimed with some exultation that perhaps after all he had done well to come."

Now, I ask—except that the Bible narrative is infinitely beautiful, dramatic, and suggestive—what is the difference in point of veracity between these two ways of stating the same facts. Why will we persist in thinking that the colouring of modern thought is the only medium through which they can be regarded? And why is it necessary with so much labour and forcing to try to get rid of a history which pleads the cause of its own truthfulness with all the eloquence of unconscious sincerity? If some later Jew invented that story then he has accomplished more than Shakespeare, for he has produced a character which sensible men nearly 3000 years afterwards persist in believing to be historical and not fictitious. Surely any attempt to preserve a narrative so unartificial, so true in all the essentials of truth, and of such permanent moral interest ought to be welcomed with pleasure. Not one atom of religious truth is lost if the facts occurred as I have represented them. Not one atom of scientific truth again is sacrificed if we believe that to Balaam they bore the meaning that came natural to the mind of an Oriental believer in God. Religion like art may represent her objects in ways very unlike the mere reproduction of bare outlines and tame colours. She does not photograph, but paints.*

* If the account given above be true, then it disposes of the argument against the authenticity of the narrative derived from its supernatural character. But it may be well briefly to discuss the other line of argument, because it affords an excellent instance of the extreme difficulty of arriving at a satisfactory conclusion. The whole story is referred to a much later time, because it contains an obvious reference to Assyrian and Hellenic conquests. Now, it is no answer to say that God might, if He pleased, cause His prophets to know all

The Miracles of Man. 195

The explanation of the plague is still more easy, and we may accept Ewald's account of it as probable and satisfactory. The object of the king may have been connected with some intention to organise the nation under a closer despotism, possibly for increased taxation or more rigorous military service. Anyhow it was secular, and was resented by the popular mind as a departure from the religious basis

or anything about the future history of nations, then unknown to them except (if even that) by name. It is sufficient to observe that there is no satisfactory evidence that such stupendous inspiration took place, and we are bound to assume that Balaam spoke in intelligible language, and that his references were such as those who heard them could understand. But then the contrary assumption that the narrative was foisted upon the Jewish sacred books at a much later period lands us in difficulties at least as great. All the internal evidence, such as the allusion to the "gardens by the river side" and the "two buckets of water" (obvious references to life by the Euphrates), is in favour of authenticity, nor are we entitled upon any ground of rational criticism to attribute gross falsification to writers who seem very patterns of ingenuous veracity. But more than this. It is difficult to see at what later time the prophecy could have been written. If we postpone it—a most daring proposition—to the dawn of Grecian power in its effects upon the East, then how are we to account for the omission of all reference to Persia and Babylon? and what marvellously delicate tact the forger (for so in this case he must have been) has displayed in his brief, obscure, almost incorrect allusions to Asshur and Eber! Further, every atom of spiritual truth, moral value, and even poetic impressiveness vanishes if the story be regarded as an ingenious legend. In such a strait one would sacrifice some days of one's life to know the actual truth. Three possible explanations occur to me :—1st. The mere fact of the existence of the unknown western world may have been enough to suggest its future power to one who knew that he was face to face with God, and that the words which rushed to his lips were no mere human fancies and delusions. Then, as in the middle of last century, a prophetic spirit might feel that "westward, the star of empire takes its way."

Secondly. Some great events entirely unknown to us may at that time have powerfully impressed the leading minds of the age. Our knowledge of Aryan migrations and their traditions in general, and of the ebbs and flows of different races at that time in particular (adopting the earlier date of the Exodus), is such mere ignorance that there is nothing to preclude the possibility of this.

Thirdly. If we accept the later date of the Exodus, that of Rameses II. and his son, then it seems probable that the names of western nations were already known. Egypt had repelled an European invasion.

upon which their national life was built. And so then, as ever, there came from the heart of the people the prophetic voice, secure in the consciousness that nature and history were God's, and that He would punish the wrong. Then comes the plague, the king's repentance, the dramatic scene at the threshing-floor of Araunah, where once more the religious imagination saw the angel of God with sword drawn against the devoted city. What would be gained supposing it could be shown that the pestilence was due, as very possibly it was, to the defective drainage of Eastern towns, if we stopped there and refused to see anything more? The course of history is the reverse of this. Men were taught to realise the idea of a personal God as the governor of the world and cause of all things, in order that the secondary or natural causes, when discovered, might be attributed to Him. David's expression, "Let me fall into the hands of God, for His mercies are great," represents the religious aspect of the occurrence, and might, as it seems to me, be with equal propriety used by a modern man of science engaged in tracing an invasion of cholera to the violation of law, the existence and persuasion of which then becomes an incentive to the employment of means of deliverance. "A moral will and not inexorable fate is the cause of this;" so thought David, and fought the battle of religion. "Intelligible law and not mysterious chance is the cause of this;" so thinks the modern physician, and fights the battle of science. And yet are not these two fundamentally the same? And is not defective drainage ungodliness now, as the taking of the census was then, because both are departures from the known or, at any rate, from the knowable will of God?

The Miracles of Man.

These two instances will suffice to illustrate the general law to which a great number of miraculous occurrences may probably be reduced. They were natural events occurring at critical moments and with decisive results, interpreted by a prophetic mind, and recounted by narrators to whom the divine, the religious, the objective, was the one element of real importance, and God was literally all in all. But it may be urged that this theory leaves a gap between ancient and modern modes of thought, which requires to be filled up. It may be that the two are absolutely contradictory one of another; it may be that they are only parts of a continuous and orderly development. Now, the test of this is, are there instances in which the two are found in combination? Can we anywhere discern the process by which the former passed into the latter? Or are we to submit to the existence of tremendous intervals in the history of the human mind, similar to those by which geology works such mischief in the doctrine of evolution? Fortunately not. There is a story which contains, as I believe, the secret of the meaning of this class of miracles, which exhibits science and religion at one with each other, and marks the precise way in which the modern method of regarding things supersedes the ancient. Beautifully enough this story is also the latest in point of time recorded in the Bible; after which I need not say that I am referring to St Paul's voyage to Rome, or more especially to Malta.

I confess that the admiration with which I regard this narrative is such that the full expression of it would be hardly suited to this volume. It might have been written by Thucydides if he had been an officer in the Mediterranean Fleet, with a sailor's natural religious trust in the protection of Almighty God. In it nearly every object of human interest seems to converge—nature, science, intellectual observation, moral grandeur, religious faith. It is now fully understood by those who have examined the subject, that every nautical and geographical detail is not only practically, but technically, correct. No modern man of science during the brief agony of an eclipse ever noted down with keener and more accurate observation the phenomena before him than did St Luke—himself one of the scientific class—note the details of the storm, the disposition of the sailors to meet it, the direction of their course, the soundings, the locality, the nature of the beach, the method of escape. Again, side by side with this, consider the display of human character delineated by single graphic touches—the selfishness of the sailors, who would desert the ship to save their own lives—the no less characteristic selfishness of the soldiers, who, caring little for anything else save doing their duty, gave it as their counsel to kill the prisoners — the calm, controlling authority of the centurion, "willing to save Paul," himself sustained and directed by a will more powerful than his own—and last, St Paul himself displaying exactly the same characteristics from exactly the same motives as in the midst of another sea, upon a still more awful night, Moses, the founder, so to speak, of the miraculous, evinced many centuries before. Everything passes in regular and natural order, and yet the prophetic mind understands it, uses it, masters it. He begins by fearing danger, not merely for the ship, but for their own lives. Then, as the crisis deepens, the faith that he should preach Christ at Rome,

The Miracles of Man.

as God had promised, elevates him into the certainty that come what would his life was safe. But then from this and from his intense communion with God there springs another certainty as well. These men were his companions; common danger and hardship had made them dear to him; it was impossible that he should be saved and they lost; in a most real sense, God had given him the lives of "all that sailed with him." Then comes the exhortation not to fear, and the suggestion of the means of escape—"we must be cast on a certain island." Then the rebuke of the sailors' selfishness with its one invaluable lesson, that God will not save the lives even of those dearest to Him unless men do their duty—"unless these abide in the ship we cannot be saved." Then follows the courageous and wise advice to take food, himself, in the very spirit that we English like to see in our captains, setting the example by cheerful words and grateful actions, not omitting the simple, religious profession, "he gave thanks to God in presence of them all." And lastly, the literal fulfilment of the prophecy, "they escaped all safe to land." It is thus that in one brief moment the old world of the supernatural, of which Christ was the consummation, is seen passing into the new world of the natural, of which He was the founder; with its soundings of twenty and fifteen fathoms; its practical wisdom, "they ran the ship aground in a place where two seas met;" its recognition of secondary causes, "some on boards and some on broken pieces of the ship." Is all this miraculous? But it is most human. Is it then all natural? But it is most divine. Assuredly of this narrative it may be said that in it nature and miracle have met together, and science and religion have kissed each other.

It may be convenient to sum up at this point the conclusions at which we have arrived. There are then three distinct classes of miracles which may be described as follows. First, those which God works alone, that is, those events in which He approaches the minds of His servants, and makes Himself and His designs known to them by evidence, concerning the precise nature of which, whether objective or not, it is futile to inquire.

Second, those in which man co-operates with God by interpreting, and, in a measure, controlling the powers of nature that do His will. Here once more it is also futile to inquire whether these operations of nature are special or ordinary, the whole subject lying beyond the range of our experience. Only let us beware, in the interests of science no less than of religion, in ascribing them to what we are pleased to call chance.

Thirdly, those done by man of his own free will and energy, in which class I place the works of Jesus Christ alone. Here, most certainly, if we receive the history, we can have no doubt that the miracles He wrought were not merely the results of an interpreting mind, but of an originating will. In short, upon the hypothesis of Christ being more than man, we have just the phenomena described in His life that we should have anticipated. By His beneficent life and triumph over death He fulfils prophetically that law whose interpreter is science, and whose *summum bonum* is the attainment of the greatest perfection by the greatest number.

It is necessary, however, to note an apparent exception, not hitherto touched upon. The miracles attributed to Elisha do not come strictly within any of these classes.

The Miracles of Man.

In his case the miracles are the man. He is of little importance in the history save as a doer of wonderful works; and it concerns us at any rate to discover the idea which underlies the history of this, the last of the miraculous spirits of the Old Testament. What is presented to us is a life spent in doing good by supernatural means. Some of the stories look like undoubted legends; others, such as the healing of Naaman, must be founded on fact, unless the whole history is a pious fraud. Much, however, that seems to us improbable, and even monstrous, would, no doubt, disappear if the history were told in our modes of thought and use of language: and in the place thereof might arise simply a man gifted with extraordinary endowments of skill, knowledge, benevolence, and assiduity in helping his fellow creatures. Around the life of one to whom men habitually resorted for advice and healing might easily grow up a halo which prevents us from seeing him distinctly, though enough remains to reveal a man constantly employed in relieving his fellow-creatures in famine, anxiety, sickness, and even apparent death itself. And thus he closes fitly the course of Old Testament miracles, announcing by the whole tenor of his life that henceforth the domain of religion was to be individual rather than national, in the spirit rather than in nature, in deeds of personal beneficence rather than of historical grandeur. And so he, too, becomes a worthy representative of One who went about doing good, and whose earliest description of the purpose of His earthly life was this (preceding a reference to this very same Elisha): "The spirit of the Lord is upon Me, because He hath anointed Me to preach the gospel to the poor; He hath sent Me to heal the broken-hearted, to preach deliverance to the captives, and recovering of sight to the blind, to set at liberty them that are bruised, to preach the acceptable year of the Lord."

There remains one other subject to be touched upon of vital importance, I mean the investigation of the times at which miraculous agencies were manifested, and the discovery of the law, if there be any, to which these periodical appearances were subject. The importance lies in this. People are accustomed with the full approbation of religious teaching, to speak of the Jews as though their history was one prolonged record of supernatural interferences culminating in the life of Jesus Christ, and then for ever withdrawn. I believe that half of whatever prejudice against the Bible exists is due to this, and to no other cause. If the Jews were an exceptional people altogether, then the student of human nature ceases to take an interest in them; if their history be nothing but a series of marvels, then it becomes distasteful to those who have a wholesome dislike of the merely wonderful. Moreover, the sudden cessation of a continuous miraculous history creates as much intellectual discomfort as does also its limitation to one particular race. And yet it is hardly too much to say that the moment we examine the history itself, difficulties of the sort begin at once to fade away beneath a closer scrutiny and clearer apprehensions of the facts.

As we survey the long drama of Jewish history we see that there were in it three decisive epochs at which supernatural agency is said to have been powerfully manifested, and three men only who, in the strict sense of the words, were gifted with original miraculous power. Who these three were it is not difficult to determine. They are the

The Miracles of Man.   203

men who founded the spiritual greatness of Israel; who held mysterious communion with God for forty days in the wilderness, and there learned the secrets of true religion; whose deaths, so says the history, were not like those of other men; who met in awful mysteriousness on the Mount of Transfiguration; the Lawgiver, Prophet, and Redeemer, Moses, Elijah, and Jesus Christ.

No sooner do we realise this than the mass of recorded miracles begins to arrange and group itself, and we begin to see a kind of law running through the epochs of manifestation. But before discussing it it may be well to explain why Abraham is not included in the list as one of the founders of religion. It is simply because, in the strictest sense of the word, no miracle occurs in his history or in the Book of Genesis; by that I mean, that the distinction between special interferences of God and the ordinary occurrences of life is so entirely non-existent in the minds of the writers that we have no data by which to define the miraculous element. Mysterious messengers come and go, mystic voices are heard in men's minds urging them to do the will of God and holding out far-reaching promises of reward; visions occur which are related as facts, and facts which are but as dreams to those who saw them. And yet even so early as this, the thoroughly Jewish appreciation of facts shows itself in the vivid realistic story of Joseph, with whom nothing that can be reasonably called supernatural is ever associated. Strange old world that rests so securely upon its foundation of simple facts, and yet associates them with a divine will and presence, making them speak of God ! We can as little realise it as we can re-animate an extinct geological epoch, and yet we are joined to it by closest ties of spiritual descent. But it is well that those who dislike or disregard the Book of Genesis should seriously consider how different all this is from the earliest history of other nations, which is for the most part buried beneath an accretion of fables and legends, so that the lives and characters of real men fade away beneath the unnatural glow of actions attributed to heroes and other semi-divine beings.

With the Jews, on the contrary, the rise of miracles coincides with the dawn and with the fulness of substantial history. Moses is, of course, the one great originating miraculous power of this period. The account as presented to us is that God, in order to work out His eternal purposes of benevolence towards mankind, gave to one man a command over nature which enabled him to fulfil the counsels of Jehovah, and further to make His Being and attributes a living object of faith to the Jewish people. This done, the miraculous dies away, all that is left being merely as a few flashes of lightning out of a departing storm. Joshua, like Elisha and the Apostles, was set apart for his work by special outward "ordination." Whatever he did, he did because the spirit of Moses was upon him, and in the two or three occasional miracles recorded of him there are plain traces that the historical basis of fact is somewhat overmastered by the marvellous element. Thus we have an imitation of the crossing of the Red Sea, picturesque and dramatic effects at the Jordan and at Jericho, and poetical embellishments, such as the standing still of the sun and moon. And it is most necessary to remark that in whatever light we regard these incidents, they do not, as in the case of Moses, belong to the essence of the history, which, in all its details of victorious invasion, might be told equally well without them. Great events and wonderful successes were invested with supernatural colouring by minds fresh from the life of Moses and the deliverance from Egypt. And this miraculous element, doubtful and occasional under Joshua, dies away almost to nothing in the time of the Judges, and ceases altogether under the Kings. God did at times communicate with the spirits of men, but not so as to elevate them into the sphere of the miraculous. As to that wonderful period of Jewish history, from the call of Samuel to the death of Solomon, how many have realised that for all practical purposes it is destitute of recorded miracles? Who sufficiently considers that the life of David, the most eminent representative of the Jewish race and of the world's Messiah, is free from any supernatural intervention? Let us realise the evidential value of this statement. It shows that the Jews conceived of the most splendid period of their history under purely natural ideas. If so, then why did they revert to the supernatural under Ahab, unless they were constrained by the force of facts? How else are we to account for what we find recorded, that to Moses and Elijah were attributed supernatural gifts, while Samuel and David " did no miracle?"* This is a question that requires a serious answer.

The second outburst of the miraculous spirit followed the same law. It was caused by another revolution in religious thought, by another crisis in the history of the people, by another revelation of God's will, by the rise of another institution—the school of the later prophets. The rise of Elijah is accompanied by full and authentic histori-

* The exceptions are such as only prove the rule.

cal details; his one decisive miracle is of the most public character, and explains the course of future events. If at the close of the day the assembled multitude on Mount Carmel did not believe that fire had descended upon the sacrifice from heaven, and if they did not act under the inspiration of that belief, then I see no available distinction by which any narrative in the Old Testament can be rescued from the region of fable. How it happened, once more I repeat, we have no means of deciding, the one point of vital historical importance being, that those present believed that something had taken place which was due to the direct action of God. Elijah's spirit also falls upon a successor, and then dies away as suddenly as it arose. Henceforward we have that which he was sent to teach and to found, namely, the prophetic spirit understanding and thereby controlling history, just as Moses had controlled nature. But for eight or nine centuries onwards no real miracle marks the course of Jewish history, though God still speaks to the spirits of the prophets in ways which do not purport to be miraculous; and yet in another sense they might be called so, because they were only rendered possible and effectual by the national belief in the works of Moses and Elijah. In short, religion, like art and science, has its great eras of discovery and invention, whereby its life is sustained and prolonged.

Again, and for the last time, when the final dominion of God over man's inmost spirit, personal life, and future destiny was to be asserted, the working of the miraculous spirit was beheld, displaying the abiding purpose of God against sin, disease, suffering, and death. We need not for the purpose of this essay, examine the miracles of

Christ; they tell their own tale of goodness and power, and can by no possible means be explained away, except by denying the historical nature of the documents that relate them. The age was a scientific rather than a religious one; the distinction between miracles and nature was clearly established; the old prepossession in favour of miracles had yielded by virtue of their long cessation to a prejudice against them; the events were recorded in just the same spirit and with the same attention to outward details and inward impressions as mark the writings of veracious and accurate historians, the very discrepancies being signs of truth rather than of forgery; lastly, the most important biographer (from our present point of view) was a member of a scientific profession, Luke, the beloved physician. Here we are compelled definitely to choose between two alternatives. If the books were written by the men and at the time to which they are assigned, then there is an end of the matter, and the fact of God's intervention in the world by supernatural means must be recognised. If they were compilations of two or three generations later, then equally there is an end of the matter, and of some other very serious matters as well. But I pass from this to point out that the law to which I have called attention is found working here also. For a while the spirit of Christ's power lingered among the apostles, whose faith in Him now and then enabled them to do the works that He had done. Yet even here, and in so sober a writer as St Luke, we find traces of that exaggerated way of regarding things which seems to be the link between the genuine actions of the original worker and the purely fabulous stories of his religious descendants in later generations. Statements like that of Acts xix. 11, 12, do not however belong to the history as component and essential parts of it, as do the miracles of Christ, and one feels how easily general descriptions of this character may be influenced by popular excitement. Still less need we trouble ourselves with the fictions of later ages. It is enough to say that when examined, the law of miraculous appearances is completely against their credibility instead of forming an *à priori* reason in their favour. There is not much encouragement given to the invention of miracles in a history which limits the power practically to three persons, and consummates it in the person of the Son of God, whose works are a prophecy and a foundation of that spirit of beneficent working in which the youthful spirit of science and the ancient wisdom of religion find a common sphere for labour and usefulness.

I shall now attempt to illustrate and gather up all that has been said by sketching the history of Moses, because that is the crucial instance for deciding upon the reality and the meaning of the supernatural. The case stands thus.

The sojourn of the children of Israel in Egypt is neither more nor less true than the Roman occupation of Britain. No reasonable man doubts that the Jews were a race of bondsmen in Egypt, that they made their escape by some means or other, wandered in the wilderness for a term of years, settled in Canaan, and practised, with more or less foreign admixture, the worship of Jehovah, to whose intervention on their behalf they ascribed their redemption, their victory, and their institutions. Now the question we have to answer is this—How did this escape from Egypt with its accompanying foundation of the national life take place? The later we place the Exodus, the more difficult does the problem become. It has been remarked by Mr Zincke, in his book on Egypt, that owing to its geographical configuration, the country presents unusual facilities to the *de facto* ruler for suppressing all rebellious resistance to his power. And if we adopt the later date, which the present tendency of modern research is tending to fix for the Exodus (a more than doubtful result), then we are to suppose that a tribe of bondsmen made good their escape from the power of the then mightiest nation upon earth, the Egypt of Rameses and his successors. The Egyptians admit the fact, and account for it by a legend which is the obvious production of national pride. The Jews also account for it in a history which, if it were not in part supernatural, would enforce not only consideration but assent by its antiquity, its local colouring, its accurate details, its artistic beauty, its moral sublimity, its religious spirit, above all by its perfect adequacy to account for the phenomena to be explained. Yet, even apart from the supernatural, there are things in it—for instance, its dramatic arrangement, doubtful chronology, inconsistency with human nature, and the like,—which challenge closer scrutiny and require some rational explanation. How then, supposing that we do not reject the supernatural upon *à priori* grounds, are we to reconcile these conflicting elements, and render the miraculous reasonable, and therefore credible?

We picture to ourselves, first of all, Moses as the self-elected deliverer of his people. We see him driven into the wilderness by failure, the narrative of which, though wonderfully true to human nature, and resting upon a clear basis of fact, seems to suggest, what would appear to nineteenth century modes of thought, a kind of ideal treatment of the facts, in order to bring out the permanent religious and human value. He remains in exile, still hoping for deliverance, but destitute of that absolute certainty as to God's designs by which men are impelled *themselves* to undertake the work which they see is to be done. So hesitating there comes to him the scene at the burning bush, in which by outward signs that seemed to him to bespeak the presence of God, and by an inward intimation that he took for the voice of God, he is told that the eternal Jehovah designs him to be the deliverer of Israel. Practically this is all the miracle that is required. God being what He is, can and will save His covenant people from the power of their enemies, and so, secure in this confidence, he returns to Egypt. The methods of God's working are suggested to him by the most obvious facts; in the plagues to which the land was from time to time subject were to be found the ministers of the purpose of Jehovah, to whom they belonged. The discovery that the nine plagues were natural to Egypt (even to the ninth, darkness, which appears at first sight well-nigh incredible), is a striking confirmation of the historical truthfulness of the Bible, and creates at least as strong a presumption in its favour as any difficulty that modern research has created against it. Thus we have a picture of a succession of plagues *natural in themselves*, but interpreted for a moral purpose by what we may call a miraculous spirit. Moses rides as it were upon the storm that bursts upon the devoted land, foretells its approach, its duration, its departure, proclaiming in the ear of king and court, "This is come upon you from the eternal justice of the supreme God, whose laws you are breaking in your treatment of His people. Your divine river, your divine cattle, your priests, your possessions, the sun you worship, all are instruments in the hand of a moral Being, whose will is righteousness, mercy, and judgment for sin."* So far we can account for all the circumstances, the hesitation of Pharaoh, his alternations of fear and pride, his doubts as to the cause of these accumulated disasters, the growing power and urgency of Moses as the heart of Egypt waxed fainter and fainter.

Then we come to the tenth plague. Shocking as it seems to our ideas, and unfitted to display the character of God as we conceive it, yet I should accept it if there were no other difficulty than an *à priori* prejudice as to what God ought to do under a given set of circumstances, the true bearings of which we most imperfectly comprehend. But the difficulty lies in quite another direction. How, again I must ask, could human life be carried on under such conditions? How is it possible that no true trace of such a catastrophe should be found in the Egyptian annals? Or when we contemplate the remains of Egyptian civilisation and survey the grand wise heads that look down upon us from temple and tomb, how can we picture to ourselves the infatuation which could gather an army to pursue an enemy whose God had smitten with instantaneous death the first-born child of every soldier in its ranks? May we not also ask what is meant by the "first-born?" Is it eldest sons whose fathers were yet alive? If so, then the warlike strength of the nation must have perished. And when we hear of the destruction of the first-born of cattle (a practical impossibility), then we know that the sacred historian is

* This thought is, I need not say, familiar to all readers of Mr Maurice.

drawing for us not a representation of literal fact, but such a conception of the stupendous event to which Israel's emancipation was due, as would be taken by a religious mind of that or of a somewhat later time.

And when we come to inquire what the literal fact might be, our only difficulty is that of making a choice between two theories, either of which is probable and adequate. The Jews, as Dr Stanley has pointed out, attributed their deliverance to a pestilence, the Egyptians to a foreign invasion; and if to disbelieve the narrative, literally taken, be rationalism, then it is a comfort to remember that rationalism is of earlier origin than the Christian era, and finds a place in the Bible itself. Twice over we have the simple statement: "He smote the first-born of Egypt, *the chief of all their strength.*" And this is the best commentary upon the story. In a moment of prostration and alarm, caused by some terrible national disaster, the Israelites made good their escape; with returning strength and pride came the resolution to pursue them. Moses acted, under the influence of religious faith, exactly as any modern man of science would have done if he could calculate to a nicety the force and laws of winds, currents, tides, and storms. What he did was natural, his power to do it was miraculous. He knew that God was master of the sea, and that across the sea lay the only hope of the salvation solemnly promised to him. If ever there be a story which, upon the face of it, rejects any marvellous interference with nature, this is the one. The idea of the Egyptians plunging madly into a sea miraculously divided before their eyes in order that their enemies might escape, passes the bounds of human credulity, and reminds us of certain words of St

Paul's, "Be not children in understanding; howbeit be children in malice, but in understanding be men."

The actions of Moses in the wilderness are all susceptible of a similar explanation. The man was miraculous, all else was natural. Nature once more waits upon the servant of God in thunderings and lightnings, and a terrible loud voice as of the trumpet of God, while under the inspiration of her awful voice he lays the foundation of the first great code of national law, and plants deep in the heart of humanity the worship of God and the knowledge of goodness. Just as all the plagues of Egypt were natural to the country, so were the blessings of the desert. To "discover the springs of waters," to give manna for food, to foretell the flight of quails, to predict military disaster, to restore health by restoring faith and courage—all this is at once the work of a divinely-inspired man, and yet in itself is no more than a scientific man could accomplish, if he knew all the necessary laws, movements, and conditions of external phenomena. There may have been, for what we can tell, more of an originating power of Moses than I think it necessary to suppose; what is required to be believed is the working of a mind inspired by communications from God in and through nature, and therefore enabled to overrule all natural events and agencies for the work that lay before him of saving Israel and teaching them religion. Beyond all question his achievements were such as to convince the people by plain, palpable works of help and deliverance that God was indeed with him and amongst them: this much at least is attested by history and poetry for many a succeeding generation. They made no nice inquiries as to the limits of the natural and the miraculous; nor can we, with the materials at our disposal, do better than imitate their silence. Let it be enough if where they saw nature obeying the *will* of God for their good we can see nature obeying the *law* of God for ours. And as moral beings let us call the result of this perception by its one appropriate name—faith.

I have already transgressed the limits I had imposed upon myself, but there are two remarks which it is necessary to make in order to obviate criticism that comes from two very different quarters. In the first place I should like to point out that what is required and has been here attempted is not the employment of a mere critical destructiveness, but the attainment of some positive result: we want to know not what did not happen but what did. And if it is at present impossible to explain minutely the method of miraculous working, we must look to further discoveries in the pathway of science as our only means of learning more about the subject. And meanwhile, we can at least point out, as I have endeavoured to do, some of the links that bind sound science and true religion together. The time may come when in the increased knowledge of mind and matter, subject and object, together with their mutual independence, any theories that may be adopted now will be regarded as mere vague, tentative advances in the direction where truth will ultimately be found. Or it may equally come when supernatural events, explained in some such way as we have been considering, will be accepted as historically true (though intellectually inexplicable) because the moral predispositions of mankind will have decided in their favour. Or they may vanish out of history altogether, and with them the religion to which they have given birth.

In the second place I desire to ask those who are dissatisfied with the meagreness or doubtfulness of the results attained this simple question—Upon what basis is it proposed to found religious belief? In religion as in other matters possession is nine-tenths of the law, and men who have inherited a beneficent, venerable, and beautiful system, may be content to accept the goods provided for them without any too curious inquiry into the validity of their title-deeds. "The Bible must be true;" "the Church cannot be wrong;" "Christianity is perfectly adapted to men's moral wants;" "it is the best account yet given of the unknowable"—any or all of these positions are sufficient for men whose religious belief is not seriously threatened. But in law, if a serious action is brought against the possessor of property he is bound to make good his title; and so in religion, if his position is actually assaulted, he must be prepared to give some rational defence of it. Why is the Bible infallible? Why in religion alone does common opinion or a majority of votes decide what is and is not true? How do we know that the Christian morality is the best possible for all ages? Are we sure that science cannot give a better account of things? These are pleas to which a man must find an answer, and come into court, and take some trouble if he means to retain his estate. And I suspect that the arguments and positions of his counsel are as unsatisfactory to the mind of an ardent and self-confident religionist, as are the unimpassioned statements of an advocate to the client who does not like to feel that his title to his paternal heritage depends upon the right legal construction of old documents and bygone transactions. If this be so, both will discover their mistake only when their cause is lost.

Practically, indeed, there is but one defensible basis of religious belief apart from actual facts. In defiance, as I think, of history, and in opposition, I am sure, to the best conclusions of modern thought, men may assert that the knowledge of God is intuitional and immediate, independent of experience, and obtained by a spiritual faculty designed for this purpose. This may be the case, but truth obliges us to say that the process and the faculty are themselves that which science would call supernatural, and the God thus attained nothing better in her mind than an idol. In calling them supernatural, we mean to say that all human thought is receptive not creative ; and so the legitimate or natural province of the religious faculty is to accept or deny, to combine or disentangle, to appreciate, verify, and judge the objects presented to human consciousness. And if man can reach the knowledge of God by innate intuitions, then is there a kind of discordant dualism at the very root of his reasoning powers. But the fact is that as men in the natural world work with and upon existing materials without any power of creating new ones; so in religion man cannot attain to a permanent belief in a personal God of love and goodness merely by surveying the operations of nature or the workings of his own soul. He turns anxious eyes Heavenwards, but there is "no voice, nor any to answer, nor any that regards." And, furthermore, call the object of our belief what we will and worship it as we may, it is but of the earth, earthy, or at best but of man, human. We are worshipping ultimately the work of our own minds, the creature, not the Creator, of our own imaginations, whether it be an image, or the highest type of human character, or the aggregation of all humanity become subjective. It is, I suspect, this subtle taint of idolatry that sets scientific men so resolutely against religion, because they see the productions of man's genius or his folly elevated into the rank of gods, and clothed with a dignity and power that belong not to them, and that too often impede the march of truth. It is this which drives them into the opposite and, upon the face of it, unscientific extreme of acquiescing in the existence of an unknown God, in preference to worshipping an idol. I agree with them; but because the office of science is to *know*, I go on to inquire into that history which claims to reveal the unknowable to man by facts that fall within his experience. The results of that inquiry I affirm to be as follows. God has displayed Himself as a living personal Being in acts of love, justice, and over-ruling power. These acts are not incompatible with the scientific idea of law, but present remarkable affinities not only with it but with the domain of science in general. They give power and reality to all the choicest hopes and noblest speculations of the human mind Godwards, and do not rob the world of a single religious intuition or idea. They account for the fact that Christianity has become the religion of civilised humanity. Finally, they require as the condition of being believed a moral predisposition in the age or in the individual which does not reject the supernatural as such, but is willing to accept any revelation of God that can be legitimately proved, rationally explained, and beneficially employed.

I venture to express a hope before I close that some of my readers will be induced to compare for themselves the method and the results of natural and revealed theology respectively. In spite of the ability which marks the writings of the former, I am compelled to assert that as to method it seems to me to cast about high-sounding words and phrases which have no reality in the world of facts and things: while as to results, it has not practically advanced one step beyond the most commonplace, but by no means satisfactory, positions of such a book as Paley's "Natural Theology." If, indeed, any one cares to see what Natural and Revealed Religion respectively can accomplish in the way of advancing truth by persuading the minds of men, let him read Paley's "Natural Theology," and then his "Evidences of Christianity," together with the "Horæ Paulinæ." I am greatly mistaken if he do not come to the conclusion that the value, indeed the very meaning, of the first varies with every shifting shadow of metaphysical belief, while the latter remain just as true, as substantial, and as convincing as when they first saw the light. I am very far from denying that Natural Religion has its own proper sphere of usefulness, but I do deny that this is the sphere which Paley himself claimed for it—namely, to demonstrate by intellectual process the existence of God, and thus prepare the way for a future Revelation of God to man. On the contrary, I believe the right and reasonable method to be this. When the mind has become convinced that Revelation conveys a true account of the otherwise unknown God by facts that fall within man's experience, it will then turn to Natural Religion for proof that the existence of such a God is not inconsistent with nature, but is rather the one thing needed to give life, meaning, and beauty to the universe in which we find ourselves placed.

Since the above essay was written a passage has occurred to me which seems to throw immense light upon the origin and nature of Hebrew theism, upon the effect of the inspiration which comes from nature, and upon the real meaning of the earliest Scriptural phraseology. Let me quote the words in their archaic simplicity. After a solemn sacrifice, in which the people entered into eternal covenant with Jehovah, we read in Exodus xxiv. 9-11, as follows: "Then went up Moses and Aaron, Nadab and Abihu, and seventy of the elders of Israel; and they saw the Lord God of Israel: and there was under His feet as it were a paved work of a sapphire stone, and as it were the body of heaven in his clearness. And upon the nobles of the children of Israel He laid not His hand: also they saw God, and did eat and drink."

Upon this passage I desire to ask two simple questions.

1. Will any reasonable man deny that this is a faithful tradition of some real event? Not unless we are to apply totally different tests to the Bible from those by which historical criticism judges other books.

2. Will any reasonable man assert that the words are to be understood literally? Not unless he is prepared to assert that man can see God and live. Now, the explanation of this event lets a shaft of light deep into the hidden sources of Jewish religion.

After the most solemn and awe-inspiring ceremonies—being nothing less than the national dedication to Jehovah—the elders of Israel are led up by what they believe to be the summons of God to the mount, where His presence was attested by natural wonders all around them. Upon their eyes, the eyes of men accustomed to Egyptian flatness, and expecting a vision of the Almighty, there bursts that glorious desert view, clear, blue, expanded, arched, radiant. And to them it was the very God who was with them. Not precisely visible, yet not wholly invisible. Here was the God, their God, who was greater than all the gods of the earth, who comprehended the world, who rode on the wings of the wind, whose path was in the waters, who made the winds His messengers and flames of fire His ministers, of whose majesty and creative power, thus realised, the 104th Psalm is the latest and most complete description. This conception was at once a vast step upwards above all other ideas of God, and yet still a step in the natural evolution of religious belief, not an unnatural break in it. It was akin to Pantheism, it was consistent with Polytheism, and these two modes of thought formed an element in the future religion that warred against the truth. But it was preserved from the first by their unquenchable belief in a God who had performed personal actions towards them, from the second by their belief that the One Righteous God *must* be Lord of all, be the others what they would.

I do not know how far this explanation may satisfy the theology or the philosophy of the day. Of one thing I am very sure, that in method it will satisfy science, because it attempts to explain the origin and nature of Jewish religion by and from the recorded facts of their history. Perhaps, indeed, that religion might have seemed a more excellent thing, and more adapted for the purposes of nineteenth-century controversies, if these awe-stricken Bedouins had exclaimed one to another, "Brothers, let our God henceforward be 'a power not ourselves that makes for righteousness.'" But, alas! poor people, they were not Mr Matthew Arnolds!

A SCIENTIFIC ACCOUNT OF INSPIRATION.

THE subject of Inspiration is beyond all contradiction the most important of the many religious questions that now agitate men's minds, and it may be taken as a sign of the worthlessness of common religious thought that so little of the attention abundantly bestowed on minor points of doctrine is turned in this direction. In the most general terms it may be defined as the communication of the spirit of God to that of man, and its importance lies in this : that it covers the meeting-point of religion and science. No doubt there are many who would prefer that the two lines of thought should be drawn parallel to each other and so never meet. But I am afraid that the principle of competition so dear to mercantile instincts will not avail where the journey is that of the human mind towards truth ; or rather, it is more correct to say that it will avail, and that the traffic of human thought will prefer the swiftest, easiest, and most commodious route. Up to a certain point, which may be described as the consciousness of being able to think, science claims, and justifies her claim, to be able to conduct the intellect by her own methods exclusively; beyond it lies that region of the unknown cause or author of the human consciousness which is the province of religion. The point, therefore, at which this unknown cause makes itself felt within the limits of common experience is the junction between science and religion, and belongs to both alike so far as use is concerned. But to which of the two does it belong to give an account of it? Hitherto religion has claimed the right for herself and undertaken the duty with no other resources than her own to keep her. It may be worth while to point out the very deplorably meagre and indefinite results which have been attained.

For instance, how inspiration operates; within what limits and to what extent; whether there is or has been any special manifestation in a particular book or among a chosen people; how far, if at all, it is to be distinguished as a religious influence from the inspiration of the artist or the mathematician; what authority it carries with it, wherein that authority resides, and upon what evidence it rests,— these and many similar questions are still the subjects of interminable controversy. Everybody wants to have the authority of Inspiration on his side, few will condescend to examine its real nature with the view of ascertaining from that source alone what its legitimate authority is. In short, every school of Christian thought accepts Inspiration as an ultimate fact, and from it derives with equal assurance of conviction, vehemence of assertion, confusion of thought, and absence of solid proof, the authority of Pope, Church, Bible, and private judgment. But the dictum of science is that wherever opposing or various theories are formed concerning the operation of any given force, it is a pretty clear proof that the real nature of that force remains yet to be discovered. And so she goes on building up her impregnable rampart of facts, much as the Roman army built their wall around the Holy City while the defenders were exhausting their rage upon each other. Thank God, in the last resort religious truth always escapes with the Christians to Pella !

Again it is a noteworthy fact that while the authority of Inspiration is abundantly claimed, the thing itself has never been authoritatively defined. Thus it is frequently asserted as a proof of the admirable wisdom of the English Church that she has nowhere defined the exact nature and extent of Scriptural Inspiration. Upon the moral side this admiration is perfectly justifiable. To define by dogmatic authority what the teachers of a national church are to believe upon such a subject is no doubt a grievous wrong, fatal to truth, because fatal to sincerity and inquiry. Nor is the reason of this reticence at all difficult to discover. There was at the time of the Reformation no method by which reasonable men, such as were the English reformers, could arrive at any positive conclusion upon the subject. But that which is right and befitting in the articles of a national church, or in a pre-scientific age, may, viewed in another aspect, become entirely unworthy of rational religion. Explanations which theology may very properly decline to lay down as essential to a right belief may, nevertheless, be clearly demonstrated by the ordinary methods of investigation as they are adopted by positive thought. Science is justly impatient of open questions : a thing is either true in this way or in that way, and the question remains open only until some man solves it or, more accurately, till some man persuades the world that he has solved it. And of all religious questions that of inspiration is the very last that men should acquiesce in leaving open. It falls in its phenomena strictly within the limits of human experience, and it forms the basis of all practical religion. No doubt in the last resort it is incomprehensible, just as is the law of gravitation, but like this and every other law it may be, and ought to be expressed in scientific terms and be capable, to speak generally, of scientific treatment. Failing this, there is no other course left for it but to disappear with all convenient speed from the number of the things that are admitted as suitable and fruitful objects of human thought.

It is generally observed that just in proportion as the mass of men have no definite or accurate information about a given fact, so much the more positively do they dogmatise concerning it, and so much the more resolutely do they seek to enforce the necessity of a belief in it upon other people. They call it a mystery and bow down before it with a delight as genuine and as unaffected as ever filled the heart of a savage contemplating his idol of shapeless wood and stone. It has so fared with the Inspiration of the Bible. Together with the kindred and no less important truth of the Divinity of our Lord it has become the standard of orthodoxy, the test by which opinions are measured, the object of just admiration, of real eloquence, of elaborate discussion, but not of serious and rational explanation. A book on Inspiration was indeed published some years ago by the Rev. C. A. Row, which honestly undertook not indeed so much to ascertain the nature of inspiration as to define its sphere and to describe its effects by the inductive method. But though warmly praised by the few who were capable of entering into the author's spirit, it did not, I believe, obtain a very wide acceptance in the general religious world—one more proof that the popular religious mind cares little or nothing at present for serious subjects that lie outside, or rather underneath, the topics of party contention and passing popular interest. What, indeed, popular religion chiefly hates is a new method of treatment. New opinions, it can answer, or failing that can persecute, or failing that can meet by fresh definitions of the faith, by revivals of ancient errors that from long lying by have almost the gloss and air of novel truths, or by a clamorous and more persistent assertion of its undying belief in the authority which it has set up over itself. But it sees with the instinctive perception of fear that a new method such as the application of scientific thought to religious phenomena cuts away the ground from all parties alike, forces them to consider ultimate truths, puts the whole question in a new light, and makes useless much of the old machinery, formulæ, definitions, and dogmas. With the men of the new method it has but one way of dealing—to take as little notice as possible of their existence, and to weigh their conclusions in the old balance, stigmatising them as mere revivals of ancient heresies. And when it is no longer safe or possible to ignore the new spirit, then it only remains to turn round and affirm stoutly that orthodoxy all along meant and said the same. I have no doubt that the popular theologians of the next generation will be chiefly occupied in singing the praises of the scientific method, and in finding, amidst the chance rhetoric of the popular theologians of the present, intimations that they too were the precursors, the prophets, and the enraptured admirers of that tendency of thought which they are straining every nerve to repel from the field of religion.

It is best, however, to let the facts of the case speak for themselves, and I go on, therefore, to inquire what is the received account of inspiration. I cannot find that it amounts to anything more definite than this: that the Spirit of God has entered into the minds of certain men— whether Jewish chroniclers or Christian bishops or the successor of the Pontifex Maximus—in such a way as to make them infallible under certain conditions, as to which there is the very widest difference of opinion. It is, however, agreed that this influence was and is supernatural and overmastering, so that in some way the words they spoke (and speak) must be taken to express the mind and judgment of the Almighty, who interfered to secure this express result. Now, surely what one instinctively asks for is some verification of a phenomenon so extraordinary. No one denies that this or any other astounding occurrence may take place if God so wills it; but this concession so far from dispensing with the necessity of proof only makes the conceder more rigorous in his demands for it. It is, indeed, a very fair remark that men may require evidence that, either in amount or kind, cannot possibly be obtained, but in the case before us the evidence is practically *nil.* Let us, however, examine this account of inspiration more in detail.

1. In itself it explains nothing. It is the mere description of a mystery in terms of religion, and reminds one somehow of an unsolved equation. It takes the fact (admitted *pro hac vice*) that communication from a personal God to the spirit of man is possible, and upon this foundation goes on by a simple dogmatic process to build up the inspiration of whatever authority it selects. But it fails to

give any reasonable description of the thing itself, because it does not attempt to distinguish it from other things that resemble it or to adjust its relations with them. To be particular, it is justly chargeable with these two capital omissions. It does not distinguish religious inspiration from other communications of God in poetry, art, or science; and it does not distinguish the inspiration of the Jews and early Christians from that of other nations and religions. And if we are met by the vague proposition that the difference is in degree and not in kind then another remark is at once suggested.

2. Why—to take the one instance upon which there is the most general agreement—is the Bible said to be inspired so as to become an authority, indeed an infallible authority, upon religious subjects? Why is it to be accepted as true? There are, for instance, elements in it—such as the discourses of our Lord in St John—that transcend the ordinary powers of human memory. Why are we to believe these to be true? Generally the answer is that we know the Bible to be true because it is inspired, to which a more rational school of thought replies that we know it to be inspired because we know it to be true. But then why once more do we believe it to be true, or, more pertinently, if it be true, why do we need theories of special supernatural inspiration to sustain the burden of truths which have been satisfactorily proved to our reason by other means? But in point of fact this assumption that what seems true to me, or my age, or my church, or my family of nations, is therefore true, is only the right of private judgment, however skilfully disguised, pushed to the extreme that ends in absurdity. Far be it from me to speak with anything but

respect of that Protestant form of it to which we owe the most precious privileges of spiritual freedom, but it is impossible not to discern the destructive effects of scientific thought upon that corner-stone of Protestantism, the right of private judgment. No man has any real right to think what is wrong, and to believe what is untrue, merely because he likes it. Ultimately the question resolves itself into the nature of the authority that shall decide the faith and practice of mankind. Catholicism sets up one authority purporting, and that falsely, to be based upon a specific revelation of God. Science sets up another claiming, and that truly, to be derived from the acquisition of positive truth ascertained from time to time by the reason which God has given us. And between this upper and lower mill-stone Protestantism is likely to be crushed to atoms unless it elects frankly to make common cause with the latter, to set up no authority as final, and to allow no authority at all except such as can be verified by reasonable evidence, and satisfy the progressive moral instincts of mankind.

3. I am, however, well aware that logical victories of this kind do not decide the matter for what may be called the practical purposes of life. It will be answered that the Bible as a mere fact in itself, previous to and in spite of any analysis, carries its own conviction to the practical religious mind as speaking the mind of God. It is its own authority for its own inspiration. At the risk of seeming to abate somewhat from the rigour of scientific demonstration, I must confess that this seems a *practically* valid position to take up. After all, no argument for the authenticity of St John's Gospel is half so convincing as the

fact that the man who was capable of writing that book gives his readers to understand that he was no other than St John himself. But even after this very considerable concession is made, we are no whit nearer either to a demonstration or an account of the special inspiration, the existence of which we have admitted. No such proof, no such account, is given in the Bible itself. It is impossible to do justice to the strength of this position in a few sentences, but fortunately the facts are well known, and the deductions to be derived from them as obvious as candid minds can require.

The plain truth is that the Jews found themselves possessed of a national literature of the most exalted character, and, in a time of religious feebleness and decay, learned to attach an extraordinary and to a certain extent artifical value to it; and that the early Christian Church followed their example. They adopted this literature without any critical discrimination of its contents apparently upon no other system than that of receiving all the fragments of early Jewish writings, and writings that were supposed to belong to apostolic times. They erected no test of inspiration, for the very simple reason that the books themselves afforded none. These range over the whole compass of literature, come before us in the most natural manner as records of what has been done or said, deal with the most insignificant no less than with the most important events in the same tone and spirit, make no claim to authority, much less to infallibility. The utmost that can be said is, that just as the Jews regarded God as the author of every good thing which they enjoyed, so they regarded Him as the inspirer of every good thought which they possessed. Exactly as men fell away from inspiration itself did they begin to perceive the necessity of theories, definitions, and a recognised canon. I entirely agree with them in believing in this necessity, but I affirm that a reasonable account of inspiration must be derived, not from the authority of the Bible, which nowhere pretends to give it, but from the methods of science investigating the nature and the history of man.

It may be well before leaving this part of our subject to consider the supreme wisdom with which St Paul treated this question. It was brought before him in the most direct way by the difficulties of the Corinthian Church concerning "spiritual gifts." His position may be summarily stated as follows :—

1. All these gifts alike are to be traced to one and the self-same Spirit, so that no distinction between the greatest and the least of them is to be made in point of origin.— 1 Cor. xii. 11.

2. The most ordinary and fundamental Christian thought, namely the recognition of Jesus as the Christ, is equally due to the direct influence of the Holy Ghost.—1 Cor. xii. 3.

3. In deciding a plain question of moral expediency, that of marriage and re-marriage, he claims to have, and feels the need of, the help of the Spirit of God.— 1 Cor. vii. 40.

4. But this spiritual power may be expressed in ordinary moral terms, for it is also described as his "giving judgment as one that hath obtained mercy of the Lord to be found faithful."—1 Cor. vii. 25.

5. Lastly this spiritual power is to be regarded in a natural sense, because the spirits of the prophets are subject

to the prophets, God being the author, not of confusion, but of peace.—1 Cor. xiv. 32.

It is thus that inspired wisdom deals with theories of inspiration. No attempt is made to go beyond the line of strict deduction from facts then ascertained, but at the same time a prophetic intimation is given which it is the business of science to realise. For if the spirit be subject to the prophets simply as men, then since everything that is natural and human falls within the sphere of science, it is clear that the mental sciences, in taking cognisance of man as a thinking being, take cognisance also of that inspiration which in time and in history has been wrought in man in such a way as to be subject to him. Furthermore, if God be the author, not of confusion that defies analysis, but of an order that invites knowledge, then it is possible to discover the law upon which that order reposes. All which is plainly the work of scientific investigation.

Following, then, the spirit of St Paul, we turn from the region of dubious authority, confused beliefs, and half-concealed ignorance, which make up theology, and we go on to inquire whether it is not possible to obtain a reasonable meaning for inspiration, and a definite place for it in the domain of facts by the ordinary methods of inquiry. And as it is of the greatest importance to know what the requirements of science are, I will lay down the eight following propositions which I think, it will be confessed, are as stringent, and, at the same time, as impartial as can fairly be desired.

1. The communication of the Spirit of God to man may be accepted as an hypothesis to be proved or disproved by evidence, and tested by time.

2. It may be granted that this communication, supposing it to be possible, operated to an unusual degree and in a remarkable manner among the Jewish people at various periods, up to the final destruction of the national life.

3. It is not necessary that this communication should be apprehended by sensible means, but only that it should be demonstrated by the phenomena it presents: these would then be the results of a cause, the absolute nature of which is beyond our faculties. No one has seen or touched that power of attraction called gravitation: thought is real but not perceptible by the senses: the moral emotions are cognisable only by the effect they produce.

4. But though positive demonstration is by the nature of the case excluded, yet it is absolutely essential that a clear, definite account of inspiration should be given in plain, intelligible language. It must be assigned a place in the number of facts, and must be distinguished from other facts, not by being dismissed as supernatural, but by having its place in nature scientifically defined. It must be in accordance with all known analogy in other spheres of thought, and must not introduce disturbing forces into the course of ascertained law.

5. A scientific account of inspiration must explain all the phenomena that fall legitimately within its scope, and must be expected to clear up difficulties as yet unsolved. The immoral conduct of religious people and the moral conduct of non-religious people is a case in point.

6. It must derive its authority from no other source than that of truth ascertained by inquiry and capable of recommending itself to men's minds. And it must exercise none

except by persuasion and by the penalties which befal those who disregard proved facts.

7. It must on no account take sides in any discussions still pending, for instance, the existence of free will, or the nature of morality. To be true it must be capable of being harmonised with any doubtful opinion that may ultimately turn out to be the right one. On the other hand it cannot be expected to be more precise in its conclusions than are the mental sciences with which it is connected and upon which it depends. It must be content to share the uncertainty or the ignorance which characterise these, provided that it is always enabled to keep pace with their improvement in certainty and knowledge. In the present state of these sciences any account of inspiration must of necessity be superficial and tentative, but not therefore useless or untrue.

8. In an inquiry of this description it is obvious that words descriptive of abstract realities must be employed. Now, of these science has one set, such as nature, law, experience; and religion has another, such as God, will, faith. Hence it is necessary that the propositions should be so framed as to suit both classes of words and of ideas expressed by them; that is to say, that supposing the propositions are drawn up with the signs x, y, and z, then it must be possible to substitute for these letters either the religious or scientific terms. I shall use the former of course, but (I hope) in such a way as not to make any assertion that would be untrue if stated in the phraseology of the latter. No more rigorous or satisfactory test could I think be employed.

It is then with these trammels, treading every step upon explosive missiles, threading a doubtful path amongst old but not exhausted controversies, blinded by the dust and rubbish of metaphysical discussions, hated by theology and slighted by science, that the men who are to re-form religion upon the basis and by the methods of science, must make their way to truth and contumely.

And yet, when we come to deal with the facts of the case, difficulties, however real, are apt to disappear speedily under the powerful solvent of some principles recognised in other branches of knowledge, but of novel application to the one under discussion. This is ever the way with truth. By means of statements so obvious that people do not only accept them but even try to persuade themselves that they have all along held them, light and order immediately begin to drive away the doubts and mysteries that only derive an apparent reality from the darkness in which they are enveloped. The simple affirmation of facts is much like striking a match in the dark. Accordingly all that I feel called upon to do is to give an account of the being of man so framed as to enable us to include in it that one of his faculties called religion.

Now, the first fact presented to consciousness as constituting man is the power of thought. Mind comes to him as something from without, which he owns in company with other men, which he cannot originate himself, nor discover the origin of outside himself. Whether we describe it in the language of science or religion it remains incomprehensible, because thoughts are not the essence but the actions of the mind, of that which religion calls the divine in man, and from which it endeavours, laboriously or intuitively, to frame its own idea of God. It is true in a sense, and false in a sense, if we say either that man thinks with the brain, or that the brain thinks. All we can be certain of is a succession of thoughts, suggested to us, coming upon us, taking possession of us, blowing like the wind where they list. They are primarily independent of us though subject to us the moment they become our thoughts. In sleep, indeed, all control by the will vanishes, and thought, as a thing outside of us and presented to us, is plainly apparent. It is not at all necessary to draw any line of distinction between men and the other animals; the bare fact that we share with other creatures a power of thinking, which it is not ours to create, is enough for our present purpose. Religion, while leaving to science the analysis and examination of the phenomena of thought, would call the fact itself the gift of God, and would claim for those who possess it a share of the divine essence.

The next fact that belongs to us is the material organisation with which this power of thought is connected, by which, and through which, alone it has for us any positive existence. The general power of thinking is conditioned and shaped into various faculties by the varying bodies of different individuals. Of the general truth of this proposition no scientific man will, I presume, entertain any doubt, though we are as yet merely upon the threshold of the sciences that deal with the subject. At present all that can be said for certain is, that no other explanation of the phenomenon presented by the existence of widely different intellectual gifts, has been suggested or appears to be comprehensible. Not, indeed, that we are without more direct evidence than this. It is certain that human reasoning requires a certain amount of brain, that it varies with the size and formation of the brain, and grows with its growth from childhood to age. Moreover, children are born with certain mental faculties in an extraordinary state of development, for which no possible reason can be assigned, except, to use the widest phrase, the physical arrangement or condition of their bodies. Some are musical, others artistic, others literary. Some have prodigious gifts of memory, or surpassing capacities of reflection, or an innate power of acquiring languages, or special moral aptitudes. In some the mind seems to proceed naturally by an elaborate process of association of ideas, in others it leaps to its conclusion or performs its work by a process so swift and unforeseen as to deserve the name of intuition. How all this comes about, by what laws of inheritance, by what variations (small or large) of nature, by what union of parental temperaments, by what local, national, or climatic influences, to what part of our cerebral, nervous, or, more widely, our physical organisation each mental faculty is allied, remains the secret of to-day, the inquiry of to-morrow, the discovery, so men dare to hope, of days to come. All I need to affirm is that the mind is distributed into its various channels by the disposition of the atoms of the body, and that this disposition comes to each individual from without, that it is a gift of that power which religion calls God. Science once more explains by the operation of natural laws that arrangement which religion attributes to the providential order of a beneficent Creator. Both mean the same thing, and both confess that thing to be in its essence incomprehensible.

So far for man's mental and bodily nature; there remains, to complete the description, his history. Circumstances, events, surroundings come to him and fashion him as by the impression of an external moulding instrument. He does not make his history any more than he makes his mind or his body. All his faculties are discovered, educated, and wrought upon by the things that come to him. Village Hampdens die, and unknown Miltons remain mute and inglorious, because nothing occurs to call their faculties into action. To what extent, indeed, the lack of opportunity operates in preventing the development of individuals remains, and perhaps must remain, uncertain; it is one of those negative questions of which wise men fight shy, for wisdom occupies herself in discovering the causes of the things that are, not the reason why things are not. But the positive assertion that the gift of opportunity exercises the greatest influence in altering the whole course of men's intellectual lives is true beyond a doubt. By opportunity I mean all that ranges between the startling events in human life called crises, and the daily press of surrounding circumstances that stimulate the mind in one direction and train it for a special work. The things that are, and the events that happen are the only known source of special inspiration. Each faculty of the mind, in short, energises by feeding upon these, and thrives by the work which it performs.

And here, with every intention to be impartial, I must confess that in my opinion religion can give an adequate account and a reasonable name for this state of things, whereas science can do neither. What is the cause of either the striking events or the overwhelming pressure of circumstances which are producing at every moment such tremendous effects upon the mind of man, and through him upon the universe? The work of science may be not unfairly described as the undertaking to explain why a thing is, and must be, in this way rather than in that. It, or rather the common sense of which it is the outcome, can, for instance, tell us why the discovery of a heathen idol washed from the Atlantic (by the way is the story true?), stirred up within the mind of Columbus new and stronger thoughts of a world beyond the sea, but it cannot so much as form to itself an intelligible reason why the little image was brought within his view, instead of being picked up by some incurious passer by. And yet all the instincts of our nature proclaim that there must be some reason for this as for anything else, we have here a *vera causa* if only we can discover it. The mere existence of such words as fortune, luck, fate, chance, proclaims the necessity under which, as a mere matter of fact, we find ourselves, of attaching some word to a notion that rests upon a real something. If, indeed, science could prove that this something was nothing, or even if it could rid itself, not to say the human mind, of the necessity of accepting it as a fact, and of applying some description to it, then there would cease to be an absolute necessity for religious conceptions, though the room for them would remain as ample as before. But this is not the case, as can be shown by a recent instance. An article recently appeared in one of the reviews in which the evolution of man is attributed to "a chain of antecedent events not provably elaborated under supreme guidance but probably simply from *that uncalculating necessity of sequence inherent in the very existence of matter*"—words in which the negation of thought, together with the necessity of thinking, is expressed in pretentious language that seeks in vain to avoid those ugly words fate and chance by an unmeaning combination of the two. For these religion substitutes the designing will of an overruling and omniscient Creator, by whose arrangement the circumstances of men are correlated to their faculties and their work by unerring and unvarying law. And thus as I maintain, history, that is revelation, is the true domain of religion, because it is the only sphere in which religious ideas are needed to give a rational account of admitted facts. Mind and matter may and must be admitted by religion, as well as by science, as ultimate facts of conciousness that do not require, or rather that do not suggest the possibility of explanation; no one ever actually asks why they are of this sort rather than of another: they admit the possibility, but do not demand the existence of God. Whereas the events and circumstances that make up individual history, and form the connecting link between subject and object, just because they fall within experience, are for ever demanding explanation; a man cannot choose but ask why a given grave event has happened to him or to some one else in a particular way. In short, just as mind is known only by its thoughts, matter by its qualities, so is God (and man also) recognised primarily, if not solely, by His actions. The first and truest revelation of God is then in history and not in nature, exactly as we realise a man by what he does and not by what he has made.

In abandoning, however, for the moment a position of neutrality, I have run some risk of losing the chain of argument which it is above all things necessary to keep clearly before us. To sum up, then, we have seen that man is the result of three factors, each of which may be expressed in religious or scientific terms—these are God or mind; creation or matter; government or—what shall I call it?—the fortuitous combination of accidents. It follows next to trace the relation of man as an independent, self-conditioned being with the three elements which he derives from an external and, as religion would say, a superior power.

Thus, then, we are brought to the subject of the will, concerning which I do not mean to make a single statement that goes beyond the clear and admitted facts of human consciousness. These, I express in the words of Locke. "This at least I think evident that we find in ourselves a power to begin or forbear, continue or end several actions of our minds and motions of our bodies barely by a thought or preference of the mind, ordering or, as it were, commanding the doing or not doing such or such a particular action; this power which the mind has thus to order the consideration of any idea, or the forbearing to consider it, or to prefer the motion of any part of the body to its rest, and *vice versâ* in any particular instance, is that which we call the will; the actual exercise of that power by directing any particular action or its forbearance, is that which we call volition or willing; the forbearance of that action, consequent to such order or command of the mind, is called voluntary; and whatsoever action is performed without such thought of the mind is called involuntary."

Beyond this description it is not necessary for me to advance a single step, however firmly I may believe that Locke's further account of the will contains the substance of all true and possible philosophy of human free agency. It is enough to say that man does not know either that his will is free or that it is bound. The one fact presented to my consciousness is this—I know that I do not know that I am compelled to act in any particular way. Practically, therefore, man finds himself an independent (I avoid the use of the word free) agent, mediating, as it were, amidst the three elements that make up his existence. To hazard a passing definition, the will is the balance of mind, body, and circumstance. Each of these comes to us from without, and is primarily beyond our control. But, secondarily, they may be manipulated by us to an illimitable extent The power of thought itself may be educated, may be fashioned by application, may be diverted into channels prescribed for it. The body itself is susceptible of change, improvement, or deterioration, according to the way in which we treat it. And events may be moulded to an incalculable extent in various directions. We might, indeed, be tempted to say that they can be originated, but this is not the case. For instance, Wordsworth's character and poetry were influenced enormously by the fact of his living in the Lake district, still he did but select one out of many possible alternatives; ultimately to him as to all men circumstances exist independently. The most important, however, of the different directions in which events may be moulded, or of the modes in which they may be used, are those which the common consciousness of mankind has agreed to call good and evil.

Here, again, I must decline as entirely unnecessary for our present inquiry all consideration of the amount and reasonableness of the blame and censure to be awarded to the human agent. As a mere matter of fact we know that men may produce good or bad results by means of their treatment of their lives and history. We can distinguish, indeed, roughly between productions of man's faculties and moral

A Scientific Account of Inspiration. 241

actions strictly so called. An artist or a poet may make good or bad art, good or bad poetry according to the use to which he puts his powers or his materials. The fault, if fault there be, may be ascribed either to the pernicious tendencies of his age, to his own defects of character, or to both combined. Different schools of philosophy will attach more importance to one cause of failure or the other; wiser people may decline the dangerous, if not impossible, task of awarding moral praise or blame to any man at all, except in the broadest and most sweeping outlines, for any *productions* of his faculties, and may limit these words to his actions. But the exact relations of morality and inspiration will have to be discussed separately. For the present it is enough to say that men may make good or bad use of their various faculties according to the "orders" of their wills.

We have thus then described, and, I think, with reasonable clearness and precision, what inspiration is in general. It is the power of thought, conditioned by the peculiarities of each man's physical nature, directed by the government of God over events, and applied by man's will in each of his various faculties to the objects with which these faculties severally have to do. These belong to all men more or less, but to some men they belong in an unusual measure, so that one is musical, another scientific, political, or philosophical. Thus, then, in the operation of human faculties we have divine thought in human fashion, seeking to discern, appropriate, and reproduce the spiritual realities of the universe, that is, the divine thoughts of beauty, goodness, and order, which underlie its various phenomena.

If it should seem to any that the way has been long and tedious towards a very simple conclusion, yet the trouble may be forgotten if it can be shown that a single further step will lead us to the definition of religious as distinguished from general inspiration. That step consists merely in the statement that as there are faculties of art, science, and the rest, so is there a specific faculty of religion. I believe that this assertion ought to carry its own conviction with it, but as confusion of thought upon this subject is general, and prejudice inveterate, I will proceed to prove it by a further account of the nature of the faculties.

I have already said that of the essential nature of these we are in ignorance, and that the utmost we can hope is that, perhaps, in some yet distant day, light may be thrown upon them. Plainly they are the result to a considerable extent of natural bodily organisation, and it may be that the artistic, speculative, and practical faculties represent three broadly different conditions of the human brain. On the other hand, they are equally plainly acquired, to a considerable extent, under the stress of circumstances, so that, perhaps, within the above-named genera there may be species so closely allied as to allow the mind to be turned into various channels by events that happen. This appears certain when we remark the affinities that subsist between various gifts, so that it seems a mere chance in which way the possessor of them distinguishes himself. In the present state, then, of our knowledge, all we can do is to fall back upon the phenomena which the faculties present, and distinguish and describe them by these alone. These are mainly twofold, the materials upon which the faculties are employed, and the productions which they severally bring forth. The mind is drawn off to the study of nature, humanity, God; here are distinct spheres of thought and operation. We call that, then, a faculty which has its own definite object, and produces its own special results. Tried by this test it is easy to prove that religion is as much a distinct faculty as music or mathematics.

1. Religion has its own special object of thought, the unknown element in things. Where the province of the other faculties ends that of religion begins. The unknown cause of life and matter, the unknown world that lies beyond the grave, that which comes before and that which comes after experience, in fine, God and immortality are the two poles towards which religious thought gravitates. And we gain a reasonable and legitimate explanation of the saying that theology is the crown of sciences, while yet distinguished from them. It deals with that element which is common to them all and underlies them all, by which, if ever at all, they are to be combined in one harmonious whole. But it must be observed that this is in no ways contradictory to the position elsewhere adopted, that the religious faculty has no immediate, intuitive knowledge of God or of immortality, but apprehends them through the medium of facts.

2. Religion has its own special instrument—faith. It is by this that we take an interest in the unknown. That general power of mind which, in the various faculties, discerns and realises the objects presented to it, may be properly called the imagination. This is that which forms a picture or an idea of things, such as beauty, law, truth, goodness. In none of the faculties, so much as in religion, does this imagination deserve a special name and perform appropriate functions. Elsewhere we speak vaguely of the sense of harmony, or of the discernment of the relations of

numbers, or of logical power. But in religion the imaginative power which realises God and immortality, and forces us to act as though they were the most essential of verities, is itself one of the most obvious of existing facts. The definition in the book of Hebrews is scientifically accurate—"it is the substance of things hoped for, the evidence of things not seen." I do not, however, deny that closer analysis might show that faith, as thus described, exists also in the operation of other faculties besides religion. But such analysis is, I think, at present hardly possible ; it is not certainly possible to me nor necessary for my purpose. It may, however, show, what is probable in itself, that the faculties are composed of the same elements, though combined in different proportions, as determined by the physical or external conditions with which the mind is correlated. Thus, a musician may be said to have the essential element of faith because he is haunted by the presence of an unapproachable beauty and harmony. Plainly, however, the musical faculty can be scientifically differentiated from the religious, even if we admitted that it ultimately led up to it. Religion would, in that case, have the same kind of relation to other faculties that pure mathematics have to mixed.

3. Religion has its own special production—prayer. The score of one of Beethoven's symphonies is not more truly the creation of the musical, nor the differential calculus of the mathematical, nor the doctrine of evolution of the scientific faculty, than is the prayer of Moses, the man of God, the distinctive product of religion. The power of composing a prayer (I will not say the power of praying) belongs to a man in proportion as he is religious, just as

the power of painting a picture belongs to him so far as he is an artist. Nor is this all. Religion creates a special type of those productions which it has in common with other faculties. Hymns, as Mr Matthew Arnold with cruel candour pointed out, are very different from poetry; sermons are not like speeches; the Vedas, Old Testament, New Testament, and the Koran, however much they may differ from each other, have something in common, an undefinable air or tone which separates them from other books. And, not to multiply instances, the religious spirit has called into being special types of music, art, and architecture; the latter especially being made subservient to religious uses, and adapted to express religious ideas. If the name and memory of religion could be supposed blotted from the earth, sacred music and pictures would still be intelligible to mankind, but the cause and meaning of Pagan temples or Christian cathedrals would become an insoluble mystery.

4. Religion has its own special heroes and masters. There are men whose genius takes from their cradle a religious bent; the emotions, actions, and aspirations peculiar to religion come as naturally to such men as those of science or literature to others. There are others in whom the inspiration of religion is so absorbing and marvellous a power, that we should as soon think of imitating Newton or Handel as them. St Francis of Assisi may be taken as a type of religious genius, and so may John Wesley, the more so as morally he is by no means so attractive a character as St Francis. The whole bent and form of the mind of St Francis, his prophetical power of utterance, his scheme of life and duty, his principles of action, his peculiar virtues, in short, the whole nature of

the man was instinct with a genius of religion, which we stand afar off and admire. Moreover, the rule is, though St Francis is hardly a case in point, that this genius is apparent in extreme youth, and is therefore in all probability connected with natural, physical temperament. It is, too, especially connected with parental and, above all, maternal care.

5. It follows from this that religion has its own special epochs. In religion, as in other departments of thought and action, certain traceable causes produce great developments, and lead to new discoveries or even inventions. There was a time when the men of the most religious people ever known were not taught to pray; the highest conception of the eternal God as a Father of men is a Christian, and therefore a comparatively modern, idea. Moreover, the same law holds good here as elsewhere, that the greatest men come first in each successive period of development. The cause of this is obvious. It is only one man who can be the first to climb a mountain, many may follow his steps with more ease and rapidity, but none with the same original daring and success. To take modern times, there is one Luther, just as there is one Shakespeare, one Newton, one Handel, and one Columbus. Of course these men have their companions, and even their rivals, but the general law plainly holds good.

6. It follows once more from this that religion should have its special varieties of type and variations of history. The religion of any given nation is just as truly part of its general history as its art or science. The forms that religion may assume are almost infinite, but each is adapted to the general culture, politics, and position of the

A Scientific Account of Inspiration. 247

nation in which it exists. There is, no doubt, an ideal form to which the various types seek, with more or less success, to approximate, but men are beginning to catch some faint glimpse of the absurdity of supposing that their religion is the only true one because they may chance to have been born Protestants at Geneva, Catholics at Madrid, or Anglicans at Oxford. Whether Christianity itself may be said to be true in any pre-eminent sense depends entirely upon our belief as to the nature and person of its Founder. Again, religion shares the fate of other faculties in such respects as the following. It never attains to existence at all amidst savages of extraordinary brutality. It sometimes, on the other hand, reaches a strange beauty and power under what seem abnormal conditions; as, for instance, among some tribes of American Indians. It dies out in individuals, and almost in whole generations, so that men cease to devote thought or care to God and immortality. Elsewhere it grows to excess and ends in the wildest fanaticism. Everywhere it is capable of the less and more, the true and false, the useful and the pernicious.

7. It follows from this, finally, that religion should have its special moral phenomena. We may assert confidently that these are the same in kind, but not in degree, as those presented by other faculties. The facts which go to prove this are so abundant and so notorious, that to record them would be to rewrite some of the best known pages of religious history. Briefly, they may be summed up as follows:—Like other faculties religion may have the most noble or the most degraded conceptions of its objects, its instrument, and its productions. The idea of God may range from a fetish to a Father; immortality may be con-

ceived as the realisation of the kingdom of goodness or as a happy Paradise; faith may be the yearning of the heart after the eternal Spirit, or a superstitious reliance upon outward machinery, such as the Apostolical Succession; prayer may be the 17th chapter of St John, an imprecation of vengeance, or a Chinese wheel. Religion again calls into being special virtues and vices of its own, just as a certain moral character belongs to the artist, thinker, and statesman as such; humility and philanthrophy are practically Christian virtues, as being the products of Christian thought; fatalism and sectarianism have a distinctively religious flavour. And, what is still more conclusive, true religion may exist in thoroughly bad men, as in the instance of Rochester's prayer quoted by Lord Macaulay, and false religion may turn the qualities of good men into evil, as all history bears but too sad testimony. The mere faculty of religion is not in itself moral or immoral, but neutral.

I submit, then, that with these facts before us, unless in religion we refuse to attribute like effects to similar causes, merely because they are religious, we have no choice but to describe religion as one out of the faculties belonging to man, the constitution of which has been before described. And thus our definition of religious inspiration emerges in some such shape as this: it is the power of thought (that is, mind) united with certain inherited, physical conditions and outward circumstances, directed towards thinking about the unknown, and towards the performance of all the actions which such thinking inspires.

Thus far for inspiration in general, and religious inspiration in particular. There remains a branch of the subject too essential to be omitted, too vast to be attempted with much hope of success; I mean moral inspiration or the communication of the Spirit of God to man in the direction of those common actions of life called moral. This includes what men feel and say, no less than what they actually do.

Now, to begin with, we are here brought face to face with the source and nature of evil, and with the existence and nature of conscience, two things of which it is impossible to give even the most superficial and neutral account without offending some school of thought or other. But, sticking as closely as I can to simple facts, I can trace the workings of inspiration as follows—

Conscience is thought applied to the decision of the rightness or wrongness of any proposed course of action. But thought being the one divine or perfect thing in man has an inherent attraction towards discerning what is right and desiring to do it. Let us reflect on this for a moment. Pure thought is pure goodness; we may call God himself perfect thought or absolute goodness. If we could imagine thought set free from all personal conditions, we could only imagine it as purely and essentially right, without taint of selfishness, corruption, or falsehood. Humanity seems to mean the upward progress of thought in combination with those material and outward elements which make up man. The attraction of thought, therefore, towards correctness of action is as natural as that of the tongue for what is palatable, or the ear for harmony of sound, and the authority of conscience is at once real and legitimate.

Again evil is, according to the profound instinct of the first pages of the Bible, a thing that comes afterwards. It seems to be essentially involved in the idea of progress and education which is suggested by the combination of mind and matter in time. Whether it is due primarily to defect of individual will, to stress of circumstances, or to inherited fault of character, or to all combined, does not affect our present purpose. It is enough to say that we find it in existence and closely allied with thought itself in all the operations of all the faculties, religion included.

Neither does it matter what view we take or whether we take any view at all of the nature of the standard by which conscience decides. These views are mainly three, and are probably all in a measure real, and possibly all ultimately identical. They vary according as men refer things to their judgment of what is right for themselves as individuals, or to their sense of duty towards mankind, or to their responsibility to the unknown, unattainable truth of things, which we call divine art, heavenly knowledge, God himself.

Now conscience acts on all the faculties alike, and within the sphere of each the conscience of each is supreme. The artist paints, the philosopher thinks, the statesman rules, primarily because the voice of his artistic, philosophic, or political conscience impels him to do so; it is a mere theological impertinence, a gross intellectual inaccuracy, and a deplorable misrendering of facts, to call the duty so performed religious in any distinctive sense. But it is quite within the limits of truth to point out that religion begins at this point to exercise a special moral influence above and beyond that of the other faculties. No doubt, the moral influence of all the faculties is closely interdependent; there is something artistically right, for instance, in the pursuit of science after truth. But whereas the influence of any two of the above-mentioned faculties (art, philosophy, politics) · upon the actions of the third is so vague and visionary as to be almost a matter of words, that of religion upon all three of them is manifest and decisive. It may exist for good or for evil, but of the fact of its existence as a deepening, intensifying, encouraging power there is no question at all. This power religion owes to her position as the "crown of sciences," as before described. I do not, however, dwell further upon this, partly because it is abundantly clear in itself, partly because it comes out more strongly still in the class of actions which now claim our attention—those I mean that make up ordinary human conduct, and cannot be attributed to any special faculty, but are described merely as the duties we perform as men among men.

Now it is possible that closer analysis might prove that there was an element belonging to all the human faculties in every action of life. Assuredly, art has represented, poetry described, science defined, and religion consecrated the very commonest and most homely duties of man to man. But certain it is that the moral power of the other faculties in helping the will to do what is right is incomparably less effectual than religion. No doubt, a well-trained and truthfully-working faculty, whatever it be, establishes a general disposition towards goodness, which, as a rule, enables a man to walk uprightly and in the spirit of self-sacrifice. An enthusiastic love of beauty, or an intense yearning after justice, or an ardent pursuit of law creates a moral tendency to which we owe some of the noblest and purest lives. But it is a mere truism that the moral force of religion, whether in a good or evil direction, is infinitely stronger than any or all of them. Taking only the good side, and remembering that every bright part of the picture has its dark and shameful counterpart, the testimony of history and experience to this effect may be summarised as follows:—

In no faculty so much as in religion does thought find so easy and direct a channel for moral influences, and in none do events exercise so strong an inspiration towards good. I may have to recur to this again in speaking of the morality of the Jews, and therefore leaving it, I go on to say, that religion has been much more universal in its effects, because it has reached hearts and minds to which science and philosophy were closed doors. It has shown an especial power of protesting against a narrow, exclusive morality engendered by a too-absorbing cultivation of one faculty, though none alas can be so narrow and exclusive as religion itself. It has created transcendent bursts of enthusiasm, and yet has directed a constant, minute, penetrating pressure towards goodness. It has brought into being a vast array of rules, guides, outward helps, for the special purpose of enabling people to be and to do good. It has produced the best accounts of morality, the highest precepts, the noblest spirits, the most beneficent lives. It can reach the conscience from the intuitional, utilitarian, and religious side. Thus it can say to people, and has said to them with marked effect, You must do your best in art and science, peace and war, home and business, politics and philosophy, because you, the actor, are a child of God; the thought that works in you is divine and eternal, incapable of destruction, fraught with immeasurable consequences through countless ages. Or you must do your best because mankind is in very truth the brotherhood that your insight teaches you to call it; men are children of a common family, whose Father is God. Or you must do your best because the truth and beauty which you desire are a part of the life of God, and to every other motive we can add this constraining one, "whatever you do in word or deed, do all to the glory of God."

I would fain spare myself the saddening reflection that religion has also taught men that they are half animal, half devil; that only a chosen few are the objects of God's favour; that His glory demands the everlasting torments of myriads of His children. But after all it is consoling to remember that the inherent, moral power of religion has been strong enough to survive these doctrines, and to make some of those who have held them to rank among the most beneficent and unselfish of men. And it is still more consoling to hope that these doctrines are vanishing before that general progress of mankind towards which religion has contributed so much in times past, and may yet contribute so much more in times to come. Her ability to do so will increase just in proportion as she claims for herself that supreme power of influencing men for good which will be produced whenever she identifies herself with goodness, teaches art, philosophy, and science to do the same, and proclaims that the unknown will of God has been revealed as the salvation of men from evil here and hereafter.

Thus, then, our definition of moral inspiration takes this form. It is thought exercising itself in and through all the faculties, but pre-eminently in and through religion, towards the right appreciation and due performance of the various actions of life, which make up human conduct.

That this agrees with all our personal experience I

venture to affirm. What do we mean by our own inspiration? It seems that we mean this. Thoughts come to us in connection with our various faculties that prompt us to goodness; habits are founded upon them that keep us in the right way; sobriety and health of body are a natural restraint upon evil and an instrument of good; circumstances and events fill the soul with the desire to do right, with the deepest appreciation of the will and love of God. It is, indeed, thus that we may ascertain whether this account (it makes no pretension to be anything more) of inspiration is a true one. Does it explain the phenomena of religion in persons, in nations, and in history? Not one of the chief of these, so far as I know, has been omitted in this necessarily rapid survey, though it still remains to write the history and account for the facts of Jewish inspiration upon the data and by the method thus described. For the present I content myself with asking—Do the facts agree with the account here given of them? All results beyond this are immaterial to me, for I am now simply an inquirer after scientific truth in the field of religion. If it be asserted that the principles here enunciated lead to Ultramontanism, Infidelity, or Anglicanism, it would not affect my mind unless the statements could be proved inaccurate in point of fact. If, indeed, I were asked my own opinion, I would say frankly that I think the position here taken up is one more forward step in that reconstitution of theology by scientific method which is likely to exercise so profound and destructive an effect upon the present creeds and received opinions of the Christian religion. At present between these two, religion and science, there yawns a gulf across which men hurl defiance and contempt at each other.

A Scientific Account of Inspiration. 255

Years hence when that gulf is crossed by many a secure line of acknowledged truth, men will easily forget then, as they readily ignore now, the few who were the first to stretch a frail and trembling bridge of rope above the abyss, and to trust their lives and hopes along that perilous pathway. So be it—but for all that God is just.

THE INSPIRATION OF THE JEWS.

THE object of this and the following essay is to give a scientific account of the special form of religious inspiration that produced the Jewish and Christian religions. Or to speak more correctly and more modestly, it is to make an effort in that direction; a direction to which modern thought is steadily tending, though for the present with imperfect knowledge and insufficient materials. The religion of the Jews (the dawn of Christianity being included) must not be separated from the other religions of humanity, but must be regarded as the type to which they all approach with more or less success, the standard by which they are to be judged, the best illustration of the laws and the most perfect embodiment of the truths common to all religions alike. If we desire to study the highest form of law we go to Rome; or of philosophy, to Greece; or of music, to Germany; or of natural science, to England; in the same way the national religion best worth studying is that of the Jews before the downfall of their country. In all these departments of thought the various nations here mentioned may or may not be surpassed in the course of time by others: but to them belongs the inalienable glory of having laid the foundation upon which others must build. This is emphatically the case with the Jews in the province of religion.

The special task before us is then to explain the most remarkable phenomenon in history—the Jewish nation, their history, their beliefs, and their literature. I remember reading somewhere the assertion that the causes of the outburst of Grecian intellect remain yet to be discovered. So, too, do the causes of Jewish religion, though the inquiry is by no means so difficult, and is much more practical in itself. But in spite of all the attempts that have been made, it is, I think, clear that men are very far indeed from realising either the importance of the phenomenon or the difficulty of accounting for it by ordinary means. And it may well be that repeated failures will drive men to the necessity of accepting the events, supernatural though they be, which do account for things otherwise insoluble. If so, then the supernatural element must be reasonable in itself, and consistent with general experience. It becomes therefore the task of liberal theology to define this element, and provide a sphere for it. Hitherto it has been represented especially by the word inspiration, which is always associated with the idea of something supernatural. This is the point I shall now proceed to discuss.

Recurring to the former essay, it will be found that our apparatus for attempting this task is as follows. Inspiration is thought working in the various faculties which are produced by material or external circumstances. Religious inspiration is thought working in the religious faculty. Moral inspiration is thought working through the various faculties towards rightness of conduct and action. Jewish inspiration is thought working through a specially developed religious faculty. We examine first the thought, then the external organisation, then the nature of the events, these three being the constituent elements of that which I have called "faculty."

The origin of Jewish religion, the growth of the constituent thought by which it was dominated throughout its long career, and which it has implanted in the heart of humanity, can be traced with more or less distinctness, even though we should be compelled to reject the details of the narrative. It was born into the world at that great seed-time of human thought, concerning which we must look to the study of comparative religion for future disclosures. (As I write these words the *Times* of the day contains Mr George Smith's paper on the Chaldean account of the Deluge.) Long before this men awaking from a savage existence had found themselves capable of reasoning, and reason had impelled them to ask whence they came, whither they were going, who and what was the dread mysterious element in themselves and in nature? We know something of the nature of the conclusions to which they had been brought, though it would be foreign to the purpose of this essay to do more than indicate the sources from which our information is derived. The Assyrian and Egyptian empires had settled forms of belief and worship; the causes that produced the Vedas, and not so many centuries afterwards the Homeric mythology, must have been in strong operation; the civilisation of the Bronze age represents a parallel stage of religious development. I have certainly no right to pass an opinion upon the question of the origin of the belief in the Unity of God: whether, that is, it was the original

religious idea of the human mind which was afterwards
corrupted, or the result of increasing mental growth and
knowledge. But this much at least is certain, that with
Abraham monotheism became a possession of the human
mind. In his age the mind of God, which we call reason,
was moving mightily upon the souls of men. And the
first efforts of reason in any new direction are always of
transcendent power and truthfulness. Genius shines out at
the beginning of the new order of things which it is sent
into the world to create. And Abraham was a religious
genius, as were in other faculties Socrates, Bacon, and
Æschylus. As Socrates to the sophists, Bacon to the
schoolmen, Æschylus to the old satiric drama, so was
Abraham to the representatives of religious thought in the
time at which he lived. Into his soul came the thought,
straight from the original mind, that God was one, and that
God was holy. And if so, then the one holy God must
needs have no false gods to share His dominion : truth of
this kind cannot die ; to him it was given, childless as he
was, to found a people who should bear witness to it ; upon
him it was incumbent to go forth in the direction in which
thought, like the sun, has ever travelled, westward, to the
very verge of the sea, there to live and rule apart from
those who were unable to realise the new thoughts. No
miracle was needed in an age when the minds of men were
steeped with the thought of the Divine, dawning more and
more clearly upon their awakening reason : every event and
every thought were His alone. That the faith of Abraham
was created in a time of intense religious excitement is
surely more than reasonable ; man's business was to believe
in God, his righteousness was to believe in the one holy

God of Abraham. In due course of time came the birth of the son, which set the seal and assurance of truth upon his faith, and told him that the God he worshipped was able to raise up children from the very stones in place of the son of promise, if needs must that he should be sacrificed. The tone of the Book of Genesis, its utter obliviousness to the distinction between natural and supernatural, its testimony to Abraham's faith as consisting in the inward thought of his mind about God and the reliance of his soul upon Him, make all this as natural and as probable as can be imagined. To me the religious genius of Abraham does not appear nearly so startling or supernatural a phenomenon as the poetic genius of Homer or Shakespeare—that is to say, I can account for it much more easily. In an age when everybody was beginning to think more and more about God, he caught the true expression of the divine mind, and believed with a reverential awe that sent him forth alone into a lonely land, that the true God would not suffer His truth to fail for want of witnesses and worshippers. Did true genius, when discovering, revealing, beginning, inventing, ever act or believe otherwise?

Now, such a thought as this possesses, in common with other dominant ideas, the power of transmitting itself from generation to generation, by natural descent from parent to child. By what means this is accomplished it is at present nearly useless to inquire, though I cannot help but think that the nature and origin of the various faculties proper to man present the one great field of research upon which the human mind will ere long exercise itself. Of the fact itself, however, there can be no doubt, and, so far as religion is concerned, the strong impressions received in early education are quite enough to account for the transmission of any specific type of belief and worship. And yet, if we were to hazard the assertion that Jewish children were born with some innate predisposition to the national religion, Locke himself, in view of the tendency of physiological inquiry, would hardly demur to the statement. This at least is certain, that the special thought was accompanied (and if so, why may we not say correlated?) by a physical type, perhaps the most pronounced that any one nation has ever been distinguished by. The thought, moreover, so transmitted and so accompanied was wrought into the very texture of the race by the physical facts that surrounded and moulded them. Their sojourn in Egypt taught them the vileness of nature-worship ; their wanderings in the desert brought them face to face with the living God, unknown, spiritual, Lord of the created world, of national existence, of human life ; their narrow strip of territory, infertile save to an eye accustomed to the barrenness of the Sinaitic peninsula, intensified their religion, and kept them apart, "a holy and peculiar people." It is striking to observe how soon the tribes east of Jordan drifted away from the national faith, and sank to the level of the surrounding nations, apparently because they were deprived of the material help provided by the physical geography of Canaan proper. It is striking also to observe at the other extreme how the sea was to them almost alone of nations that have dwelt upon its shore a barrier and not a pathway. There is a touch almost of pathos—there is certainly a true "inspiration"—in the simple statement in which the annalist seems to confess that, in spite of a period of delusive splendour, the genius of his country was not to find its expression in maritime ascendency. "Jehoshaphat made ships of Tharshish to go to Ophir for gold, but they went not, for the ships were broken at Ezion-geber." But I need not pursue a well-known tale. Whatever of redemption from evil, of association in the bonds of national unity, of successful conquests, victorious struggles, regal glories, return from captivity, and ultimate independence crowned their history, was due to the faith in the God of Abraham, which Abraham had bequeathed to them. That thought never died; when it seemed at death's door, then it revived with a new and more exalted life. Our Lord could find no more serious and overwhelming reproof than this, "If ye were Abraham's children ye would do the works of Abraham;" and it explains another saying of His, so difficult to our practical mind, "Your father Abraham rejoiced to see my day, and he saw it and was glad." St Paul, when building the bridge that was to connect the Jewish religion with the Gentile world, laid the foundation in the truth that the promise was given, "not to the seed which is of the law, but to that also which is of the faith of Abraham, who is the father of us all." The truth of the belief that God was the one holy covenant God was proved to them by the only method of proof possible to man—an experience ranging over, perhaps, 2000 years. In a people so constituted, with such thoughts and such a faculty, their history being internally and externally what it was, the divine mind poured forth its inspiration abundantly. God thought in them the thoughts that make up the highest truths of religion. They were, as has been over and over again observed, an inspired people, inspired in religion as other nations in war, commerce, law, philosophy, and art. But this brings us to the special inspiration represented by their literature, and to the events by which this was produced.

Now, all the highest forms of inspiration, in every faculty alike, come to humanity through certain chosen instruments. Amongst a people in whom any faculty is widely spread, there arise from time to time men in whom that faculty attains an extraordinary elevation. These are, in one sense, the outcome of the age in which they live; they are, in another, instances of the abrupt changes in which, whether intellectually or physically, nature rejoices, and which she refuses to surrender to theories of gradual variation of type and imperceptible modification of tendencies. They are at once creatures and creators of events and circumstances, and there is always a strict correlation between them and the history of their times. Now, the history of Jewish religion presents a remarkable exemplification of the influence of the greatest minds; it concerns itself almost exclusively with them, and by a curious instinct the people invariably attributed their national literature to their national heroes. The instinct is a true one, for it points to the fact that the one source of special inspiration, whether of works, actions, or books, were the events which kindled the flame of religious thought in the minds of their great men.

That the Jewish writers derived their inspiration from events, whether of special occurrence or derived from the general condition and history of the people, is true beyond a doubt. I have said in a previous essay that the true sphere of divine operation, *recognised as specifically divine*, is in events; so assuredly the Jews believed. They were compelled, by the instincts of humanity, to ask why things happened to them in such and such a way: they were taught by the tradition of their fathers, and by the assertions and testimony of their leading minds, that it was the hand of God. God was dealing with them in a special way because He was in covenant with them, because He had made them what they were, had a favour unto them, and designs on their behalf, transcending the utmost power of the prophetic spirit to discern, though the vague outline was always being filled up by new touches, and the oft-thwarted hope never ceased to exert its overpowering fascination. Under this inspiration they thought and wrote, sang and prayed; and they needed no other. The earliest songs of the desert at the marching of the host, or the digging of a well, down to the last psalm of the Maccabæan uprising, bear ample testimony to the truth of this assertion. The mind of God flashed itself upon them in the things that happened. It was as the reflection of the sun upon the brightest mirror. Some of the events might be deemed miraculous, others accepted as natural; some were the heroic actions of great men, others the punishment of their sins and follies: some were material, some visionary, some usual, others extraordinary. But all alike were believed to be the actions of God, and the Jews understood that which men are so slow to perceive even now, that if we want to know the will and character of any person, and therefore of God, we must find them in the things He is believed or known to be doing for us and towards us; and this knowledge was their inspiration.

I do not wish to disguise the effect of this position upon accepted theories of inspiration. It is common ground, as we know, to all of them alike, that thoughts were and are supernaturally infused into men's minds; that certain men were thus miraculously preserved from error on at least certain points, and were enabled to declare truths that were beyond the unaided intelligence of mankind. All my life I have been disturbed by the difficulties inherent in this view, and have felt that they presented an insuperable barrier to the reconciliation of religion and science. The received accounts of inspiration have appeared to me untenable, because they explain nothing, are incapable of verification, intrude into the province of reason, cannot be expressed in intelligible language, rest upon no basis of fact, and are capable of being wrested to support any authority that it may please the believer in them to set up. And regarding, in common with all Christians, the Bible as containing the chief results and loftiest productions of religious inspiration, I believe that we mean no more than to say that it is the perfectly natural play of human thought about events and facts believed to come from God. Whether this definition can be shown to be true and sufficient remains now to be ascertained.

This can be done in two ways. First, we may inquire whether it is in agreement with the facts of the case as presented in the Bible itself; secondly, we may inquire whether it is in harmony with the operations of inspiration elsewhere. The first of these questions must be answered in a separate essay, the second has been answered already to a great extent, and in a general way by the comparison of the religious with the other faculties. It remains however to say something more upon what may be called the inspiring power of facts.

Now, the end of the religious faculty is to have right thoughts about God and about His relations towards mankind. If such thoughts, supposing them to be possessed by any person, are plainly the results of other people's experience and instruction, then no question arises as to his being inspired in any special way. Meditation and education are rightly set down as sufficient to account for their existence. But the question does arise at once in those cases in which the thoughts are new, and we are entitled to ask whence they came. To say that they are supernaturally inspired says nothing; this is equally true of all new thoughts in every faculty, unless we can discover some test by which they may be distinguished. By what possible means can any person decide that a given thought in his mind comes from God in a way that other thoughts do not? Of course I readily grant, or rather insist, that all religious thoughts of thankfulness or sorrow or prayer in every individual life, are caused by the action of God upon the soul through facts or events, and that in this sense our "hearts are cleansed by the inspiration of His Spirit." But I am seeking now for some test which shall enable us to distinguish between the special inspiration which we attribute to the Jews, and the general inspiration which we claim for all religious persons. Why has an almost universal Christian instinct attached the idea of supernatural interference to the results of Jewish religious thought? Why was St Paul inspired in a sense in which Luther was not? Unless scientific theology can discover the reason on which this instinct rests, so as to be able to account for it, we must be content to submit to the strangest opinions upon the subject, to verbal or plenary inspiration, or still worse that which comes from dreams, oracles, ecstasies, and poetic extravagancies. The thing then that we have got to inquire about is the phenomenon presented by the existence of those great, original, and absolutely true ideas about God, which have passed from the Jews to humanity itself, and which constitute their claim to special inspiration.

I must not allow myself to be led astray from this inquiry by the temptation of enlarging upon the genesis of all new ideas. But I repeat what I have said elsewhere, that all genius is the application of the mind to facts, whence it brings back new discoveries and civilising truths. The word Revelation may be quite correctly applied by religion to this process in every human faculty, to the discovery of evolution, or of the nature of God as contained in the word Jehovah. But the methods by which the process is carried on are of course innumerable, varying with the nature of the facts under investigation. Science again may, with equal correctness, be the name applied to the process on the human side; it is trained reason exercising itself upon phenomena: still the scientific method assumes very different forms in, *e.g.*, history, music, and natural science properly so called.

Now, religion is the science of God—that is, of a personal being; and whereas the natural science which discovered evolution consisted in the play of thought about facts of nature called material phenomena, the religious science (if so it is to be called) which discovered the name Jehovah, was due to the play of thought about facts of history, called events. Increased knowledge of a person is derived from what he does; things that happen produce new ideas in the mind, because they form a new experience concerning the source from which they come. From them I learn that any given man is selfish, good tempered, favourable or unfriendly to myself. Hence it is that though it is possible to give a scientific account of a person's character, it is not possibel that such account should be exhaustive, because some new phenomenon, or a new action, may upset all our previous calculations and conclusions. Accordingly, our only method of growing in the knowledge of God is by receiving and pondering over the actions in which He reveals Himself to us. This is exactly what the Jews were always doing. Believing, rightly or wrongly, that all their national history proceeded from the will of God, they were enabled to conceive and to utter those new ideas which were suggested to them by the actions of the Person concerning whom they were thinking. The character and purpose of God stood revealed in their history. Events believed to be supernatural —that is, to come direct from God—created ideas which seemed to them entirely natural and obvious. Nor is there any reason that I can discover why they should not seem the same to us.

But while making this claim on behalf of these ideas, it must not be forgotten that their supernatural appearance, the *something* about them which has given rise to a belief in special inspiration, can be easily accounted for. A new revelation lays hold of the minds of its first recipients with an overmastering power. It is as though something of the reverent awe which we attach to the power of God as the author of the beginning of Creation, accompanied every fresh manifestation of creative energy displayed in the uprising of new ideas. Men are carried away beyond themselves, they overpass the limits which before this seemed to have been set for them by nature. Even natural science in her majestic way feels this overpowering influence, and men are carried away by a boundless enthusiasm when the discovery of such laws as gravitation or evolution, and of such facts as the movement of the earth or the circulation of the blood, starts scientific research upon new and hitherto unimagined careers of investigation. So men passed into a delirium of enterprise at the discovery of the New World. So also the mind of Thucydides was saturated with those impressions of contemporary Greek life which suggested to him the philosophy of history. But, far beyond this, men are transported into new regions of thought and action by the belief that they have received some special revelation of the character and intentions of God. New thoughts seize upon them as the first acquisition of knowledge lays hold upon a child. A few dominant thoughts possess their souls and exert a transforming, intensifying influence upon their lives. Under such influences laws, poems, prophecies, histories, are poured forth abundantly; magnificent enterprises are undertaken and prosper beyond men's hopes; the very nature of the people seems as though cast into a furnace of mental heat, whence it emerges in new and strange forms. To illustrate this in the case of the Jews would be to transcribe Ewald's history, in which the spiritual life of the people is traced with unsurpassed power. What wonder, then, that as the actions of God cease to speak directly or are at least no longer believed to do so, men who inherit the ideas by ordinary laws of intellectual descent begin to regard their spiritual ancestors as recipients of a special inspiration which separates them from the crowd of ordinary men. So in truth they were, if facts, newly revealed, go for anything in the history of mankind. But everything is gained for the cause of rational religion, if it can be shown that inspiration itself is the same in every faculty, and is in its essence—that is, as a mental impulse—no more supernatural in religion than in politics or philosophy.

It would be possible, I think, to draw an instructive parallel between the prophetic writers and the author whose book presents the strongest points of contrast to them, I mean Thucydides. He was inspired at once by the past history of his people, and by the events which were daily unfolding themselves before his eyes and suggesting to him new ideas. But whereas he described the actions and analysed the character of the nation, the Jew described the actions and realised the character of God, whom he discerned in all the events of history as truly as Thucydides perceived the genius and, so to speak, spiritual personality of Greece. Nor are the thoughts of the Jewish writers at all more difficult to account for than those of the great historian; in one there is a rush, in the other a load of thought that almost baffled expression. The inconsistencies and contradictions natural to the human intellect, when brought face to face with a new revelation, find a place in Jewish inspiration, for instance in St Paul, as in other regions of thought. I turn, however, now to point out the effect of this theory of the naturalness of inspiration upon the relations of science and religion.

Now it must be clearly understood that the quarrel of science with the received doctrine of inspiration by supernatural infusion of thought is by the nature of the case internecine. A miraculous event is not as such necessarily opposed to any fundamental law of science; it is at most a contradiction to the sum of human experience. No doubt, a strong prejudice is created against the miraculous by the scientific way of regarding things, but the prejudice may turn out to be unfounded, a mere passing result of the astonishing growth of scientific thought. And if any miraculous event can be proved by evidence enough to convince the final court of human appeal—that is, the mature and definite decision of enlightened opinion—to have taken place, then, as I have repeatedly affirmed, science will have no choice but to accept it as a fact, to find some reason for it, and to analyse its effects upon human thought. For myself, I hope I may live to see the day when such an admission will be on the whole made, upon the simple and satisfactory ground that some such cause is needed to account for phenomena otherwise inexplicable. But the case is far otherwise with the received doctrine of a supernatural inspiration conferring dogmatic authority upon those to whom it is vouchsafed, for this cuts at the very root of scientific method itself. This method rests upon the assumption that the reason of man is sufficient to ascertain by ordinary intellectual processes whatever truth can be attained from the contemplation of facts presented to consciousness. If, then, it is possible for any man to say, " This is true, not because my reason has thought it out, but because God, in a way I cannot understand myself nor explain to you, has put the idea in my mind "—then the very instrument of scientific thought is wrenched from its grasp, and truth is discoverable no longer by reason, but by authority to which reason must submit. Step by step indeed authority is yielding the ground it has invaded ; at present it may be said to have finally abandoned the domain of material phenomena over which law now reigns in place of the dethroned usurper. But the very formula by which it seeks to cover retreat and take up a new position, shows how very far the spirit of authoritative dogma is from apprehending the aim and forces of its opponent. We leave, it explains, the region of physical law to science, because God has not revealed by supernatural means truths which unaided reason can discover for itself. To which the answer is that reason is competent for the investigation of every fact, be it spiritual or material, in nature, history, or man himself; and further, that no truth deserves the name that cannot be demonstrated by argument or submitted to human judgment. Poetry, for instance, has its laws, by which poems must be judged. This assertion will cause no trouble to those who believe that all thought is essentially divine and absolutely good till it comes within the corrupting influences of individual men. To such it will appear evident that religious inspiration is only one (the chief, it is true) of the manifold workings of the Spirit of God, "who worketh in us both to will and to do according to His good pleasure."

Perhaps, however, the difference of attitude towards supernatural events and supernatural inspiration may be illustrated as follows. Science can raise no fair objection to any claim, however preposterous in itself, which is willing to be judged according to accepted methods of inquiry. If then any claim is made in these days, as indeed is very commonly made by spiritualists and others, to the possession of miraculous powers, science can at once put such claims to the proof, and, as in the well-known case of Faraday, expose and annihilate them. But the claim to the possession of supernatural inspiration, and to authoritative knowledge derived therefrom, eludes any test to which reason can submit it. If, therefore, any man claims to speak the words of God by virtue of special mental communication from Him, common sense has no means either of detecting the lie or approving the truth, unless, indeed, it is false or immoral upon the face of it. Science must therefore either admit that the reasoning powers upon which it rests are capable of being directed by supernatural agencies, and are therefore in themselves insufficient and deceptive; or it must drive these rival pretensions from the field by bending the whole force of human experience and feeling against them. If the Pope, or any writer, or any institution, or any body of men, be infallibly inspired, there is an end of reason, and therefore of science as the only authoritative leader of mankind and guide to truth. Religious minds may unconsciously seek to disguise the nature and extent of this antagonism between two mutually exclusive powers, and may wonder that science rejects with increasing confidence the various compromises from time to time suggested, and insists with what seems unjustifiable arrogance upon overstepping and obliterating the lines of demarcation so painfully traced out. But reason coming to claim her rightful kingdom is not likely to leave one of its fairest provinces in the hands of a power that persists in setting up a rival claim to the allegiance of mankind.

So much then being decided we are now brought face to face with a very serious question. The more stress we lay upon facts as being the ultimate source of inspiration, the more necessary does it become to arrive at some conclusion as to their nature. This I have attempted to investigate elsewhere with a success that no one sees more clearly than myself to be indifferent. Upon the subject of miracles there is yet much to be learnt, but it is satisfactory to remember that as they purport to be facts, they court the closest scrutiny that reason can apply to them. For our present purpose, however, no such scrutiny is required. It is enough to say, first, that the Jews thoroughly and honestly believed that they received communications from God through outward events, either in the call of their great men, or in the providential circumstances of their history; second, that these events did as a matter of fact create certain ideas about God and life and goodness; third, that the ideas so created were legitimate results of the facts, supposing them to be true. Of these three propositions there can, I suppose, be no doubt. If God was that which they believed Him to be, if He had acted and was acting as they supposed Him to be acting, then their conclusions about the divine nature and human duty were warranted by the plainest considerations of reason and common sense. I shall have, however, to allude in my next essay to the connection of Jewish inspiration with the revelation which they supposed had been granted to them. But though it is impossible to foretell what will be the ultimate verdict of men upon the truth or error of the Jews' belief in God's special dealings with them, yet it is very possible indeed to foresee what will be the effect of that verdict upon the future of Christianity. It may take one of two forms. Either the Jewish mind imagined, honestly enough, though mistakenly, the occurrence of miraculous events, and then derived its religious ideas from them; or such events did actually from time to time occur, and so created, kept alive, guided and developed that type of religion which God intended to be the universal religion of subsequent ages. Let us examine the effect of these alternatives separately.

If the first be the true one—if, that is, there was no such intervention in the history of the Jews as could be clearly and decisively traced to the power of God—then it requires but small power of prophecy to discern that Christianity will perish, probably amidst such an outburst of human wrath as will throw into shade the wildest excesses of the Reformation or the Revolution. Just in proportion as its religious ideas are strong, decisive, and predominant, so will its errors appear gross and injurious. If the Jews and early Christians were the victims of delusions upon which they founded their faith, then it will be argued that they went astray exactly in proportion to the strength of the religious faculty which they possessed. At present the faults of Christian teaching are condoned, and much more than condoned, for the sake of the invaluable truths derived from the facts to which Christianity bears continuous testimony. Nay, I will go further and assert that in spite of appearances to the contrary, very few scientific men really believe these facts to be devoid of substantial foundation. No doubt it falls in best with the natural tendencies of positive thought to accept them as untrue, just as it is natural to the religious faculty to accept them as real. But for the most part, a few enthusiasts excepted, men are contented with this lazy, indifferent attitude, and do not care to advance to the more serious task of *proving* them to be false to their own satisfaction, and with the intention of convincing others. They are so bound up with the opinions, traditions, and institutions of modern human life, that men instinctively prefer to leave them alone, lest society, and themselves with it, should be cast adrift into a shoreless sea of darkness and despair. They cling to the idea while nominally rejecting the facts which alone give the ideas any vitality. But if men believed with the inward assurance of positive faith that the facts of Christianity were untrue, their attitude would soon be changed from the negative, scornful, half-silence of the present day into that which Christian apologists are fond of attributing to them—a resolute, combined, unswerving hatred of superstitious falsehood, ending in a determination to uproot it at whatever cost of human agony and suffering. And to this cold-blooded resolution of intellectual men would soon be added the passionate fury of the common crowd, red-hot with justifiable anger at the reflection that they had been deceived and traded upon in matters that concerned their dearest hopes. This is what they would say—

"For all these long centuries, then, we toilers and sufferers have been victims of gross imposture. We have been taught to look forward to immortality because one man has vanquished death—death which to common experience vanquishes man; we find now that death vanquished Him also, and that He was Himself a victim to His own delusions. We have been taught to pray to a common Father of whose existence we have no positive proof, except what He, who chose to call Himself His Son, has thought fit to give us, drawn from the depths of a bewildered self-consciousness. Let us think of the immeasurable waste of time, of wealth, of thought which might have been applied to temporal and human ends, but which have gone to aid the purposes and swell the power of those who have profited by our superstitions. Above all let us remember that we, reasonable creatures, have been lavishing our best thoughts and deepest feelings in prayer that was mere idle breath cast to the scoffing winds." He must indeed have a strangely constituted mind who believes that any part of the Christian religion would survive the discovery that the history of Jesus of Nazareth was a series of well-intentioned fables, and Himself an impostor with or without His own connivance. In that outbreak of human indignation against the religion and the teachers by whom the world had been so long enslaved, short work would be made of all that appertained to the name of Christianity. Churches would share the fate of monasteries, and clergyman become as hateful a word as priest. And in my opinion quite rightly.

But then we are told that the ideas would remain because they are eternally true, or true to the individual conscience. I am not sure that I know what this means, or how an idea can be true to me which is independent of facts, and cannot be demonstrated to any one else. No doubt ideas that concerned the duty of man towards man might remain—the law of self-sacrifice, for instance, might take its place in the great code of human duty as part of the experience of mankind. But in what practical vital sense God could be considered my Father, who had never done to me an action that I knew to be fatherly, passes my understanding. As, however, we are in the region of the future, there is no power of hindering people from prophesying whatever their personal inclinations predispose them to desire. Only I take leave to call the attention of any who may be tempted to " prophesy out of their own hearts, who follow their own spirits and have seen nothing,". to three of those simple, obvious facts which are to plain people the true " word of the Lord."

First, truth that is true to me is no truth at all, unless I can convey it to my neighbour in some such way as will convince him, unless he himself is in fault. And in the sphere of religion I have no other means of doing this except by reasoning founded upon the facts of the case. In vain do I urge that the truths in which I believe are very consoling and animating to myself; they may not be so to other people. One man's truth is another man's lie, and perishes with the idiosyncrasy or the selfishness which gave it birth, or made it attractive. Such truths therefore have no inherent power of self-propagation—nothing but their correspondence with some outward reality can enable them to be transferred from one mind to another. False ideas either invent a fictitious reality or impose themselves upon people by an appeal to their enthusiasm or their credulity. Therefore a religion which rests upon a supposed intuitional apprehension of truths that have nothing to recommend them to other people save the satisfaction which they give to the person who apprehends them, cannot in the long run subsist. Hence it is that speculative religions invariably perish or sink to the level of man's selfish desires. Truth in religion, as elsewhere, is that common property of mankind which reason has thought out, time tested, experience approved, so that the human intellect has set to its seal that it is true. This by no means excludes the operation of the heart or emotions of man: their province is to afford the motive power required for actions, and furthermore to compel the mind, by the strong craving of the desires, to do its work. My desire for a heavenly Father is no proof of His existence, but it is a very strong reason why I should endeavour to search if there be not proof to be found.

Secondly, if Christianity as a revelation to man through facts were to perish, it must be remembered that there would be theories of life, of duty, of expediency and morality, which would neither require nor leave room for religious ideas, not even in the form of Positivism. Such theories, call them materialistic or scientific, are in existence now; they claim to be workable, to be sufficient, to be satisfactory. Nothing stands between them and victory save man's belief in the events by which God has made Himself known. But by degrees the spiritual instincts would fade away with the facts to which they owe all their vitality, and men would more and more find their only goodness in duty to the race, their highest wisdom within the limits of experience, their supreme happiness in the negation of God and immortality. What chance in the present temper of mankind would intuitions have when brought into conflict with facts?

For, thirdly, that some such conflict must of necessity arise between the recognised theories of life and the religious instinct is abundantly apparent. History tells us that it did arise once, and that thought and virtue went one way with philosophy, devotion, or rather superstition, another way with the mass of men. But seeing that Christianity has gained an empire over men's minds infinitely stronger and more enduring than Paganism, it is reasonable to suppose that the new philosophy, based as it would be upon ascertained facts, would be compelled to hunt religion out of life altogether, perhaps with sharp and systematic persecution. The very gist of the charge against the old religion would be then, as it is now, that it calls men away from sensible realities and obvious duties into an imaginary and delusive region of faith. No heretic would be half so detestable as the man who, without the shadow of a fact to rely on, persisted in doing what the community thought wrong, because he felt sure that the sufferings he received at their hands would be made up to him in a future life. This and similar ideas might be allowed to linger in the minds of certain men, like the odour of cedar in old fashioned rooms, provided it did not interfere with the course of life by leading to practical results. Not indeed that it would much matter. Ideas that are true only because true to me, are very seldom practical to anybody else.

Let us now see how the adoption of the other alternative would affect our views of the nature and authority of inspiration. There is good reason for believing that there were three distinct miraculous epochs in the history of the Jews, from which they derived their certainty that their history was the result of God's direct action upon their affairs. But it is important to observe that, so far as we are at present concerned, the acceptance of any one miraculous event is sufficient. Let that event be the Resurrection, because it is the best authenticated and the most intrinsically probable. If this be accepted, then it follows not only that there is no antecedent improbability for any miracle, but that the Jews were right in attributing to God's over-mastering will the whole course of their history, miraculous or otherwise. If God raised Jesus Christ from the dead, that fact puts the crown of reality upon all their beliefs and hopes. If, to put it strongly, every atom of miracles could be removed from the Old Testament, the life of Christ would still be sufficient to show that the finger of God was visible in all that befell them from Egypt to the destruction of Jerusalem. They were in a special way the subjects of divine government, and their national instinct, that they could discern the character and purposes of God in events that happened, is proved to be a true one. And thus the mainspring, so to speak, of all the complicated machinery of inspiration is furnished to them.

And the dynamic force of this mainspring is simply incalculable. All that men were required to do was to receive and detail the facts with tolerable accuracy, and to think concerning them with powers of mind that were up to a fair average when contrasted with other nations. History, poetry, statesmanship, and that vast amount of literature which is in one form or another practically preaching (the declaration, that is, of truths and their consequences), occupy themselves chiefly with the actions of living beings, of man and of men. This is the main source of their work and use; it is their glory and delight. Now let us for an instant imagine the effects upon a religious faculty, strong in native genius, traditionary instincts, and individual enthusiasm, of the thought that God was acting towards the nation by deeds of mercy, judgment, redemption, and chastisement. The utterances of such a faculty carry with them the same kind of authority as those of other faculties under analogous circumstances. There is no need of supernatural infusion or overpowering guidance in one case more than another. Events inspired Moses as they inspired Homer—the difference lay in the nature of the events. Brought face to face, as they believed, with the will and deeds of God, the Jewish writers believed that the thoughts that rose spontaneously to their minds came from Him. There may be much in them that is wanting in knowledge, inaccurate in fact, defective in argument. They may share to the full the idiosyncrasies, bad or good, of their nation. The Psalmist may give utterance to uncharitable maledictions, St Paul may "hebraize," St Peter "judaize." Their opinions may be open to correction and criticism. But when all this is granted, there will remain, instead of the old artificial non-human authority which aroused opposition because it repelled intellectual sympathy, that genuine reverence which man pays to the greatest and wisest spirits of his race, to the recipients and preachers of new truths, to God's chosen servants, according to the exquisite Jewish conception of great men. And if—which may God grant—the prejudice against these actions of God called miracles disappears before our growing knowledge and a fairer spirit of inquiry, then science herself will bring her ungrudging homage, the homage that all that is best in positive thought seems to me so ready to bring now if difficulties could be removed. One of those difficulties is the feeling of repulsion felt by religious minds towards the scientific method of inquiry in a province that they conscientiously believe to be alien from it. But how gladly St Paul would have accepted that homage in his Master's name, those who have realised his character may be permitted to picture to themselves. And, on the other hand, were he to be offered the spurious deference paid to supernatural or semi-divine beings (for such upon the ordinary theory of inspiration he becomes), we may imagine how swiftly he would run in among the people, "crying out and saying, Sirs, why do ye these things? We are men of like passions with you, and preach unto you that you should turn from these vanities unto the living God."

An objection may be raised to the foregoing view that facts cannot prove spiritual truths or, as I have seen it stated, that it is absurd to ask for a purely intellectual proof of the existence of an all-loving Father. Now there is a sense in which this statement is true, and, as I shall show presently, in agreement with what I have maintained throughout these essays. But as, taken literally, it reduces them to an absurdity, I must go on to show in what sense an intellectual proof can be given of even this ultimate spiritual verity.

Now, the only proof that can be given in such a case must be derived from the performance of fatherly actions. If faith without works is dead, much more is love. And if we eliminate from history the possibility of any direct personal action of the unknown Being whom we call God, I am at a loss to know how we are to believe that He is our Father, or what good that belief would confer upon us. It seems to me not easily distinguishable in kind (though raised far above it, if by nothing else, at least by its pathetic unselfishness), from the caresses and pleadings which the savage lavishes upon his insensible idol. But granting the historical truthfulness of the life and person of Christ, then its effect in affording intellectual demonstration of the fatherhood of God may be made clear by the following illustration.

Intellectual proof means nothing more than arguments appropriate to the nature of the case, and sufficient to convince reasonable people that the thing in question is true. Legal proof is one thing, scientific (in physics) another, historical (perhaps) a third. Now, let us suppose a child brought up in ignorance of his father, who was obliged to live a long way off. The child would know that he owed his existence to a father, but whether he was alive and loving him would be quite an open question—the balance of probability inclining towards the negative. Let us imagine next a man presenting himself, bearing a strong family likeness, and claiming to be an elder brother. He informs the child of his father's existence and character, tells him that he has come thousands of miles to make this clear, gives ample explanation of the necessity for living apart, proves to him that all his education and comforts have been due to his father's care, loads him with benefits and good advice, and departs promising a speedy meeting in the father's home. Is not such proof as this intellectually convincing, none the less so because, being in the sphere of the feelings, it takes care to address itself to them as well as to reason properly so called. But it is the kind of proof which, *mutatis mutandis*, Christians believe that they possess in the life of Christ, who declared, amongst many similar assertions, "My Father worketh hitherto and I work," as though He would say, "My Father has all along been working on your behalf, and my works are but His works, evidently done among you, that you may know Him that sent me."

What, however, I suspect to be the meaning of the assertion above quoted is merely this—that no intellectual proof of spiritual truths can be given except to those who are morally predisposed towards them. This is what I have insisted on throughout these essays; indeed, the right understanding of it is necessary to a right conception of my position. To repeat it once more, it is this: all proof in religion as elsewhere must be primarily addressed to the reason, must be itself therefore rational, based upon facts, and capable of historical verification. But the actual proofs, as we have them, are such that men may—at any rate at the present time—honestly accept or honestly reject them; and the turning point in their decision will be whether the facts sought to be established are in agreement with man's moral nature and requirements. And, on the other hand, any attempt to establish religious truths by appeals to the inner self-consciousness, or the voice of nature, or *à priori* considerations of causation and design, or the hopes and wishes of mankind, will end in confusion and scepticism. Such appeals, it must be added, have their invaluable but still lower office. They may be suitably made in conjunction with the arguments derived from revelation, and may either prepare the way for it by creating an antecedent probability, or supplement its force by conclusions derived from wider and further-reaching premises. But considering how total has been the failure of " natural" religion in past ages, and how entirely religion is now the creature of revelation, I am inclined to think that the use of the former is mainly supplementary, and suitable for speculative minds to whom religion is an excuse (often the only one they have) for embarking upon comprehensive inquiries.

Once more an illustration will make my meaning clear. The authority of the fourth Gospel is one of those questions upon which the arguments for and against hang at present evenly balanced, so far as purely intellectual proof can go. Hence, the judgment of each man now, and of all men finally, will turn upon personal predispositions. A man's love for the Christ he finds there, his moral yearnings after God, may be so intense as to sway his judgment in one way rather than another; and this, whether right or not, is, I am very sure, the way in which all the practical affairs of life are ordered. But a certain class of minds find the cultus of the Virgin Mary equally attractive, and, as they think, essential to them. Yet, as that cultus is absolutely devoid of proof that could be based on facts, or called reasonable, to believe in the Roman view of the character and position of the Virgin, because it is lovable and attractive, is simply to ignore the intellect and do despite to facts. Nevertheless, I do not see what answer those who accept an opinion, because it suits them, can give to the votaries of the legend of the mother of God.

This, then, is the conclusion of the whole matter. The Jews, who were the religious nation *par excellence*, were inspired by events exactly as religious persons, *par excellence*, are inspired now. Once more I appeal to common experience. Let a man be fully persuaded, by any means whatever, that he is in the hands of an overruling God, and then the events of life inspire his mind with the thoughts, the feelings, the words, and the actions which make up his religion. Daily cares, sorrows, blessings, occurrences, and above all sins, make him think in a certain way about God, and address Him in certain words. Religion is not and ought not to be a perpetual straining of the religious emotions, or an artificial inspiration that comes of ceremonies and outward observances. It is the wholesome reflection of serious minds about the daily experience of lives believed to be ordered and guided by God here, and subject to His judgment hereafter, and, therefore, now as in the days of old, may men pray with full assurance of faith for the inspiration of God's Holy Spirit.

So then, inspiration is neither above thought or independent of fact. Rather it is one out of the many ways in which thought may regard facts, and with the special events the special Christian inspiration must stand or fall. If they fall Christianity expires with them, and with Christianity dies religion, as one of the powers that rule the hearts of men. One other possible alternative there is, so at least some persons are found to think. It is that the spirit of philosophy should sit in judgment upon the mass of hopes, desires, beliefs, and words in which the religious instinct has found expression, and should, after careful balancing and earnest scrutiny, agree to recommend some of them as on the whole the most suitable, useful, and becoming; concerning which religion I can only say that I hope I may be comfortably in my grave before I am obliged, by the tendency of thought or the progress of knowledge, to accept and practise it.

THE INSPIRATION OF THE BIBLE.

IT is impossible to begin this essay without once more calling attention to the difficulties which surround this and similar inquiries. In the first place, those who agree with me that there is no such thing as supernatural infusion of thought, deny also that there has been in history anything that can be called a specific revelation from God. Those, on the other hand, who believe that God has intervened by certain personal actions in the affairs of man, have no sympathy with the doctrine that He has not, and thought being what it is, cannot have supernaturally interfered with their thoughts. I have no right therefore to expect sympathy from any quarter beyond, I hope, that of candid minds who are willing to recognise what seems to be on the face of it an honest investigation, be its results what they may. And this would be fatal if my object were to convert a certain number of persons to a given set of opinions—to construct a system of religious belief in its relations to scientific thought. But I have no such ambition. This book is not, it must be remembered, after all so much a reconciliation of religion and science, but "Essays" or attempts in that direction. It aims at throwing some light upon the conditions of the problem to be solved, and at suggesting a new method of approaching them. What we want is a *novum organon* of theology, the application, that is, of rigorous scientific tests to the phenomena of revelation—*i.e.*, of historical religions in general, and of Christianity as the crown of them in particular. And the first condition of such a task must be the absence of any *à priori* opinion for and against the supernatural. No inquiry can be satisfactorily conducted in which the main point at issue is assumed, not provisionally, but as an absolute not-to-be-questioned truth, beforehand. I fear it must be confessed that theological animus has crept (a mild word!) into scientific thought when brought into contact with religious questions. Hence the impossibility of reconciliation.

It is not, however, merely want of sympathy which I have to fear, but also the unfeigned aversion felt by religious minds towards an investigation of the phenomena of the divine life in man. Men demand a "margin for mystery," and Science, by the mouth of her wisest interpreters, confesses the reasonableness of the demand and the reality of the fact demanded. But the question arises, "Where is the line to be drawn?" The dictum of science is plain, and in my judgment incontestable. The Bible, view it in whatever way you please, comes within experience, and is therefore capable of rational treatment. Everything about it—its composition, facts, thoughts—has a meaning which that trained common-sense of mankind called science can discover and explain.

But it is said that the special grace and power of religion perishes under such treatment. Thus, if we dissect a flower, we gain, indeed, some knowledge, but at the cost of its fragrance and beauty. But the facts of Jewish history are rather to be compared to geological formations which lie deep down in the constitution of things, and may be explained, but never explained away. And so they grow in dignity and worth the more closely they are examined. It is one of the many points of resemblance between the Christianity of the first and the science of the two last centuries, between the genius of St Paul and Newton, that they set themselves to reduce the sphere of the unknown within limits which are felt to be legitimate only because they are pushed as far back as the faculties of man can reach. In the mind of St Paul religion was no longer mysterious: in the clear light of the revelation of Jesus Christ, God's character and purposes towards man, man's duty and relations towards God, shone transfigured as with celestial glory, in which every feature and outline might be traced, not of necessity all at once, but in time and with patience. No man of science, when grasping the key with which to unlock the door of many mysteries, ever felt a deeper gladness than St Paul when it became apparent to him that in the life and person of Jesus Christ every question that the religious mind could reasonably ask would be without fail rationally answered. We must remember that St Paul is in no sense answerable for that other method of dealing with religious questions which delights to draw distinct outlines of vague impalpable realities, to label them as "mysteries," and propound them authoritatively for the acceptance of mankind. Who wrote the Athanasian Creed may be very uncertain; one thing at least is certain, that St Paul did not.

For myself I must take leave to assert that no one can approach the history of the Jews from Abraham to St

John with so real an appreciation of its sanctity as they who, in the humble spirit of scientific research, seek to discover the secret workings which produced results so unusual and so entrancing. The spirit of Voltaire is indeed very far from being extinct, and there are even signs that it may revive. But I attribute this partly to the determination of the dominant school of religious thought to treat the Bible in an unnatural way, partly to the perverted theories—such, for instance, as the whole theology of types—to which the most popular among them still adhere. But upon the whole, if we may judge by some of the utterances of the leaders of science, the Bible still leaves upon the minds of even "advanced thinkers" an impression of genuine sanctity. Events that would be commonplace in any other history, challenge our reverence here from the way in which they are treated with a constant reference to the will of an overruling God. Here is an instance. The fall of Athaliah is in one sense a very ordinary Eastern palace revolution, yet listen to the story especially as told in Mendelssohn's immortal music, which it in turn inspired, and a strange feeling of the awfulness of Jewish life creeps upon the mind. Put it as you will, here were a people alone among nations who believed that they were living in the presence and under the controlling power of one holy and Almighty God, and who somehow or other depicted His character and attributes in a way that no other nation has ever even attempted. Not the vulgar awe that comes of gazing at mysteries, but the profound reverence that enchains the human mind when searching into facts that seem to speak closely and clearly of God, is the spirit with which the Bible must be approached.

The theory of Scriptural Inspiration which this essay is intended to maintain, is, to repeat it once more, that it was the result of the play of human thought according to its natural ordinary methods about the events that made up Jewish national and individual life. The advantages thus obtained for the cause of rational religion have been in part already pointed out, and will appear still more clearly as we proceed. They may be summed up in the simple statement, that human life becomes possible to the Jews and their experience useful for us. What we have to ask, then, is whether it is possible thus to account for those special features of Jewish life and thought which distinguish them from other people? To this we now address ourselves.

At the outset it is necessary to recall what has been already said as to the events by which God was believed to have "called" all the chief persons of Hebrew history, and to have given them a commission to perform the work He had in hand. The more I think of it, the more sure I feel that in these calls lies the root of all that is special in the Bible. I have attempted in its proper place to give some account of them regarded as divine actions; but it is obvious that, regarding them as we do now in their effects upon the recipients, we may adopt any account of their external reality that seems good to us. Either they occurred as related, or the recipients honestly believed so, or the narrators honestly thought so, or the people honestly so accepted them. If they were mistaken, that does not alter the fact that they derived their special ideas about God from their mistake. The inspiration remains, *valeat quantum*, whether the events were real or not.

And it is distinctly as an inspiration that the events come

before us. In all of them, no matter what their outward form, or whether they were represented as supernatural or not, the voice of God is represented as making itself heard by man. The effect upon Moses or St Paul was as though words had been addressed to their understandings. Whether the voice was objective or no seems to me the idlest of inquiries, so long as it is admitted to be real in its effects upon the mind. It concerns us, however, to inquire a little more closely into the nature of that pregnant word voice.

Voice is simply the external utterance of the inner spirit. It is, therefore, the most spiritual thing of which we can have a sensible perception. But a kind of prejudice is felt, that even so it is not spiritual enough adequately to represent the communications of God with man. I suppose that such reasoning means, that God being a Spirit can only approach men through their thoughts or moral emotions. No doubt any method of representing God's communications to man must be inadequate, but I contend that the voice is the most purely spiritual thing that can be imagined; and thus we are led to a question of the most serious importance, What, in plain words, is the meaning of "spirit"?

For hundreds of years the world, as it seems to me, has been haunted by the notion of a spirit as a house is plagued by ghosts. It has been regarded as an immaterial something, a substance, because separable from the body, nowhere discoverable, everywhere present. It has affected philosophy with vain inquiries as to the nature of that which being incapable of analysis is beyond knowledge. It has driven men to Atheism by the sheer impossibility of discovering its existence, or it has conducted them to Pantheism by the determination to believe in that for which no separate existence could be found. It has plunged theology into wild speculations as to the origin of "souls," whether they are specially created or derived by inheritance. It has taught men to speak of the immortality of the soul instead of the immortality of persons, and has made them desire to save their souls as a thing separate from themselves, instead of saving themselves as moral and rational beings; and this although the great Teacher Himself uses the two phrases loss of self and loss of soul as synonymous (St Luke ix. 25). It has created dreams of purgatory, intermediate states, spiritual manifestations, ghosts, devils, and witches. It has filled men's minds with Manichæan contempt and hatred of matter, and Gnostic fables concerning the nature of Christ. And now men tremble and despair of religion because science begins to declare, "This spirit of yours, I can nowhere find it: matter I know, life I know, and thought I know; but what is this which is and is not, which exists for your purposes but not for mine, and which digs a wide impassable gulf between knowledge and faith?"

Of all the benefits that science is conferring upon religion, and, I must add, of all the testimonies that it is bearing to the truth of revelation, none, I think, are so great and so searching as this destruction of the old notion about spirit, and the consequent necessity of finding a new one. What, then, did Christ mean when he said that God was a Spirit —a declaration which M. Renan is good enough to honour with special approbation? He meant to declare authoritatively that which throughout the whole history of the Jews He —the Word of God—had been engaged in making known to them, that God is a Person. Personality is consciousness of self, spirit is self-consciousness regarded in its effects upon, or relations towards, others; it is therefore the more complete and fuller expression. The true antithesis, therefore, to spirit is not matter, but unconscious impersonal existence. It is a moral and not a metaphysical word. Are we really to be told that Jesus Christ entered upon subtle metaphysical discussions, when from this premise He drew the conclusion that men were to worship God in spirit? The addition of the words " and in truth "—that is, sincerity of self—shows that He meant to declare that God, being a Personal Being, was to be worshipped with personal love and devotion, irrespective of place and circumstance. How easily the language of religion lends itself to this idea of spirit may be seen in the words of the prayer in which "we offer and present unto God ourselves, our souls and bodies, to be a reasonable, holy, and lively sacrifice,"—spirit being here regarded as the personality which is the result of the combination of mind and body. And thus a real basis is laid for the permanent union of science and religion. The former asserts that only in the ultimate incomprehensibility, called the power of thought, is there room for any conception of God; the latter affirms that this power of thought resides in a person. The former insists that no positive conception of God can be formed from the contemplation of mind and matter in nature; the latter proclaims that He has made Himself known by His voice, the one only means by which beings like ourselves are primarily and directly reached by spiritual influences from other persons. It only remains that each should examine the facts upon which the other relies—science reverently and religion rationally—for this union to become an accomplished fact.

The difficulty of making an assertion, such as the preceding definition of spirit, lies in one's knowledge of the different ways in which it will be received. To some it will appear as though with much parade I had stated the alphabet of science. To some it will appear as though the essence of religion had been then and there destroyed. And there are some of whose opinion it is impossible to form even a conjecture. Thus one of the leaders of contemporary English theology, after describing with great eloquence and power the self-conscious personality of man as constituting his spiritual being, goes on, apparently under the constraint of an exacting orthodoxy, to say that "God is perpetually creating souls out of nothing and infusing [!] them into bodies. He creates each soul at the moment when the body which is destined for it enters really and properly on its inheritance of life." Surely the pleasure of quoting Jerome as a psychological authority in the nineteenth century is dearly purchased at the price of such inconsistency as this. However, be the opinion received as it may, I wish to point out that it has been reached from no metaphysical predilections, and quite irrespective of the conclusions of modern psychology. It has forced itself upon my mind as the only rational means of explaining the history of the actions of God as detailed in the Bible, and if it agrees with the scientific conception of spirit, so much the better for me. As, however, I have unwillingly strayed into the domain of metaphysics, it may be well to digress for a moment, in order to show how the truth that spirit is simply self-conscious personality enables us to harmonise the needful requirements of religion with the conclusions of science. Let us take as instances free-will and immortality.

It is essential to religion, as being based upon the responsibility of man to God—not that the will should be demonstratively known to be free, but that it should not be known to be bound. Consciousness testifies to an apparent freedom beyond which it is impossible for knowledge to pass. We are not justified, therefore, in founding a religious system upon man's free agency, as though that were an absolutely positive fact; on the other hand, if the consciousness of freedom were rendered impossible, then all religion perishes at once, and those who will have brought about so vast a revolution must be left to say how morality, or, indeed, human action of any sort, can survive. The latest and most complete philosophy of science affirms that man is a succession of psychical states produced by physical conditions, arising from the circumstances which "environ" him. If this be true (and I neither deny nor affirm it, it lies beyond my scope), then it is plain that spirit as a separate entity can have no existence; but it is by no means so plain that spirit as self-conscious personality, involving the consciousness of free agency, is at all affected. For it is a simple fact that I know myself as a being with a continuous history past, present, and to come. Consequently, in addition to all other psychical states that determine my action at any given moment, there is one which does not result from my environment, but from my direct apprehension of myself as a being to whom something is due, whom something may hurt or advantage, not necessarily now, but ten years hence. So far, therefore, as the consciousness of personal identity enters as a motive into my actions, so far they are not determined by external agencies exclusively. No doubt by far the greater part of our actions are not free in any real sense of the word. If, for instance, food is set before me when I am hungry, I eat it with no more actual consciousness of freedom than an animal. But if I decline it upon the plea that it may in some small degree prejudice my health hereafter, the consciousness of self and its dues becomes the deciding motive of what I do, and this even though my knowledge is (like all memory in this philosophy) a psychical state; and if this be so, then virtue is essentially a rightful consciousness of personality, of what is due to and from one's self. Evil, on the contrary, is that which men do to their own harm and the hurt of other people, because they do not think rightly of what is due to and from themselves. (I say "to and from," because both views of the nature of morality are thus included.) Evil has therefore its primary root, as men have been long tending to think, in the intellect: it is in its lowest forms want of thought about self, and in its more refined forms the misapplication of thought from mistaken selfish predispositions. And thus thought, becoming conscious of self,[*] is the one divine thing in mankind, that which answers to the idea of the creation of man. I think—that is, I exist.

Next, it is essential to religion that the hope of immortality should not be quenched. What men desire is not that any part of their friends should exist after death, but that the persons themselves should continue a self-conscious life. In this sense the spirits of the dead live even upon earth for a little while. What they were still strives, so to speak, amongst those who knew them. But let us trace this idea of spirit in its bearings upon the fact of evolution.

---

[*] As this self-consciousness is due to the correlation of thought with various bodily conditions, the body is seen to be an essential part of each man's personality.

A certain unknowable entity called mind is correlated with a certain unknowable entity called matter. By slow process through countless generations a being is formed who thinks—that is, becomes conscious of himself. The question, whether this final step is due to natural evolution, or requires to be accounted for by some special creative act, is purely a scientific and not a religious one. This being, so compounded, dies with every fibre of his personality crying aloud for life. If he has but a doubtful metaphysical theory to rely on—namely, that spirit is an entity separable from matter—he is, indeed, in a sorry plight. If he rejects with disdain evidence merely because it is supernatural, for a belief—*i.e.*, in his own immortality—which belief involves, if true, the most supernatural thing that can be imagined, his reasoning must be in as sorry a condition as his hopes. Driven by the impossibility of drawing a line anywhere between man and animals, he is compelled to assert that if spirit lives after death, then animals, though no glimpse of the idea can be known to have crossed their minds, also are immortal. He exclaims in defiance, My body is not me but mine, just at the moment that science is more and more clearly discovering that body is neither more nor less an essential part of ourselves than soul, life, will, or anything else that a person can call his own. But let him grasp firmly the idea that spirit is merely self-consciousness, and then he may go with safety into the furthest extreme of Materialism, far further, indeed, than sober science would carry him. Supposing my body is not mine but me, what then? The same power which by chemical action, molecular combination, call it what you will, built up my personality, and made phosphorus to live my rational life, and kept my personal identity safe amid the perpetual change and flux of the matter which composes me, can do so after my death if it pleases, as it pleases, when it pleases. But if I am asked why a bare possibility should become positive fact, and how I know anything of what this power is and what it pleases to do, I answer that the resurrection of one Person under circumstances that make it a crucial test converts this potentiality into actuality, verifies an hypothesis, and substantiates faith. This was the reconstitution of a personality that, so far as we know, perished at death. His body was the same yet different, adapted to those spiritual functions which become a Person who knew no sin, and whose body, therefore, knew no corruption. More than this I do not know, but to know this is more than enough.

We return now, after this long digression, to the consideration of Inspiration viewed in its origin as the communication of thought from God to man. To quote what I have already said, "A voice from a living God made itself heard by methods sufficient to satisfy rational and sober minds of its reality, and thus revealed the abiding character and present designs of Almighty God." And again, "The men thus convinced acquired a mental certainty that the thoughts which came and went were not the mere chance workings of their own minds, but the inspiration of God." In what way, then, these thoughts operated we are now to inquire, with reasonable prospect of success.

That which distinguishes the history of the Jews from every other nation is the recurrence of the expressions "God did this" and "God said so;" the former of these phrases describes the miraculous element, which I have already considered, the latter contains the claim to distinctive Inspiration. Under any circumstances, the mere existence of such a claim, with all its past pregnant consequences upon humanity, would demand the most earnest attention. Here were a people whose statesmen, poets, historians, and writers deliberately asserted and confidently believed that the words they uttered expressed the mind of God. If, to take one instance, a reformer had any abuse to point out, he did not say that he had discovered either the abuse or the remedy, but that God had sent him with a message. What, then, did they mean? To answer this question all I can hope to do is to give the briefest sketch of the meaning and the working of the various formulæ of Inspiration. These are as follows:—

There are two sets of phrases to describe first, the communication of God to the individual directly; and, secondly, of God to the people through the first recipient. And then there are four sets, so to speak, of these phrases.

1. "God spake unto," with its corresponding phrase "I am the Lord."

2. "The word of the Lord came unto," and "thus saith the Lord."

3. "The Spirit of the Lord came upon," and "such a man did or said so and so."

4. The word of Jesus Christ "I say unto you," who spoke of His own authority as we might imagine God speaking among men. This, therefore, does not strictly belong to inspiration, but rather to the consideration of His person and character. I shall confine myself therefore to the first three, and show how each of them is consistent with the theory that inspiration is the result of the working of the mind about events believed to come from God.

The first formula belongs to the legal period of Jewish

history, and is confined almost entirely to the Mosaic legislation. Speaking of the expression "I am the Lord," which is used to sanction certain of the laws, Ewald says: "These words considered as to their outward form serve only to mark the declaration as coming from Jehovah Himself; but considered as to their inner meaning, they flow out of that strong simple feeling, according to which the true prophet announces what he receives not humanly but divinely. In the earliest times this feeling was most direct and powerful, so that the human being seemed wholly to disappear in presence of the God who spoke through him; and the language corresponded with the feeling, expressing in the strongest way that God alone spoke, and spoke, moreover, as God—that is, simply commanding : wherefore the irresistible power of His word was announced by the expression 'I am Jehovah' either preceding or closing it."

This contains the sum of the whole matter. Let it be granted that Moses composed in the desert some at least of the laws that bear his name, and especially the Ten Commandments. Let it be further granted that he believed himself to have been called by God to the work of making Israel into a nation in the way that has been described. Then the laws were simply such as might have occurred to any great and original genius under the given circumstances. They grew out of the events, the beliefs, and the wants of the times. It rests with those who believe in a supernatural infusion of thought to show what there is in them that cannot be accounted for naturally. The evidence for such infusion must be found either in the statements of the narrative or in the nature of the results produced. Let us look at each of these for a moment.

The words "God spake" need imply no more than the use of a common Eastern expression, nor is there any hint given that anything more was intended than that the lawgiver felt himself entitled to proclaim his enactments as containing the will of God. On the contrary, there is much to show that this explanation is the true one. The phrase is used with an indiscriminate profusion, that shows how general and universal its application must have been. Can we seriously suppose that the minute and trivial regulations concerning dress, ritual, and the like were spelt out to Moses by the Divine voice, so that he, one of the greatest of men, becomes a mere registering machine? Again we ask our old question, Is human life, intelligent life, possible under such conditions? Nor is this all. The appointment of elders is in one case (Exod. xviii. 24) attributed to the advice of Jethro, in another (Num. xi. 16) to the express command of God; nor is the force of the argument much diminished if we make the accounts to refer to two different occasions, instead of being reminiscences, as surely they are, of the same. Again, how can we account for the record of long conversations between God and Moses except upon the supposition that they are dramatic narratives of the thoughts that swayed to and fro in the prophet's mind? It is, however, far more from a general survey of the use of the phrase itself that we are irresistibly driven to conclude that a natural intelligible meaning must be found for it.

Nor are there any claims in the narrative itself to lead us to any other conclusion. It is most true that it is shrouded in mystery and accompanied by awful manifestations of divine power—none the less awful because they are now known to be natural to that awe-inspiring land. I do not wish to take refuge in the idea that these were accessories added by later hands; this is to sacrifice what purports to be history for the sake of a theory. It may or may not be so, but unless we are to make a clean sweep of the whole narrative, we must admit that the "law was given" under external circumstances that seemed to attest the presence of Jehovah, and were calculated to inspire the mind with the sense of His will and character. The surrounding scenery, the attending storms, the sound as of a trumpet, the withdrawal of Moses, all the phenomena of that rugged, desolate, silent land, so strange to a people that had just come forth from Egypt, so useful to a people that were destined to conquer Canaan, must be in their general outlines frankly accepted if we are to preserve an historical basis. But all this is compatible with the fact that Moses, inspired by the tremendous solemnity of what had happened and was happening around him, filled with the presence of God, composed those laws which have come down to us from the desert life. The one exception proves the rule. God is said to have written the Commandments on the tables of stone. But this, whatever view we may take of it, is not inspiration but miracle, not a supernatural infusion of thought but an action of God. More than this I for one cannot take upon myself to say.

But let us now look at the results of this inspiration, and ask whether there is anything in them transcending the natural powers of the human mind, the circumstances being granted. The giving of the law itself follows in natural sequence, partly because laws are the necessary instruments for giving form and duration to the free-will dedication of the people to God; partly because the drawing near to

God for direction and government is nothing else than the wish for a better ordering of their newly acquired national life. But the laws themselves must plainly have existed in germ before, just as the Lord's Prayer itself is adapted from partially existing materials. Assuredly the people of Israel must have been accustomed to most, at least, of the Ten Commandments; certainly to the fourth, and probably to all the rest, unless, what seems more than likely, the addition of the tenth marked an upward step in the great code of human morals. Then, again, there are others which seem to refer specially to the old life in Egypt. But that the whole code is founded upon one or two great ideas, which ideas, again, spring naturally out of their history, has been abundantly proved by Professor Ewald. God the Holy One, the Personal Being, the God of their fathers, above all the God who had delivered and would deliver them yet again—these were the animating thoughts. What I affirm is that the laws were natural, in the sense that they followed from the men, the events, and the national character, being what they were. And if it be argued that the divine origin of, say, the Ten Commandments is proved by the fact that they alone of ancient codes have passed unchanged into the morality of mankind, I answer that I admit this very cheerfully. But divine origin does not imply supernatural infusion of thought into the minds of men, but only a controlling influence, recognised as coming from God, over their actions.

The second formula, "the word of the Lord came unto," belongs to the prophetic period, and extends from Samuel to John the Baptist. All that need be said upon it in connection with our present subject, can be reduced within a small compass. On the one hand, it is clear that the prophets believed themselves to be in communication with a personal God; on the other, it is capable of proof that the results of this belief, as contained in their spoken words, can be accounted for by what we know of the ordinary workings of the human mind. Until some proof to the contrary is alleged, we may be contented to believe that prophecy is a natural product of Jewish life, thought, and history; and is explicable by some such account of the religious faculty as was attempted in a previous essay. The prophets performed the functions of public writers and speakers; they were critics, preachers, originators, advisers, and forewarners. In what way the prophetic influence first came to them is not very easy to determine, except that in the best known cases their vocation was generally determined by something partaking of the nature of an objective occurrence. But it is clear that they were men gifted with a strong religious faculty, men in whom the genius of the people found its fullest expression. One unfailing proof of this is that they sprang from every class of society, as, to take one instance, the English poets have shown how deeply seated the poetic faculty has been in the very heart of the race. They knew what God had done, and what He had promised; they believed that all good thoughts came from Him; they saw the sins of the nation reflected in the holiness of God; and their mistakes, whether of policy, worship, government, or administration, were made apparent by contrast with what the prophets knew from the law and the history to be in consonance with God's will and character. Above all, they realised, what the mass of the people must have felt very faintly indeed, that God was in covenant with them, and was a very present help in time of trouble. Then came the impulse to speak or to write which they felt within them, and with noble faith declared to be the Word of the Lord. We observe that the growing intelligence of the people no longer rested satisfied with the simpler expression " God spake;" room must be left for the play of individual thought, and the human no longer superseded by the divine. They did not claim any authority for their declarations upon the plea that they felt a supernatural interference with their thoughts; it was because the thoughts were natural, orderly, and suitable that they were felt to be divine. In short, the inner consciousness of the prophet responded to external religious truth, just as the mind of the Greek artist drank in the laws of beauty, and reproduced them in the forms that stood to him in place of words. Their naturalness, their humanity, their truthfulness, are the best proofs that they are divine.

Nor is there anything to be found, either upon the face of the narrative or in the words uttered by the prophets, to compel us to fall back upon the theory of supernatural enlightenment of thought. Wherever the merely marvellous occurs, and it occurs very seldom, further inquiry proves that it rests upon a superficial mistake. The mention of Cyrus in Isaiah and the apocalyptic visions of Daniel are accounted for by the proved later authorship of the books which bear the names of these great prophets. The mention of Josiah by name is exactly what might be expected of a writer who witnessed Josiah's reforms, and was acquainted with the old story of the prophet who denounced Jeroboam, and foretold the consequences of the disruption from the point of view that would be natural in the kingdom of Judah. If marvels of this description were meant to be relied upon as proofs of supernatural power, it is the greatest marvel of all that there are not more and better authenticated instances of them. The really wonderful element in Hebrew prophecy is that the prophets delineated the character and work of a Person who, if the Gospels be true, appeared in history several hundred years after the last of them was dead. But then the modern view of prophecy, which may be regarded as one of the best ascertained results of later theology, fully recognises this, and adequately accounts for it without the necessity of supernatural inspiration. We know what this view is. The prophet taking his stand upon the circumstances of the times, and contrasting the national religious ideas with their realisation at any given period of history, was enabled to foretell in dim outline a Person and a Character who should answer to the idea that always was to be, and never was, fulfilled, nay, rather that grew larger the more it was fulfilled. Adopting this view, let us see what is lost and what remains.

1. For supernatural interference with reason is substituted a divine method of action, working through nearly 2000 years in and by the minds of responsible, intelligent agents.

2. For a miraculous knowledge, which it is difficult to harmonise with any possible conditions of free human life, is substituted an astonishing development of the religious faculty, which gave the Jews their peculiar character and mission.

In this way, then, history reveals God. If, to take an illustration from nature, I know that water freezes at a certain temperature in England, I know that it will do so all over the world. Similarly, if I know the character and will of God from His dealings with the Jews, I know that He is the same everywhere. Everywhere He carries forward His designs by the workings of human genius, which, no matter whether distinctively religious or not, then becomes the object of earnest and, I must be allowed to add, of *religious* investigation. The prophets remind us most of God when they are seen to be most clearly men. The stern morality—the instinctive appreciation of the divine will—the enthusiasm that could not be quenched—the hope that would not die, but that, like certain fire, burnt more intensely under the deluge of misfortunes—the unerring perception of the human heart, and of the nature, drift, and tendency of passing events—the marvellous manner in which the future was described and spoken of under the guise of the present, so that eternal truths were for ever revealing themselves concerning the Eternal God—the subtle intuitions—the faint indications—the synthetical grasp of facts—the burning diction—the words that meant at once more and less than they intended,—but where shall we stop in the enumeration of the gifts and powers of the prophetic order? In the sense that all thought is divine, their thoughts were divine, and call forth our gratitude to the Giver of all good; in the sense that all thought is natural, their thoughts were natural, and call forth the spirit of inquiry, that desires to know what they said and why they said it.

There remains for our consideration the third formula of Scriptural inspiration, "the Spirit of God came," the importance of which is discerned the moment we remember that it was the formula adapted from the Old Testament into the New to express that kind of inspiration under which we ourselves live. It occurs in its proper place of historical development. The overwhelming consciousness of divine power which sent forth the lawgiver or prophet upon their special message, more and more recedes, so as to leave room for the gradual, invisible, peaceful influence of the Spirit of God upon the lives of men. In the theology of St Paul, indeed, no accurate distinction seems to have been drawn between the spirit of man and the Spirit of God that wrought in him. The two met together in indissoluble harmony, just as the divine and human were united, never to be put asunder, in the Person of Christ.

Now, when we examine the usage of this expression in the Old Testament, we find two distinct phenomena described by it, both of which find their counterpart in the New. There is, first of all, the violent seizure by which men were elevated into an ecstatic state and were enabled to "prophesy"—that is, utter ecstatic words of prayer and praise. The instances of this are not very common, but they begin as early as the seventy elders, appear to have been a not uncommon occurrence in the schools of the prophets, and extend as late as the apostolic times in the form of the outpouring of spiritual "gifts." Now, it is necessary to say distinctly that the best minds among the Jews held these ecstasies in very little regard, and that they are of little or no value in tracing the meaning of inspiration. It may be that the thoughts uttered were wonderful, specially divine, supernatural, anything we please; but assuredly no word has been thought worthy to be preserved. On the day of Pentecost itself the results of inspiration are seen in St Peter's speech, which is as calm and rational, and, in human terms, as able and convincing, as was ever addressed to human audience. It is the more necessary to insist upon this, because it forms part and parcel of the Hebrew conception of religion. No doubt their history contains incidents of this kind; and visions, though of an exceedingly calm and rational character, occur now and then as a method of calling prophets to their work. But as a rule the whole set of the Jewish mind was against them. The law had a sharp and decisive remedy for dreamers of dreams who might be inclined to use outward tokens of spiritual possession against the inner verities of the national faith. Micah, Isaiah, Jeremiah, and Ezekiel denounced enchantments, magic, dreams, visions, divination, familiar spirits, in terms that seem to show that these were the main reliance of false prophecy in its contest with the true. And St Paul crushed the nascent growth of the same reliance upon "spiritual gifts" by his disparaging remarks addressed to the Corinthian Church. In doing so he was but faithful to the genius of his race. It must never be forgotten that the one out of the religions of antiquity which has passed into modern life was that of a practical, rational, realistic, unimaginative people, who had small fancy for frenzies, poetic extravagances, and all the metaphysical idealism which is in modern religion made to take the place and do the work of solid facts.

I am not, however, to be supposed to deny all value to these manifestations; that, with the history of the day of Pentecost before us, would be impossible. What I do deny is, that they have any bearing upon the nature of inspiration. Their real value would seem to be connected with the religious life of the individuals who were affected by them.

They represent a stage through which all religious minds pass, and which in times of excitement assumes an extraordinary form. There comes a crisis to all intensely religious persons when for the moment the human personality is overpowered by the consciousness of the divine, and God seems to take entire possession of the man in order that the sense of His abiding presence may never depart from him. Those who have passed through this stage realise for ever that they are in the hands of an overruling power. And where many persons are joined together this "spiritual power" passes from one to another by means which are probably distinctively material, due, that is, to nervous operations. That God should use this fact of man's nature as the vehicle of His actions upon one great occasion, and for a special purpose, is consistent with all we know of His methods; it is only when an almost solitary and transient event is made the excuse for all kinds of irrational excitement and supernatural views of inspiration that an outspoken protest becomes necessary.

The second use of the formula "the Spirit of God came" in the Old Testament is to express the *ordinary operations of the human intellect carried to extraordinary perfection.* A more surprising and gratifying fact there cannot be, and fortunately the proofs for it are overwhelming, and indeed not denied. The Spirit is the creator of natural life, moving upon the chaotic void before the worlds were. It is the giver of animal life, the breath or spirit of God which is in the nostrils of man (Job xxvii. 3, Gen. ii. 7). Pharaoh regards it as the source of intellectual excellence in Joseph (Gen. xli. 38). God filled Bezaleel with the spirit of architectural and mechanical skill, and Balaam's insight into the destinies of the nations was due to God's Spirit resting upon him, a Gentile and an adversary. When Othniel, Gideon, Jephtha, aroused to patriotic valour, went forth to fight and conquer, or when Samson felt the stirrings within him of great bodily prowess, it was because the Spirit of the Lord came upon them; and it was the same Spirit that anointed a later prophet (and afterwards Christ Himself) to lead a life of practical religious beneficence. Thus, then, our view of inspiration is found to be simply that of the Bible itself. It is, first of all, thought working in all human faculties. When recognised as proceeding from God it becomes religious. And lastly, it is felt to be specially or even exclusively religious in proportion as the divine Personality is seen to be overpowering the human agent. These men waxed valiant in fight, patient in suffering, skilful in art, discreet in policy, virtuous in action, wise in thought, because they believed that the Lord God of their fathers was present with them, and had distributed to each man severally as He willed.

But more than this. Though little is said upon the subject, yet it is to this kind of inspiration that, if anywhere, we are to look as the living force of Hebrew literature. We are nowhere told that God spake unto the historians, or that the word of the Lord came to the psalmists; these all write with the unconsciousness of men, to whom, as to Christians now, the thought of the habitual indwelling of the Spirit of God is an ultimate natural fact, rather than an occasional supernatural occurrence. And it is thus that we can account for all the peculiarities of Jewish historians and poets. They composed as might be expected of men who were inspired by events and facts which revealed God to them. Thus their poetry described God in nature in language which, although at times pantheistic in terms, yet never lost its hold of God as a Personal Being. Nature and history were with them subordinated to the task of declaring His actions and character, and it is thus that all our modern difficulties in understanding them arise. They, for the most part, recorded the lives of men only so far as was necessary to make God apparent, and naturally this would be done chiefly by way of moral contrast. Hence follows that essential peculiarity of Jewish history, the unswerving fidelity with which they described the sins and littleness of their greatest men, and of their nation at its greatest moments. It is, I must observe, a singularly unworthy return for this honesty to use their descriptions to disparage the characters of Jewish heroes, and at the same time to withhold all credit from the writers upon whose conscientious veracity these hostile criticisms are founded. But fairness in the mere literary assailants of the Bible is as little to be found as in the majority of its professed theological defenders.

We must, however, turn away from the tempting but too vast an undertaking thus opened to us, and content ourselves with giving one instance of the way in which all the peculiarities of Jewish literature can be accounted for by this theory of natural inspiration. Let it be the history of the creation, and let us be allowed for convenience' sake, if not for old associations' sake, to regard it as the composition or the compilation of one mind. Now, what would be the facts of the case which the author would have before him? First, the existence of the world itself, with its gradations rising from inanimate matter to intellectual life. Secondly, a number of traditions shared by at least the Semitic family. Thirdly, an irresistible belief, probably but just born into the world, in the existence of a Creating, Personal Being, Lord of all other lords, be they what they might. Now given these factors, is not the result just what might have been expected? He takes, in all the unconscious simplicity of genius, just so much of the legends as would suffice to give his account an historical form, and thus display the actions of a beneficent Creator. From the mere survey of the world around him he caught the idea of progressive development as most suitable to the designs of an overruling mind. He threw it into the form of days as the simplest mark of time, and made the days into a week probably because the Sabbath was in germ already established. He was clear of one thing, however, that everything came from the power of one Almighty God, because he caught sight of that absolute harmony in nature which it is the province of science to describe under the name of law. And then having to account for man, he gave utterance to one of the most sublime efforts of inspired genius in the declaration that man was made in the image of God, His delegate and representative upon earth, endowed with that power of self-conscious thought which we call spirit. Yet all this follows as rational conclusions from admitted facts. If God had spoken to man, had formed designs and exhibited a moral purpose, then as man also could do the same, he must be in God's image, must be like Him. Many centuries afterwards this thought received its full explanation when Jesus Christ uttered the word "Father," and crowned the fabric of God's revelation to man. Man made in the image of God is the "fact" of the Old Testament; God made in the image of man is the "fact" of the New.

Now it is precisely this mode of inspiration that our Lord and His apostles after Him selected as the most fitting to express the communication from God to man in its ultimate development. Discarding transient bursts of enthusiasm and overwhelming manifestations of divine power, they fixed upon the Old Testament belief that the Spirit of God was the author of natural gifts as the best method of explaining religious and moral inspiration for all time. In so doing they definitely asserted that this inspiration is natural also, and can be explained as in other faculties of man. But they went on to make two final assertions. First, they connected inspiration with an everabiding personal influence, the Spirit of God. Second, they definitely attached religious inspiration, as distinct from others, to the notion of goodness; this Spirit was the *Holy Ghost*. The stages through which this grew up can be easily traced from the time when our Lord began His preaching by declaring that the Spirit of God was upon Him, down to His promise that the Comforter should come in His stead. This, too, follows from a natural necessity. For as the whole object of revelation is to create permanent relations between God and men as separate yet closely allied persons, and as God in His essential being dwells apart from man's knowledge, while Christ Himself was shortly to be withdrawn from the world, the advent of the Spirit is the crown and completion of all God's dealings towards mankind. Unless science is prepared to exterminate religion, she is deeply and especially interested in proving that after this final union of God and man *in the region of natural reason*, no other revelation can be made, and that all further miraculous manifestations are a going back to "old and beggarly elements." And so the union between the divine and the natural, between religion and goodness, having been once for all cemented, we have the strongest *à priori* reasons—reasons based upon analogies drawn from universal experience—against accepting any fresh supernatural interventions, even were the evidence as strong on their behalf as it is almost grotesquely weak. Surely we have here a satisfactory answer to a difficulty which appears to puzzle many persons, that if we admit the miracles of the Bible, we are obliged to admit the possibility of the marvels of mediæval history. The mere legal evidence for the stigmata of St Francis may be as strong as that for the Resurrection (it is nothing of the sort); but the difference is, that the latter carries on the revelation of God to its supreme point, while the former is a recurrence to methods suitable, if at all, to the mere childhood of man, and nowhere paralleled in Jewish history. It is as though a man should complete the education of his children, and then, instead of starting them in life to work out their own experience by aid of what they had been taught, were to insist upon teaching them the alphabet again.

It may, however, be asked whether any room for the influence of the Holy Ghost can be found in the conclusions of scientific psychology. Now let us remember that in Him we have God dealing with us as a person with persons. As the spirit of one man conveys thought to the spirit of another, thereby influencing his character and conduct, so, are we as Christians obliged and enabled to believe, does the Spirit of God to man. As men amongst themselves, so He reminds, instructs, cautions, exhorts, consoles, suggests—in a word, makes men holy as God is holy. How can this be?

Now, in our absolute ignorance of what thought is in ultimate analysis, we might perhaps pronounce the question to be insoluble. But I am not inclined so to leave it, and think that something at least may be done towards clearing it up. I have already said that man's belief in his own free agency depends upon his consciousness of himself as a personal moral being. In the same way the possibility of receiving good thoughts from God depends upon our consciousness of His personal existence and relations towards us. We can be influenced by Him, as by any other person, only so far as we realise Him as He is, or can be, known from His dealings with us. Hence, when by any act of our own, arising from our needs or our duties, we place ourselves in communication with Him, then the religious faculty is as it were opened and enlarged to receive inspirations of goodness. This is what religion specifically consists in, and it explains all the distinctive Christian doctrines. In prayer, for instance, the spirit of man is placed in condition to receive impressions from the Person in whose presence we are kneeling; nor is there any necessity, from what we know of psychological laws, that these impressions should come there and then. In the Lord's Supper we feed upon—that is, take into our spiritual being—His life and character, which were displayed, as must be the case with all men, through a material bodily organisation, and which as a moral power culminated at His death. In meditating upon the actions of God, or reading them in the Bible and elsewhere, new thoughts and resolutions take possession of our souls. This is exactly described in Christ's own words. The Spirit takes of His goodness, and showing it to us, inspires us to be and do the same. Lastly, that shamefully abused word "grace" is seen to be not a kind of spiritual substance infused into souls, but the influx of good thoughts into minds that are in communication with the object whence goodness derives its origin. If I open my eyes towards the sun, natural light streams upon them; if I open my mind towards a friend, mental light streams upon it; so, also, if I open myself towards God, spiritual light streams upon me. And thus, I think, I can realise our Lord's promise, that the Father will give the Holy Spirit to them that ask Him.

It remains to say a word or two upon the inspiration of the New Testament in its literary aspect. This (apart from the words of Christ) consists of a simple record of events, and of moral and theological teaching founded upon them, mainly by one man, Saul of Tarsus. The first three Gospels are remarkable for being the result of general, rather than of individual, inspiration. The mind of the whole Church seems to have formed the Synoptic Gospels as we have them by an unconscious process of selection and arrangement. And all the New Testament scriptures are certainly alike in this, that they claim no power to reveal or declare truths beyond the natural intelligence of man. They do not give us to understand that they were miraculously preserved from error in details; and St Luke, in particular, gives us a most natural matter-of-fact account of the origin of his book. Neither do they claim superhuman knowledge in matters of opinion. Once more we must observe, that given the facts and the inspiration follows. There is nothing that could not be said, and would not naturally be said, by the men being what they were concerning events being as they were believed to be. All that is vital in Christian theology might almost be written now, if we preserve the historical basis of the life of Christ as recorded in the four Gospels. But, once more taking an instance, let us glance at St Paul's writings. Granted a man of his nation, education, traditionary opinions, wonderful conversion, distinctive belief as to what Christ had done, and there is not a word in his letters and speeches which is not in the highest degree natural, and divine just because natural. He writes in total unconsciousness of supernatural aid, though never ceasing to attribute all he said to the Spirit of God. His mind grows in the apprehension of spiritual verities in exact agreement with the successive experiences of his life. He falls into a most natural misapprehension about the second coming of Christ, and shakes himself free from it by degrees. He attempts no unapproachable subject of human thought, but is obliged to leave the doctrine of Predestination as he found it—a mystery. He has no special revelation upon the subject of immortality beyond the argument to be drawn from the resurrection of Christ, which he exhibits in strict logical form; for the rest he falls back on natural analogies, and upon arguments common to all who have ever thought upon the subject. He submits his statements to the test of reason, desires to be judged in what he says, declines to be "lord over their faith," argues at great length where mere dogmatic assertion would have sufficed. In short, he claims the authority of a divinely-commissioned apostle, not of a supernaturally-inspired oracle; and in his reasonableness, freedom, reliance upon facts, and conception of morality as the ultimate aim of religion, is akin to all the healthiest instincts of human nature. Some day modern scientific thought will wake up to see what it owes to St Paul.

It is time to conclude, and yet I must be permitted a few

words more, if it be only to indicate how this theory of the naturalness of Jewish and Scriptural inspiration enables us to account for the difficulties or peculiarities we find in the history or the book respectively. Thus we see why the Jews were so exclusively a religious people, and were enabled to produce, according to the flesh, the one entirely and exclusively religious man whom the world has seen. It was because the events in which they believed exercised a controlling influence that intensified their thoughts in this one direction. The same consideration enables us to see why the Jewish religion has shown the greatest power of self-propagation; the facts gave it a missionary power akin to that of positive science in these days. Again, we see why it was at once retrospective, intermittent, and progressive. It was the former, because the mind of the people recurred to revelations of old made once for all and incapable of destruction. If the promise of God to Abraham was true 2000 years, say, before Christ, it is true 2000 years after. It was the second, intermittent, because these revelations appeared at long intervals, and rekindled the flames of enthusiasm and the light of inspiration. And it was the last, progressive, because the same God was from time to time making fuller declarations of Himself, to mould their character and guide their conduct. Hence it comes that from the time of Abraham to the present day, Christianity has, at all its great crises, created fresh points of departure by going back to unfulfilled ideas, to revelations the meaning of which had not been fully realised till time and experience made them manifest. Thus Moses strives to make the people realise the Abrahamic covenant, but "adds the law." Samuel clings to the old theocracy, but anoints a

X

human king. Isaiah turns back to the glories of the reign of David only to predict a more glorious Lord. Our Lord fulfils the law and the prophets, and in so doing creates a moral and spiritual and universal religion. St Paul claims the Messiah for the Jews, but makes Christianity the religion of the Gentiles. Augustine derives his doctrines from St Paul, and yet is the chief creator of mediæval theology. Luther is inspired by Augustine, but is also the founder of Protestantism. And, finally, the new reformation will go back to Luther for his method, his free spirit, his undaunted disdain of authority, and yet will replace Protestantism by the union of religion and science.

But that which above everything else must recommend this theory to the minds of thinking persons is the fact, that it enables us to understand, and therefore to defend, the character and conduct of the heroes of Hebrew history. Anything, of course, that makes human life more natural and possible, makes the accounts which contain it easier of acceptation. At the bottom of modern unbelief in the historical truthfulness of the Bible lies the idea that theologians have been bent on turning some of the greatest men that ever lived into prodigies instead of human beings. But once accept the belief that they were men " like ourselves," who were compelled to reason out a line of conduct and a theory of duty from the contemplation of the events that made up their national or individual history, and which they accepted as coming from God, and in an instant all Voltairian shafts of ridicule at their mistakes and vices vanish into darkness. We can understand why deeds and thoughts ascribed in their minds to the inspiration of God might be very defective if tried by the standard of later morality. Religion is seen to be compatible with failures in faith, such as those of Abraham, Moses, and Peter; with fierce and even treacherous actions, such as those of Joshua, Samuel, and Jael; with a certain unscrupulous tone of character (a common temptation of men who feel intensely that God is on their side), such as we see in Jacob, David, and faintly, perhaps, even in St Paul. Religious inspiration can, in short, only develop itself according to the morality of the times and the character of the individuals to whom it comes; and religion, like every other faculty, may ally itself with much of human weakness, imperfection, and even wickedness. It was, for instance, a religious motive, pure and simple, that inspired Jael to kill Sisera, and Deborah and Barak to sing her praises. And if these words of praise were infused by direct action of God, then is God the author of imperfection, which God forbid. At the same time, I think it right to protest against the mere sentimentality which shudders at deeds of this description as outrageous breaches of ideal morality. I do not doubt that, as science familiarises men's minds more and more with the idea of the beneficent ruthlessness with which the laws of nature do their work, we shall be more inclined to see, first, that a certain ruthlessness of feeling naturally accompanies an intense faith in what was then, in Jewish belief, the one true religion; secondly, that this feeling has a definite part to play in the development of the race. A religion that in its earlier stages presents the picture of Joshua exterminating the Canaanites, or Samuel hewing Agag to pieces before the Lord, cannot fairly be discredited if these are shown to be parts of a natural development that ended in Jesus Christ.

I conclude with one other remark upon the natural affinity between the spirit of science and the spirit of religion. It is characteristic of all epochs of religious revival that men discern the overwhelming power of God so absolutely that all laws, events, words, and works are thought of as coming from Him. The free agency of man is not necessarily denied, but it is seen that this is not the thing to be insisted on; indeed, theological systems which display anxiety to secure the doctrine of man's free-will, have always been, regarded from the religious point of view, impotent and superficial. They have been useful rather as checks and safeguards, and yet even so have been apt to create those human devices, whereby men, in the exercise of their freedom, seek to come to terms with God. Now, as the next religious movement (whatever it may be) will certainly derive its motive-power from the spirit of science, it is interesting to point out that the whole tendency of positive thought is to create precisely that atmosphere of iron necessity and unchangeable law, which, when translated into the language of religion, will seem to men to mean the all-encompassing will of God, " in whom we live, and move, and have our being." And the new reformation will be fairly started as a revival of religion among the people by the man or men who, filled with the inspiration of the presence of God in nature and history, and fired by the passionate enthusiasm of redeeming men from evil through suffering, submission, and obedience, shall make God's overruling power the mainspring of man's free action, and shall be able to reutter the splendid paradox of St Paul, "Work out, therefore, your own salvation with fear and trembling; for it is God which worketh in you both to will and to do of His good pleasure."

THE DIVINITY OF CHRIST AND MODERN THOUGHT.

IT may be desirable to state at the outset in what sense I use the words "modern thought," which I have placed at the head of this essay, the more so as they are synonymous with the word that has occurred so frequently, science. I mean, then, the tendency or determination to accept nothing as true except what is derived by strict process of reasoning from facts that can be proved to exist. Science, therefore, in the sense in which I have used it, does not mean merely the investigation of natural or material phenomena, but the application of the positive method to all branches of human knowledge. And I assume that all facts can be verified or ascertained by sensible or indirect perception; one fact alone excepted, which forms the basis of all knowledge, is apprehended immediately, and is beyond the reach of scientific analysis. I mean, of course, the consciousness of one's self as a thinking, personal being.

Now there can be no question about which Christian people are so naturally and strongly interested as to know what they ought to think concerning the nature and person of Him whom we call our Lord Jesus Christ. The facts upon which our opinion must be founded are fortunately well known. They are comprised in a perfectly consistent history of His life and actions, as to which no real doubt can be entertained concerning the meaning and intention of the writers. The incarnation and resurrection of Jesus Christ, which are called supernatural, are just as distinctly realised and as plainly narrated as His death and burial. Mythical they may be, mystical they cannot be. It is open to any one to argue that these facts are due to later legendary accretions; it is not open to any unprejudiced mind to say that the writers meant to describe, or thought they were describing, something else than plain historical facts. The innate realism of the Jewish character triumphs over all suspicions of this kind, and compels every candid inquirer to confess that the Jews had at least an unusual, and upon one view very inconvenient, faculty for clothing fiction in the language of fact.

I wish, however, to observe once more, that having regard to the present state of the Christian Church, moral, theological, and ecclesiastical, and on the other hand to the daily increasing pressure of the idea of unchangeable all-enfolding law, we are not entitled to be surprised if a growing number of minds take refuge in the mythical theory of the origin of the Christian religion. Once more I must repeat that it is by moral considerations alone that the minds of men will be directed towards one of two possible conclusions. Only I hope that whoever arrives at the mythical conclusion will not tamper with the further conclusions that flow naturally from it. If a homely proverb may be excused in so serious a matter, we cannot eat our loaf and have it. We cannot retain Christianity and destroy

Christ: the faith that founds itself upon the purely human name of Jesus has another, and that an ominous, meaning in our minds. Let us honestly and avowedly cease to subscribe ourselves, who live in the nineteenth century, by the name of one who died 1800 years ago; indeed the very words "nineteenth century" are absurd. Let us not pretend to speak of Christian art, civilisation, morality, legislation, in honour of a man whose true history is wrapped up in the obscurity of legendary fables. Let us not found a religion upon the misreported or badly remembered sayings attributed to one whose words as they stand are few, are *ex hypothesi* full of error about himself, and probably represent the mind of the original man about as closely as the present cathedral at York represents the original church, vestiges of which are still seen at the foundation of the present building. It is one of the blessings attached to courageous thinking, that it puts alternatives clearly before the minds of ordinary persons who would like to spend their lives in saying that they believe one thing, and acting as though they believed the contrary. To M. Comte belongs the credit of having fairly faced the facts of the case, and forced unwilling people to do the same. And M. Renan, so far as he is critical and historical, has carried on his countryman's work; so far as he is sentimental and religious, has done his best to overthrow it.

I do not mean it to be inferred that every event connected with the life of Christ is of necessity to be accepted as historically true. By the theory of inspiration maintained in this volume we are relieved from any such obligation. Doubtful circumstances may have crept in, and are to be detected by the methods of historical criticism, without at all assuming that the supernatural cannot, as such, take place. The coming of the Magi, the description of diabolical possession, and the rising of many bodies of saints at the Crucifixion may be adduced as instances that seem to baffle reasonable explanation. For myself I can honestly say that my own belief in the great events and general tenor of His life would be greatly supported were a line to be drawn between such narratives and the plain matter-of-fact testimony to events of divine worth, intense moral significance, and deep religious importance. If mythical additions or the influence of Jewish modes of thought can be traced in a few unimportant instances, such as the above, all the more credit would then become due to the narratives in which these could not be found. Here, as ever, reasonableness is the best intellectual, and candour the best moral, support of truth.

Be this as it may, we are entitled to assume, until the weight of evidence has proved the contrary, that the facts of Christ's life happened as they are recorded. Among these facts I do not include, as bearing upon our present subject, the words that were spoken. Nothing can show more clearly the baneful effects of attaching authoritative declarations to every word of Scripture than the controversy concerning the nature of Christ. His own words would indeed be relevant facts; but, as might have been expected, they disclose very little about His essential being, and are capable of very varying explanations. Language such as "My Father and I are one," is paralleled by "My Father is greater than I." And apart from His words, the controversy has been made to turn upon chance expressions, rhetorical outbursts, the MS.

omission or insertion of a single stroke in a single letter, a disputed reading, a doubtful punctuation. The evidence is overwhelming to show that the apostles were compelled to think out their conclusions as to their Master's person from the facts of His life and character, or rather it would be more true to say that they did not feel the necessity of arriving at strict definitions at all. The words "Son of God" expressed all that they required. When every fibre was thrilling from their personal contact with the divine life, they did not seek to analyse its composition or define its nature. And if a question like this is to be decided by minute investigation of phrases scattered here and there in unconscious simplicity, then I feel sure that the divinity of Christ will never remain, and could never have become, the creed of Christendom. Happily, however, there is no need to be restrained within such limits. We have the facts before us as the apostles had. They have a meaning for us if we scrutinise them patiently. They, and they alone, can decide the question. As Christ Himself said in answer to some doubting questioners, so may we say now, "Go, show the world again those things which ye do hear and see."

This much, moreover, I must beg leave to add. However repugnant the application of scientific method to religious matters may seem to some, it is high time that not only the method but something of the spirit of science were breathed into this controversy. What one hears all around, mainly from the lips of accredited defenders of the faith, is simply shocking to reverent minds. The person of Christ is made the battle-field whereon some of the worst of human passions—hatred, contempt, schism, vituperation, calumny—are allowed to display themselves. His divinity must be "defended" as one would defend the honour of an absent friend—by challenging his assailant to fight a duel. The Church is to stand or fall with the creed which deals out everlasting perdition to those who do not indeed deny the doctrine, but who do not profess to understand the abstruse phraseology in which it is conveyed. The ark of the covenant is indeed being carried into the camp with great shouting, while humble Christians begin to weep and say, "The glory of Israel has departed, for the ark of the Lord is taken."

In order to show by an example what is the legitimate effect of the scientific spirit upon theological controversies, as well as to carry my argument a step further, I go on to indicate the reason why different opinions concerning the nature of Christ must of necessity arise, and why the Catholic doctrine was sure, the conditions being what they were, to prevail. Nothing so takes the venom out of controversies as to show that opinions are natural growths, and not, as men like to believe, the deliberate choice of a perverse and perverting mind.

What we find, then, is this, that Christians, while professing to accept the same facts and acknowledge the authority of the same books, have, notwithstanding, held the most diverse views as to His essential nature. Some have gone so far as to sink the human personality in the divine, and have invented fables to support a belief which the historical facts in no way warranted. Others, again, have denied that Christ could, in any true sense of the word, be called God, and have thought of Him as man, affirming that only as perfect man, the realisation of humanity, could He be realised in thought or regarded in history. Now this difference of opinion results from the contrast or collision of two thoughts which has appeared more than once in these essays. On the one hand, men demand that human life amongst the Jews should be rendered possible, human nature respected, human experience taken into account; on the other hand, they have demanded with even greater determination that the distinct and distinctive operations of God towards man shall be preserved. These two tendencies come to a head in the life of Christ. Everything that is precious to humanity perishes if we regard Him simply as God. Everything that is precious in the personal love of God for man perishes if we regard Him simply as created man. The difficulty meets us the moment we begin to consider the workings of His self-consciousness, His motives, conduct, and teaching; and it is one that can be got rid of only by a kind of moral appreciation of the facts, and not by any dogmatic formulæ.

It is not, however, astonishing that the opinions of those who leant more exclusively upon His divine nature should have prevailed; because, as the very office and *rationale* of religion is to maintain the belief in God's personal dealings with mankind, the divinity of Christ was seen to be essential if this belief was to be retained. But, as might have been expected from the infirmities of the human mind, every other consideration was so entirely sacrificed to this predominant necessity, that human nature, possibilities of life, common-sense, and moral example have run no small risk of being destroyed. Here is an instance. We frequently hear it stated, at least I myself have often heard and seen it, that as God Christ did something, while as man He did something else. No doubt this is the language of men of ordinary intelligence, whose duty as preachers compels them to turn abstract dogmas, the phraseology of which they adopt without grasping the purely abstract meaning, into practical thought and common language. I should imagine that such an expression can hardly be within the limits of technical orthodoxy (not that I am a judge of such matters); but it is certainly in very common use, and as certainly reduces the life of Christ to a moral and spiritual dualism, as inconceivable as the fancies of paganism itself. Against this tendency, therefore, the other school of thought has uttered an unceasing protest; and it is well for religion that this protest has been made in her name, and by Christian thinkers. Of late years, indeed, the ideas represented by the more humanitarian school have been planted in the very tissue of popular religion, though the old beliefs as to the nature of Christ remain, so far as religion is concerned, the same. The general aspect, however, of this controversy in modern times may be best surveyed by associating it with the name of one of the foremost champions of the rights and needs of human nature, the great and illustrious name of Channing.

There is hardly anything more striking in the history of modern theology than the fact that Unitarianism, as held and taught by Channing, has exercised comparatively so little direct effect upon the world, and seems to be likely to exercise less rather than more. His opinions on morality, his view of human nature, his interpretation of Scripture, his conception of God and of Christ, are, when tried by the touchstone of modern thought, far away superior to anything that can be found in theological writings during his time, and seem to forestall much that has been said of late years against the commonly accepted theology. And yet, though successful in argument and devoted in life, he has not founded any great school of thought, or left behind him successors to carry forward to future generations the legacy of wisdom and piety which he bequeathed to mankind. Unitarianism, as Channing taught it, is not a progressive creed: even in America itself it would appear that Theodore Parker is superseding him as a leader of religious thought. Channing believed, as we know, in the supernatural facts of Christ's life; and, so far from stumbling at miracles, hailed them as valuable, and indeed as essential parts of religious truth. He was willing to call Christ the Son of God, though objecting to call Him God the Son; and while exposing with singular power, ingenuity, and temper the inconsistencies of popular theology, bent his whole genius to the task of finding for Unitarianism a firm standing-ground and a definite work. But in spite of all this, the tide of thought seems to have swept past him; and that which is most effective and powerful in Unitarian theology is now in the hands of those who, by rejecting the supernatural, are much more removed from the Unitarianism of Channing than he was from Trinitarianism itself. Modern orthodoxy makes, of course, short work of this remarkable fact. The spirit which causes the Pope to see in liberal Catholicism his most hated enemies, finds many representatives elsewhere. One of the most honoured of modern English teachers speaks of Channing with a sigh as being outside the Christian Church, while to the mass of religious writers it is a matter for rejoicing that the more orthodox form of Unitarianism seems to be vanishing from the world. It is as though, when an invading enemy was upon English soil, the standing army should in a transport of professional fury fall upon the militia and volunteers, and having destroyed them, or driven them to take shelter within the enemy's lines, should then proceed, proud of their victory, to confront the foe alone and unaided. The time may come but too soon when the doctrine and spirit of Channing will be sought for in vain as a mediator, an interpreter, and a rationalising influence; and when men who, like him, have the spirit to refuse their assent to dogmatic authority while founding their faith firmly upon revealed facts, will be desired as the last hope and best defence of a tottering creed.

If, then, this description of the case, as regards the influence of Channing, be true, what is the cause of it? Why have his writings been so effective against Calvinism, so ineffective against Trinitarianism? The question must surely occur to those who read that splendid array of logic, illustration, eloquence, and devotion, "How is it that I am not a Unitarian, and why has not this form of Unitarianism become predominant?" And yet there is no real temptation to accept his creed; so that upon further analysis the question resolves itself into this, "There must be a good reason for this state of things, let me discover it." This question I propose to answer by an appeal, not to primitive antiquity, but to modern thought.

In this discussion two things will be assumed. First, no question will be raised as to the historical events of Christ's life, which Channing, no less than his most orthodox opponents, fully accepted. Second, no question will be raised as to the moral attributes of God or His relations

The Divinity of Christ and Modern Thought. 335

towards mankind. With Channing we take for granted that these attributes are the same in kind as we find in ourselves, and are absolutely and not relatively true; and further, that God stands to all men in the relation of a Father. But the question, whether it is more consonant with fact and reason to speak of Christ as divine or as entirely human, must be decided by considerations that have to do with the essential nature of God and the modes of His existence. And thus another controversy which has appeared throughout these essays once more comes before us, and will require fuller consideration than we have yet given it.

From almost the dawn of thought men have occupied themselves in the attempt to frame mental conceptions of the unknown God, to whose existence the very conditions of human thought and human nature bear testimony. They framed a number of expressions—such as Absolute, Omnipotence, Perfection, Infinite, Eternal—to describe the conceptions to which they thought they had attained. One nation, however, there was that never embarked on this hazardous undertaking, and that nation was the Jews. They assumed the existence of God because they believed that He had made Himself known to their fathers in actions of mercy, justice, and redemption. Their ideas of God were not metaphysical—that is, derived from the laborious investigation of their own minds; but historical —that is, based upon a series of events which, if true, revealed to them His character and purposes. The problems which exercised the minds of Gentile philosophers were never so much as presented to the Jewish people till the captivity. The moral difficulties, indeed, which are inherent in the relations between God and man, find ample expression, especially in the book of Job; but such a question as "Canst thou by searching find out God?" applies to His operations in nature and His dealings with man, and does not touch the essential modes of His existence. The people who believed in the God of Abraham and Moses, and whose very national existence was due to His special providence, revealed in events of the highest moral significance, could not and did not concern themselves with speculations which are to other men not merely inevitable but of surpassing interest. The fact and the cause of it are both abundantly evident.

Between the captivity and the coming of Christ there are, indeed, traces of the growth of the doctrine which culminated in St John's description of Christ as the Word. This is well known, and I need not enlarge upon it further than to remark that it was essentially historical and not metaphysical. Wisdom, already personified in the Book of Proverbs, becomes in later apocryphal books more and more separated from God himself. It was poured upon His works, was created from the beginning, is the splendour of the eternal light, is, so think some authorities, regarded dogmatically as a different Person. This is in full accord with the spirit of Jewish thought and finds its fulfilment in the New Testament: it is merely the play of the intellect upon facts in a more abstract and subtle fashion than was possible in earlier days. But, side by side with this, the Jewish mind became largely imbued with foreign elements, and I am tempted to think that the growing predominance of metaphysical speculations had done its part in withdrawing the idea of a living personal God from the heart of the people, and had created that atmosphere of worldliness tempered by superstition which Christ found at His coming. At any rate this is true, that He remained faithful to all the best traditions of His people. No metaphysical notions are permitted to darken the perfect moral splendour of His picture of God as the Father, as perfect love, justice, and goodness. His one authoritative declaration about the nature of God is, as we have seen, that He is a Personal Being—God is a Spirit; and when He is asked, in the very spirit of intellectual curiosity, "Show us the Father," His answer, "Have I been so long with you, and hast thou not known me, Philip?" is conclusive evidence that, in His opinion, the only knowledge of God possible to man must be derived from a moral manifestation of the divine Personality in history.

The apostles carried on the same idea. In one of the latest of St Paul's epistles, written in the fulness of experience, and with that sense of the limitation of human faculties which is only realised in old age, he speaks thus (1 Tim. vi. 16), "Who only hath immortality, dwelling in the light which no man can approach unto; whom no man hath seen, nor can see." Let us note how exactly this conclusion represents the truth which is veiled in the narrative of the communion of Moses with God in Exodus xxxiii. 12-23. "Thou canst not see my face, for there shall no man see my face and live," might be quite accurately expressed in the phraseology of modern thought thus, "No man can form positive conceptions of the nature of God without transcending the conditions of human thought." But though His glory might not be seen, yet He says, "I will make all my goodness to pass before thee, and I will proclaim the name of the Lord before thee, and will be gracious unto whom I will be gracious, and will show mercy on whom I will show mercy." That is to say, we have here that idea of the manifestation of the character of the unknown God by deeds of mercy in history which St John, the last of Jewish theologians, summed up in his doctrine of the Word that was made flesh. A light had been shining all along in the hearts of men which had at last become man that the glory of God might be revealed as full of grace and truth. This, too, is the invariable view of his epistles in which God is described exclusively as a moral Being revealed in the works which He had done. "God is light." "God is love." "Hereby we perceive the love of God, because He laid down His life for us." "And we know that the Son of God is come and hath given us an understanding that we may know Him that is true, and we are in Him that is true, even in His Son, Jesus Christ. This is the true God and eternal life. Little children, keep yourselves from idols."

When next the curtain of history opens wide upon the Christian Church, it discloses her in the act of setting up some of the idols against which St John had warned his readers, and which still retain a place in the mind of Christianity, waiting till some modern Hezekiah shall break them in pieces, calling them, as befits words spoken without charity, "sounding brass." For in some sort the worst of all idols are the idols formed by the mind. The mere image of wood and stone carries its own ultimate confutation written upon its passive face and helpless limbs. But the images evolved from the mind, the abstractions, not of thought, but of the negation of thinking, appeal to

The Divinity of Christ and Modern Thought. 339

the minds of even wise men, and hedge themselves in with a kind of divinity that belongs to the intangible, the mysterious, and the unintelligible. Catholic theology from the date, say, of the Nicene Council is mainly the result of Greek philosophy exercising itself upon Hebrew facts. If ever there was an idol in the world it is the word ὁμονούσιον in the Nicene Creed. If, indeed, it be granted that the question of the essential relations between the Father and the Son must by the necessity of the case have been raised, then this word may be accepted as conveying a relative truth to the minds of men at that time: that it conveys any positive truth to us now, the very conditions of human thought compel us to deny. It is a confession of ignorance in terms that have been consecrated, as it were, by long historical usage, and as such I accept it. Indeed we may discern the will of God in it exactly as we may discern the same will in the brazen serpent which Moses was commissioned to place before the eyes of the people, and Hezekiah was equally commissioned in the fulness of time to break in pieces. Of all vain things in the world, lamentations over the course of history, and of history that has lasted over 1500 years, are the most useless; and speculations as to what would have happened if some crisis or other had turned out differently, the most futile and misleading.

But none the less is it incumbent upon us to insist that the intrusion of abstract speculations into theology, after running its course of 1000 years for good and for evil, ended in the withdrawal first of God and then of Christ as moral and spiritual Powers from the hearts of men and from the life of humanity. Coincident with the decay of metaphysical speculation came the Reformation with its appeal to morality, and its resolute attempt to enshrine the Saviour as personal King of man. Between the last of the Schoolmen and the first of the Cartesians lies the period during which religion became once more a pressing reality, an intense moral power, a teacher and leader of men. Men brought into contact with forgotten facts of humanity and history were too much in earnest about the character of a living God to discuss the nature of the absolute or the infinite—they had lost their taste for inquiry into things that could only be expressed by the use of abstract adjectives. But by the nature of the case the escape was transitory and imperfect, and the old slavery recommenced from the time that Descartes announced that he had a clear mental conception of God, and that this conception was the one substantial proof of His existence. The founder of all true modern psychology is also the founder of false modern ontology—the time had not yet come when the two could be dissevered. And in the sphere of religion this teaching prevailed, while beaten in every other field of knowledge. The philosophers were determined to have a God whom they could understand and reason about—indeed this was to most of them the main object of His existence. If they could not discover Him for themselves, they would have none of Him, and yet when discovered all interest in Him there and then ceased. No doubt a strong protest was always raised within the ranks of philosophy itself. Locke maintained that men could not know substance, Berkeley confessed that he had no notion of spirit. But on the whole the theologians went against them, and through them the popular belief in the minds of men remained, that the words which described the being of God conveyed a definite meaning to their understanding, and expressed truths vital to the existence of religion itself.

Here, then, we have the explanation of the phenomenon (at all times interesting), why the man who had the best of the argument got the worst of the battle. Channing and his opponents both accepted as their major premise the belief that they could form a real conception of the nature of God by what is very improperly called natural religion. From this premise Channing arguing rightly came of necessity to a wrong conclusion, while his opponents arguing wrongly chanced upon a right one; or rather were saved from error by their adherence to the traditional faith no less than to that fundamental idea of religion which consists in the belief that God communicates with man. The faith proved much stronger than its defenders, the idea did not perish in their embrace. No one, I think, who reads Channing's arguments, can gainsay their truth, if the premise be granted—as it was. From God, thus believed to be known, he was compelled to say that Christ was separate, and that if reason were allowed to judge His person, life, and words, then He was not of the "same substance" as the eternal God. Moreover, he was greatly aided by his exposure of the perverted morality of Calvinistic theology, which, in order to prove our Lord's divinity, had resorted to such propositions as this, that sin being infinite requires infinite suffering as an atonement. (This use of the word "infinite" is an excellent illustration of the fundamental error.) In short, if the choice lay between the reasoning of Channing and that of his opponents, between his views of Christ's character and person, and those of modern defenders of His divinity, I see no escape from the conclusion to which Channing came; except, indeed, by blind submission to some authority selected to suit our own opinions.

But what if the premise be false? The dawning conviction in the minds of metaphysicians that their propositions were unthinkable, which was expressed with so much vigour by Sir W. Hamilton, was coincident with the advent of positive philosophy, as the ultimate outcome of scientific thought. All knowledge was seen to be derived from facts by process of reason; nothing else deserved the name. We can have no true conception of the unknown God, nor can we affix positive ideas to the negative terms under which we are compelled to speak of His essential nature. God is that tendency or stream of things which we perceive, but cannot understand. And thus the whole position is reversed. Channing's argument ran thus: "I have a true conception of the nature of God; but (the facts being granted) Christ was distinctly separable from the personality of God, and inferior to Him, therefore He must be described as a different Being, nor must we be allowed to escape from the conclusions of reason by taking refuge in verbal mystifications." But the reply is: "No one can have so clear a conception of the nature of God as to be enabled to found an argument upon it. We can, on the other hand, form a clear and adequate notion of man; but (the facts being granted) Christ was distinguished from man in origin, character, and destiny; therefore it is right to call Him divine, and impossible to separate Him from God." Thus, then, the traditionary belief was seen to be in harmony with the methods of modern reasoning, and so far as the logical position is concerned, the decision goes against the man whose honesty forbade him to reach true conclusions by erroneous arguments.

But logic is not everything—is indeed in religion very often a very poor thing indeed. And to stop at this point would be to lay ourselves open to a protest, that I for one feel to be quite unanswerable if only from its mere indignant authoritativeness. "This," it will be said, "is only the old puzzle. Man's ignorance is made the basis of belief and the reason for his submission to any dogma that promises to enlighten him. He is reduced to bewilderment after a fashion well known in dogmatic quarters by a series of intellectual dilemmas, from which his tormentor at last prescribes a way of escape, that, whatever else it may do, results in the ecclesiastical aggrandisement of some one. Besides, facts are fruitful, fertilising, suggestive, yet here they are used for the bare purpose of driving an opponent into a logical trap. The doctrine of the unknowable may prove Channing to be wrong; but it does not prove any one else to be right in any satisfactory, edifying, saving sense." With the tone of all this I thoroughly concur, nor would this essay have been written if the negative conclusion, above arrived at, were all that is to be desired or hoped for. Absolutely true, and absolutely essential, I believe it to be, but only by way of preparation for something more real and more useful. What this is I now proceed to inquire.

1. It is evident that although men can form no positive conception of the Unconditioned (I use this word as being the most general, and as the only one which does not beg some question or other), yet they have no difficulty in

imagining beings, agencies, actions, and manifestations of power, which are superior to natural or human conditions. Cases in point are fairy tales, story-books, religious myths, and that disagreeable class of literature in which men seek to ventilate their opinions under the fiction of future times, strange places, or marvellous agencies. I have, for instance, no difficulty in imagining a being who, for all I know, came into existence one moment and the next ceased to be by his own volition; who could, by the same volition, overrule all natural laws; who could so far transcend the conditions of space and time, as to be able to place me in a moment in the planet Jupiter, or tell me what would happen a hundred years hence. The Unconditioned is unthinkable, but the Unconditioned, manifested within my experience as superior to the conditions which my experience imposes, is not unthinkable, and therefore not impossible: for whatsoever may be conceived in the mind, may happen in fact. The most outrageous miracle is not impossible *per se*, though it is incapable of verification to minds that have learnt from experience the truth and order of things. In all this I mean no more than what I understand Professor Tyndall to have meant by his assertion, that alteration of physical laws in answer to prayer is not *per se* impossible, though not even an attempt has been, or can be made, to verify it.

2. The belief that some such manifestation of the Unconditioned has taken place, is common to every system of religion, and forms, therefore, the one distinctive religious element in human nature. Such manifestation may be made—so men have believed—either to the senses or the intellect; perhaps the word "presentation" might express

my meaning better. Here, however, we get upon hotly contested ground, and are exposed to strong antagonisms. To take the most representative of these, Mr Herbert Spencer maintains that the element underlying all religions is the recognition that the unknowable exists. This, to speak with the candour which is the surest token of respect, is a demonstrable error. The word religion is in fact tacitly defined at the outset, so as to mean this and nothing more. But the recognition of the existence of the unknowable, though common to all religious systems, does not differentiate religion itself from other things in which the same recognition is equally apparent. It belongs to man, not because he is religious, but because he is human. Science, philosophy, common-sense, even art, with wistful gaze towards unattainable beauty, proclaim the same; the first more distinctly than the rest. One need not, therefore, be religious in any possible sense which that word can bear to know that there is the unknowable.

No doubt—and from this the mistake has arisen—the relations of religion to the unknown are entirely different from those of science. The latter accepts the fact, and then ceases to be interested in it. But every system of religion has this groundwork of belief in common—that, as I have said, the Unconditioned has come within human experience in such a way as to show that it is not limited by those conditions which experience imposes upon man and nature. I am very well aware of the difficulty of finding words to express this truth accurately. It is comparatively easy to state adequately an abstract generalisation, but to make a statement which shall express the truth about a vast number of concrete facts, taxes the resources of language much more severely. Still I think the meaning of this remark is plain enough—plain and true. Take, for instance, two widely different systems of religion. The savage believes that his idol can grant his prayers by methods above the power and perception of man. The Pantheist believes that God is immanent in the universe by modes of existence which transcend knowledge. Take immortality. The Red Indian believes that Paradise in the shape of a happy hunting-ground will fall to his personal share after death. The Buddhist hopes—or hoped—for a personal annihilation after death, concerning which, nevertheless, thought refuses to think. And all the array of religious systems that lies between these two poles agrees in believing that the Unknown God has had, is having, or will have, direct relations with mankind, and has existed and operated within human experience by transcendental unconditioned modes of being and doing. Limitations in such manifestation no doubt there are, but they are imposed by the conditions which belong to the human faculties, and not to the Being who is declared in and by the manifestation itself to be superior to any conceivable limitations whatsoever.

3. This element, then, that is common to all religions, rescues religion itself from the mere passive helplessness which is the only intelligible result of a bare recognition of the existence of the unknowable; and to the science of religion belongs the work of comparing the various facts or modes in which men have believed that the Unconditioned has been manifested to experience. Such comparison is foreign to the purposes of this essay; it is enough to remark that if any religion be true in a sense in which others are not, then by common confession Christianity must be

that one. But assuming, as I have done throughout, the truth of the facts, we proceed naturally to inquire, Do they give, when examined, a worthy, reasonable, and morally useful idea of the manifestations of the Unconditioned? And with special reference to the subject of this essay, Do they entitle us to speak of Christ as divine, for the simple reason that His life and person enable us to attain a positive, though partial, conception of those negative ideas of God, which the mind of man has been constrained to form? Let us try, if not to answer this, to offer suggestions which may set people thinking in this direction. They shall be very brief, as become suggestions.

The Christian religion asserts, that in their inmost essential nature God and man are the same. "Man made in the image of God" is the root of all Scriptural teaching, just as the Personality of God is its crown. "God is a Spirit." To be conscious of self as a Personal Being is the ultimate definition of man and of God; it is the point where the divine and human become coincident. Modes of existence, conditions of action, relations of mind and matter—all these may be different, without so much as touching the essential identity of nature. Hence there is no difficulty in conceiving that the divine and human may coexist in One Person. To this truth the best instincts of Paganism bore emphatic witness.

It is always a strong presumption in favour of any doctrine, if it enables us to interpret hard sayings that have hitherto defied explanation. A case in point is afforded by some very remarkable words of our Lord's in answer to the Jewish accusation of blasphemy, "Thou, being a man, makest thyself God." He answers, "Is it not written in your law, I said, Ye are gods? If he called them gods unto whom the word of God came (and the scripture cannot be broken), say ye of Him whom the Father hath sanctified, and sent into the world, Thou blasphemest, because I said I am the Son of God." No commentary that I have yet seen has done justice to the force of this deep saying; none, indeed, has succeeded in rescuing the argument from a certain appearance of being a play upon words; but read in the light of the truth above stated it becomes clear enough. An instinct had taught the Psalmist that *they* must be in some sense gods with whom God could hold spiritual communion, " to whom His word came;" possibility of personal intercourse implies some community or likeness of nature. Hence it was no blasphemy to assert that as God had sent men into the world by what we call natural laws, so had He sent His Son by special "sanctification." If the fact of this sending be true, there is no difficulty in the inference, and no blasphemy in the statement that Christ was God. But it must be observed how definitely He adheres to that form of words in which alone these truths can be expressed within the limit of human thought—He is the Son of God. We are thus, moreover, enabled to see that the solemn assertion, "the Scripture cannot be broken," implies that there is a real substantial meaning in these lofty prophetic phrases which is not to be dismissed, *more commentatorum*, as an illustration or an argument from the less to the greater or by similar unsatisfactory devices.

Jesus Christ, then, is One Person, and so saying we express our simplest conception of God and man. But the question now arises, "Was the Personality manifested as both human and divine?" So far as the first is concerned, it would not, I suppose, be denied that Christ was subject to all the relations and displayed all the qualities that make up our definition of the essential nature of man. So far as the second is concerned, we are now to inquire whether He displayed that independence of human or natural conditions under which the mind of man has always thought of God. If He did, then ideas of God, hitherto merely negative and unthinkable, become positive and cognisable.

Let us take five of these ideas and set against them five facts of His life. The ideas are these: The absolute or independence of causation; perfection or independence of evil; omnipotence or independence of law; the infinite or independence of space; the eternal or independence of time. The facts are these:—His Incarnation, Death, Resurrection, Ascension, and Mission of the Holy Ghost.

1. The Incarnation presupposes prior existence. By this assertion we are by no means driven to take part in the unscientific subtleties of Arian speculations. To the dogma, "There was a time when the Son of God was not," we oppose, not another dogma, but the truth that all such propositions, as lying beyond experience, are unthinkable. But prior existence, an existence lying outside creation as we know it, a coming into the world by an exercise of self-determination, is *for us* the same as divine self-existence. It gives a positive conception to our negative idea conveyed in the word absolute, because it is not related to any cause with which we are or can be acquainted.

Again, the Incarnation asserts that likeness of nature between God and man which we are thus enabled to express in the language of facts. God and man are spiritual beings in the sense in which that word has been defined above. But spirit or self-conscious thought is allied in man to a number of conditions and limitations which he inherits as man, and which make him what he knows himself to be—a being conscious of the divine and yet an animal. Christ, on the other hand, is represented to us as pure spirit, joined to a sinless body. He was like God, because His Spirit wrought perfectly and without hindrance the things which He set Himself to do—*i.e.*, a life of absolute duty in fashion as a man. Spirit absolutely able to accomplish what is best as it pleases—this is God. Spirit striving to accomplish what is best through the medium of an imperfect (because perishable) bodily organisation—this is man. Spirit succeeding in accomplishing what is best through a perfect (because incorruptible) bodily organisation—this is God and man, one Person, Jesus Christ.

Thus the Incarnation is seen to lie at the root of all rational conceptions of the life and character of Christ, if, that is, we accept as true such facts as His sinlessness or His Resurrection. To believe that Christ was sinless, and yet in His origin purely human, is to believe not in a miracle, but in a monstrous prodigy—it is to believe that God will break His own laws, do violence to the reason which He has implanted in man, and become the author of irremediable confusion. The sinlessness of Christ being granted, or the Resurrection accepted, then the mind of man demands to know the cause that has set aside the laws of causation as he knows them. To this reasonable demand the Incarnation affords an adequate reply.

2. We are thus enabled to advance a step further and obtain some positive idea of that moral perfection which we

associate with God. Being in His origin free from the "environment" which is the natural condition of every man by virtue of his birth, He was able to overcome the evil that belongs to man's environment as constituting the experience of individuals. The follies of theology must not blind us to the real distinction there is between the evil that we inherit and the evil that we accumulate. Now, the life of Christ was an exhibition of moral perfection. His spirit conceived rightly of duty, willed perfectly to accomplish it, and bound the body to its sway. This perfection was fully displayed by His death, in which we see the crowning power of goodness—the self-sacrifice of God for man. This, indeed, is our highest conception of goodness—the self-conscious personality discarding all personal considerations in order to fulfil the will—that is, to act up to the character of God.

Nevertheless, I am constrained to add that the essential nature of perfect goodness seems to me to be as much beyond our knowledge as self-existence or the infinite. The death of Christ appears to me just as essentially miraculous as His resurrection, because perfect goodness is beyond our experience as much as immortality or omnipotence. Every separate trait in His character we may imagine; its love, purity, justice, and sincerity, are all such as we know them in ourselves, they fire our souls with unextinguishable sympathy and adoration. But the character itself, the harmonious combination in a divine unity of those attributes which we are compelled to regard as separate, must transcend the power of thought, and thus His character, no less than His personality or His deeds, is seen to be essentially divine. It is that which we desire to approach unto; the spirit of which may enter into us and draw us up through countless ages to itself, while yet the imperfect—the spirit that has once sinned—never becomes perfect, as, indeed, we do not understand how it could without the loss of historical self-consciousness. So, then, our idea of perfection is also seen to be negative, to consist, that is, in the absence of the conditions of evil. And Christ Himself expressly claimed to manifest to man's experience and judgment that independence of evil which we attribute to God. For when He desired to give proof drawn from His own character of the fact that He had "proceeded forth and come from God," He does not positively assert his own perfection, but asks negatively, "Which of you convinceth me of sin?" To sum up, then: our conception of God is that of freedom from evil, our experience of man testifies to His imperfection; therefore is Christ, "who did no sin," divine.

I digress at this point for a moment in order to deal with a difficult question. It has been asked, In what way specifically does the character of Christ differ from that of other men, so as to make it that spiritual influence which it has undoubtedly become? Very curious answers, indeed, have been returned by representatives of various schools of thought. We can hardly attribute it to mere intellectual perfection, when we remember that upon almost all the chief objects of human thought He remained entirely silent. Moral perfection, in the sense of negative sinlessness, is not enough to satisfy man's cravings for perfection, or to account for His all-absorbing influence upon humanity. My own impression is, that the peculiarity and significance of His character may be explained as consisting in the fact that, as the Jews among nations, so He among men was religious

The Divinity of Christ and Modern Thought. 353

to the exclusion of all other motives, faculties, or sources of inspiration. In Him the religious faculty swallowed up every other mental power. He was possessed by the divine to a degree that no other man has ever yet approached, and yet religion was in Him absolutely subservient to, or rather identical with, the interests of morality and humanity. Thus duty to Cæsar was part of duty to God. Flowers of the field bore testimony to His gracious care. The stones of the temple suggested the coming divine judgment upon the Jews. Natural objects, social relations, were parables of divine government. Social life did but present opportunities for declaring His Father's will. Every sense, every faculty, every thought, every wish, was, so the history tells us, absorbed in His religious feelings towards God. It was not because He thought wisely or truly of philosophy, art, politics, or literature, but because He did not think of them at all apart from God, that His character has been stamped as unique in history, and has been for eighteen centuries, and seems destined to remain for ever, the one religious force by which humanity is impelled. It need not be added that this peculiarity accords well with the belief that He was conscious of a special relation towards God different from that of other men.

3. Divine perfection necessitates divine omnipotence and also explains it. We may define it—again negatively— as the spirit working out its will without hindrance from bodily organisation or material surroundings. And this is just the idea presented to us by the miracles of Christ. In His conflict with evil, in His redeeming labours, in the accomplishment of the purpose that lay before Him, nothing prevented Him from doing what He pleased. "No man took His life from Him" against His will. The exact point

is brought out in His answer to the father of the demoniac boy, whose words, "if thou canst do anything," appeared to throw a doubt upon His power to help. His answer amounts to this, "The question is, Canst thou believe? there is no question as to my power. All things are possible to him that believes, but faithlessness in thee may prevent the cure, not because my power is limited, but because its exercise would then cease to be morally beneficial" (St Mark vi. 5). The other side of His omnipotence is brought out in His assertion, that if they could by so much as a grain of faith appropriate the mind and will of God, no material obstacles could prejudice their work; the mountain would at their command be removed and cast into the sea. Here, again, though the mere form of words sounds hyperbolical, a simple and intelligible thought is expressed in them.

But, on the other hand, His omnipotence did not interfere with the conditions of His human nature. He might be hungry, thirsty, tired, and mistaken *—for instance, in the fig-tree. But these limitations, again, did not prevent, but rather co-operated with the work He had to do. He had what may be called a human omnipotence, displaying itself, that is, under human conditions, in an absolute power to do own His special work in His own way, without restraint or interruption. And thus the Resurrection comes in to crown His life and works. He conquered death by

---

* It may be well to notice here the reasonable objection, that if Christ was omniscient, He must have been so unlike mankind as to make His life unnatural and His character useless as an example. The answer is, that judging from the history, His knowledge was limited by the usual conditions of human experience, of which, however, His own special birth formed part. The only exceptions seem to be the two or three occasions on which He was elevated to superhuman knowledge in order to carry on His beneficent work towards individuals—for instance, the woman of Samaria. And if the question be asked, Must He not, as divine, have known all things? I answer these wearisome puzzles by another just as irrational, Being divine, cannot He be all things, and therefore limited in point of knowledge by voluntary self-surrender?

dying. No conception that we can form of omnipotent power is higher or more complete than of One who triumphed over His own death. And this He expressly claimed for Himself: "I have power to lay my life down and power to take it again." Here, therefore, we have once more one of our negative ideas of God brought within historical experience, and right reason teaches us that He who could die and rise again is divine.

4. When we speak of God as an Infinite Being, the only conception (once more negative) that we can attach to such a statement seems to be that His spiritual influence is not limited by any conditions of place. He can and does exert His power everywhere at the same time. Now during the life of Christ no such superiority to the ordinary conditions of space is to be discovered. By this I mean that He could only hold communication with other persons by (so to speak) local intercourse. He was obliged to see and hear and ask questions. But the series of appearances after His resurrection present Him to us as placed in immediate communication with His disciples by means quite independent of the laws which govern the communications of man with man. Space no longer exists for Him as able to control His movements. The Ascension is the crown of these appearances; and whether we attach the idea of Infinity especially to this event or not, this at least is certain, that all Christians are able to believe that Christ in actual personality, as He lived on earth, is with them, may be spoken to in prayer and worshipped in praise. True Christian feeling will, I think, rather impel us to pray to God in, as it were, the presence of Christ, feeling His protecting, mediating power. Certainly any petitions which separate Christ from the Father are false and pernicious.

On the other hand, to believe that we may draw near to the Infinite Son of God, just as friends, disciples, mourners, and sufferers drew near to Him during His finite life on earth, is of the very essence of the Christian religion, and enables us to realise His promise, " Lo, I am with you always, even unto the end of the world."

5. Space and time are so closely allied to each other as modes of consciousness, that it is only by a somewhat artificial arrangement that we can so far separate them as to attach the idea of eternity especially to the coming of the Holy Ghost. Still there is a real meaning in the union of the idea and the fact. No merely human spirit can as a mere matter of fact exert its power over other spirits except for a limited time after death. In any case it cannot be transmitted as a personal influence beyond the number of those to whom the person when alive was known. No matter how strongly a person may have impressed others during his life, a few fading memories are all that remain after death. With Christ the reverse is true. His spiritual influence upon earth was transient and, judged by results, unsuccessful. This He recognised in words, such as, " It is expedient that I go away," or, " I, if I be lifted up, will draw all men unto me." Being then lifted up, the power of His Spirit becomes universal, eternal, missionary. It descends from man to man through man. The Spirit that came at Pentecost has in most simple, literal fact "taken of" Christ's life and character, and revealed it to generation after generation. Like some mighty river, the Spirit gains volume and strength the further it flows from its source, not disdaining the various rivulets that run into it from countless fountains, as it passes on its way to God bearing up the prayers and strivings and excellences of mankind.

Whatever else be doubtful, the personal power of Christ over the souls of men through sixty generations is a plain matter of undoubted fact that claims to be called divine, if to anything whatever that name may be applied by the sons of men.

This brings my argument to a close. In it two conclusions have been, so I maintain, satisfactorily proved. First, that granting the facts, the Christian instinct which speaks of Christ as divine is reasonable and true. Second, that the negative ideas under which men have been constrained to think of God have been realised within human experience, so far as that experience can render possible, in the life of Christ; or, to put it once more simply thus, God has been revealed in time in such a manner as to be seen to be superior to the conditions of time. In what way a confused mass of legends could be fused, by men ignorant alike of philosophy and history, into that harmonious revelation which is seen to meet and satisfy the deepest speculations of human thought, I must leave to be explained by those who ascribe the origin of Christianity to mythical sources. Those, again, who prefer to found their faith upon the real or the supposed testimony of their own self-consciousness, rather than upon facts that can be verified, must be permitted (they will assuredly do it, with or without permission) to ransack their minds, and urge the flagging powers of thought (as a rider urges his reluctant horse over the edge of a precipice) beyond the border of the thinkable, in order to reach that which lies close at their feet waiting to be taken up, examined, and made useful. It is indeed the old, old story. The *à priori* road to knowledge must be tried and found impassable before men will consent to travel by the humble but sure road that God has appointed. It is as though one should try to cross the Atlantic by flying. Religion is the last region of knowledge from which this fallacy will be dislodged, and men will still continue to create a God out of their own imaginations, and then, and only then, consent to recognise Him in the facts by which He has been revealed. Desperate contentions there will be as to whether the absolute, the infinite, the perfect, are thinkable terms, contentions that might be settled in an instant if any one could succeed in giving a definition of them so clear, adequate, and reasonable, that no one could refuse to accept it. How surprising that the "primary original intuitions" should be precisely those about which men agree the least! Meanwhile, instead of torturing our but too generous minds in the hopeless attempt to discover the object of thought in the thinking subject, let us reflect whether we cannot believe upon reasonable evidence, appealing to all our deepest moral cravings, that for us the Absolute was born at Bethlehem, the Perfect died on Calvary, the Omnipotent rose at Easter, the Infinite ascended from Bethany, and the Eternal came down at Pentecost.*

Let me be permitted one word more. It will be asked with some curiosity, What effect has the positive method of treating religion upon the possibility or usefulness of creeds? Some will ask it who believe that religion is useless without dogmatic formularies; others, who have taught themselves to feel that the bare idea of dogma is shocking

---

* The difference between the various conclusions that can be derived from the premise "the Finite cannot comprehend the Infinite" may be stated thus :—

Therefore, says Mr Mansel, it is our duty to believe in God as a Person.

Therefore, says Mr Herbert Spencer, it is our duty to believe in nothing that we cannot verify or understand.

Therefore, say I, it is our duty to examine without prejudice any facts which purport to reveal the Infinite to our understandings.

to their religious susceptibilities. Science, I apprehend, will agree with both of these, and with neither. A creed it will regard simply as a proposition, resulting from thinking about facts, that can, like any other proposition, be submitted to man's judgment and acceptance; and it will add, that to summarise conclusions under convenient formularies is as reasonable in religion as in science. It is wrong to seek to enforce a creed upon others by show of dogmatic authority; it is wise to have a creed of one's own, by which our religious beliefs may be formulated for the practical purposes of life.

What, then, ought such a creed to be? First, it should be historical, not metaphysical—that is, it should speak of God as He has been revealed in the facts of nature and history together. But, secondly, it should be moral and not historical—that is, it should not merely recapitulate facts, but condense from them the true spiritual relations and moral purposes of God towards mankind. By such a creed as this I have myself almost unconsciously lived, and now with equal unconsciousness I find that I have proved it to myself by inductive reasoning. I may be pardoned, therefore, for closing this attempt to reconcile religion and science in the words of the creed which expresses my inmost convictions about God. It is (with a verbal alteration) the creed which the Church of England taught me and commissioned me to teach others.

I have learnt, then, to believe in God—
 The Father, who made me and all the world.
 The Son, who redeemed me and all mankind.
 The Holy Ghost, who sanctifies me and all the people of God.—Amen.

THE CHURCH AND THE WORKING CLASSES.*

Τὸν πατέρα καὶ δημιουργὸν πάντων οὔθ' εὑρεῖν ῥᾴδιον, οὔθ' εὑρόντα εἰς πάντας εἰπεῖν ἀσφαλές· Ὃ ὁ ἡμέτερος Χριστὸς διὰ τῆς ἑαυτοῦ δυνάμεως ἔπραξε. Σωκράτει μὲν γὰρ οὐδεὶς ἐπείσθη ὑπὲρ τούτου τοῦ δόγματος ἀποθνήσκειν· Χριστῷ δε, τῷ καὶ ὑπὸ Σωκράτους ἀπὸ μέρους γνωσθέντι . . . οὐ φιλόσοφοι οὐδὲ φιλόλογοι μόνον ἐπείσθησαν ἀλλὰ καὶ χειροτέχναι καὶ παντελῶς ἰδιῶται, καὶ δόξης καὶ φόβου καὶ θανάτου καταφρονήσαντες. Ἐπειδὴ δύναμίς ἐστι τοῦ ἀρρήτου πατρὸς καὶ οὐχὶ ἀνθρωπείου λόγου κατασκευή.

JUSTIN MARTYR, Apolog. ii. cap. x. (ad fin.)

ALTHOUGH the words "The *Church* and the Working Classes" stand at the head of this essay, yet I have no intention of separating either the interests or the existence of the Church of England from the sum total of English Christianity, of which she may, for our present purpose, stand as the representative. There are indeed, as will be seen, special causes for the failure of the Establishment to attract the working classes, but on the whole that failure is not more conspicuous or more lamentable than that of other communities; while, in all probability, it is due essentially to the same deep-lying causes. The confession of a common failure may possibly do something to reunite the various branches of the Christian Church in England, if not (although in the remote future even this

* This essay is reprinted in order to show that there is a practical need for the reform of theology by scientific method. It was written in 1868.

may be hoped for) in one outward organisation, at least in the bonds of mutual sympathy and honourable rivalry. At any rate this confession is better than those exaggerated claims of success, which, while they scarcely serve the purpose of putting even a decent gloss upon failure and disaster, are nevertheless very sufficient to show the denominational jealousy and sectarian bitterness, which at once supply the motive and frustrate the designs of much of the religious working of English Christianity. We may, I think, safely prophesy that no party in England is likely to be led very far away by the intoxication of a real, or even of a fancied, success.

Now of the importance of this subject there cannot be a question. Properly speaking, indeed, it comprises all other questions that are now agitating the English Church, just as really as all political questions a year ago (in 1867) had resolved themselves into this, "How and to what extent shall the working classes be admitted to a share of political power?" The alienation of those classes from the Church of England is the one paramount fact that suggests, or rather compels, the need of a reform, and the one absorbing motive which should direct and control that reform, ought to be the desire to bring them back again. Only let it be distinctly understood that far more is at stake than the interests of one National Church. Upon the influence which Christianity is to exercise upon the democracy depends its future existence, at any rate for a century to come, as the ruling religious power of the civilised world. It is the fashion to say that Christianity is upon its trial; and sometimes a more perfect morality, again a scientific discovery, then an enlarged philosophy, are the instruments which, in the minds alike of friends and foes, are to accomplish the overthrow. Those who believe in the historical truth of the Christian revelation can afford to treat these prophecies with very scant respect, and to rest content with the assurance that all that is essential in Christian teaching will be but more completely proved to be true by the progress of knowledge, and that all that is good in Christian practice will but improve with the improvement of the world, and recommend itself more effectually to the conscience of mankind. But the continued alienation of the working classes would stretch the stoutest faith to its utmost tension. If Christianity becomes the religion of a caste, or of a race, or continues to be the religion of a civilisation instead of becoming the religion of human nature, it ceases to have any claim upon the undivided allegiance of the world. And if the democracy, including, as it will do, thousands of men of a pure though possibly imperfect morality, undoubted earnestness, considerable ability, and possessed of a large share of political power, rejects the claims of revelation, and leaves it with contemptuous indifference to the upper and middle classes, then we may be very sure that much more than Established Churches will perish in the confusion.

There is, in fact, a sense in which it is as true that the dispute between the advocates and the assailants of the Christian religion will have to be settled ultimately by the democracy, as it is that the dispute between Conservatism and Liberalism is being referred to the same tribunal: for if Christianity is, in any real effective sense of the word, true, it must be capable of being shown to be true to educated and intelligent men as a class. I say, in any real effective sense of the word, because there is, of course, another view exactly the opposite of this, which underlies alike the Catholic and the Protestant theory of religion (or to speak more accurately, the Catholic practice and the popular Protestant theory), and which is responsible for much of Christian failure and unpopularity. It would not, of course, shock the faith of those who believe that the Christian religion is a scheme for saving a few souls out of a perishing world, if they were told that the scheme would fail, on the whole, to reach the working classes. "So much the worse for them," would be the very intelligible and logical reply. But fortunately for the interests of Christendom there has never wanted a healthier and nobler feeling, though, in all candour, it must be confessed that in this, as in so many other instances, the preservation of the truth has been due to the, perhaps, extreme opinions of communities, or of men, lying outside the recognised boundaries of the Catholic Church. And to that large and increasing number who are beginning to regard Christianity as God's method of regenerating humanity, and in the literal sense of the word "saving the world," such an announcement would be the deathblow of faith, energy, and hope. We at any rate cannot afford to attach the notion of a "very small remnant" to the work of a religion, which we believe to be, as St Paul believed it to be, the religion of the "last days," the ultimate revelation—to be developed in history —of God to man. Faith in human progress is as necessary to the Liberal in religion as to the Liberal in politics, and the hope of a more universal, effective, and pure religion is to him exactly what the hope of a better government or of social improvement is to the other. And, therefore, both alike make their appeal to that vast and unknown force, that democracy of which we in England have only this last year become practically conscious, but which, we dimly see, holds within its grasp the destinies of the future, whether in the domain of politics or of religion. Our business is to absorb that mass into the still larger entity which we call the national life; and the Church of England, if she have the faintest conception of her position and responsibility, must set herself to accomplish in religion that which statesmanship has to effect in other departments of thought and action. It need hardly be observed that the influence is not one-sided, but that the Church and State in their turn must hope to be largely influenced for good by their contact with the Demos.

Now this being so, it plainly becomes of the utmost importance to know what are the prevailing sentiments of the working classes on the subject of religion. Rhetorically they may be summed up in one word—indifference. It is my object to indicate, as briefly as may be, the extent and causes of this indifference, yet so as to suggest the grounds for a better hope, and also the general direction in which practical reforms should tend. The influences for good, which in its turn the democracy will exercise upon religion, will, I hope, come out incidentally; but it does not form so distinct a part of my purpose to discuss them. I shall endeavour therefore to establish or comment on these four propositions:—

I. That the idea of an Established Church is essentially a democratic one; and yet that the working classes have no affection for the Established Church of England.

II. That attendance at public worship is essentially a

part of democratic religion, and yet that the working classes, as a rule, attended nowhere.

III. That the clergy and the democracy are naturally friends and allies, and yet that there is no friendship or alliance between the Anglican clergy and the working classes.

IV. That the Christian revelation is one eminently suited to a democracy, and yet that the working classes are indifferent to its claims upon them.

I. In a speech delivered last session in the House of Lords, the Duke of Argyll is reported to have expressed his belief that Voluntary Churches would be the religious communities of the future. Now this seems to me a curious instance of the way in which mere local or national considerations can prejudice the intellect of very able men. Familiar with the past history of the English, and still more of the Scotch Establishment, and fully sensible that their present position with respect to other Christian communities is rapidly becoming untenable, the Duke leaps at a bound to this very wide and sweeping generalisation. No doubt the past religious history of the two countries presents to us the prospect of the gradual invasion of the establishment principle by the denominational; but this resulting, as it does, from causes and from the existence of communities as old as the establishments themselves, forms but a very slender induction from which to prophesy the religious future of the world. Of course one man is as good a prophet as another until the event; still if we emancipate ourselves for a single moment from the mere passions and prejudices which encumber the question in countries like England or Scotland, and regard rather what may be called its political philosophy, we shall find reason to believe that not only is the idea of an endowed Church suitable to a democracy, but that it is the only method in which a democratic religion can develop itself. Let us consider for a moment the invariable relations of the demos to the commonwealth at large. The demos consists, broadly speaking, of those who, being obliged to maintain existence by hard bodily labour, are thereby excluded from any very large participation in the luxuries, the pleasures, and the blessings of culture and civilisation. Hence the constant and legitimate tendency of the democracy is to insist that this natural inequality shall be as far as possible redressed by spending large sums of money from the national income upon objects calculated to benefit the people; and the whole problem of practical statesmanship centres now in the difficulty of harmonising this tendency with the general interests of the nation at large. There are, however, certain cases in which the benefit to the whole commonwealth is so manifest that the claims of the demos are frankly conceded. Many instances might be quoted, but the typical one is of course national education; while on the other hand such Bills as that for improving the dwellings of artisans raise the whole problem in its most embarrassing and difficult aspect.* Now let us imagine, for the moment, that the demos becomes as interested in religion as it now is in education; let us suppose—no very incredible supposition—that the working classes are as anxious to be provided with the means of religious worship as the middle

---

* I am not sure now that there is any real difficulty in it. An expenditure of millions in buying up wretched dwellings would probably repay itself economically as well as morally. But this requires faith.

classes are at present. Of course if they remain indifferent, *cadit quæstio*; but then, as I have said, far more than the principle of endowments would fall also. Now religious institutions to be made at all capable of doing their work are very expensive things, as Dissenters, and Churchmen as well, have discovered ere this. Churches cost more than schools, clergymen than schoolmasters. Is not the conclusion therefore inevitable that this is precisely one of those common benefits which the State will be expected to provide in order to redress as far as possible the inequalities of life? Would it not be urged with irresistible force that the religion of the people is as necessary as their education, and that religion, conducing as *ex hypothesi* it does to general prosperity and good government, falls exactly within the limits of those things which in a well-ordered State are provided in part by the common fund? I pass over the distinction sometimes drawn between establishment and endowment, merely remarking that in the case of any very powerful and united Church the latter necessitates the former, in the sense at any rate in which establishment means the ultimate control by the nation of the Church it subsidises, or for whose revenue it acts as trustee. Of course I am aware that the United States may be quoted against me; but apart from the absurdity of quoting the example of a country peculiar alike in its economic condition, and in its, at best, but brief historical experience, it is enough to say that the American demos is neither very poor, nor, as yet, eminently religious. A far more real illustration of what is in fact an elementary truth in the politics of democracies, may be found in the practice of the Athenians with regard to the Theoric Fund. The Theatre, intimately bound up as it was with religious thoughts, together with public festivals and games, was to the people of Athens much what I am assuming religious institutions will be to the demos of the future; these were at any rate the shape in which their protest against the hardships of life and their craving after rest and recreation were embodied. And we know, of course, that in that wonderful and typical Periclean democracy, the Theoric Fund provided, at the common expense, for the entertainment of the poor citizens, and was regarded as one out of many legitimate ways of remedying the inequalities of the social state. And its further history, while it shows, no doubt, how the sentiment upon which it rested might become perverted and abused, is a signal proof of the extremely jealous care with which democracies regard that portion of the common fund set apart for the common use and benefit. That the middle classes would now submit to almost any privation* sooner than tamper with funds which (whether in the Established Church or in the Dissenting communities) had been set apart for religious purposes, may, I think, be taken for granted; but it gives us a very faint idea, indeed, of the horror and indignation with which such a scheme would be received by the working classes if once they were interested in the wellbeing of the national religion.

It is perhaps necessary to go a step further than this, and to assert that not only is an Established Church eminently suited to a democracy, but also that in it alone the people can exercise that controlling and regulative power which

* With our present experience this statement sounds absurd enough. But I have never been able to estimate the length to which religious animosity will go. It was not, however, religious animosity but political justice that overthrew the Irish Established Church.

belongs to them. The fatal defect of Voluntary Churches is that they become—to use an old-fashioned word—timocratic. Two men who subscribe £100 a-year can control the government of a Church consisting of three hundred men who subscribe £1 apiece. In every voluntary association those who find the money must ultimately be the governors, because they can in the last resort withdraw the support by which the association is maintained. This explains one of the worst features in modern dissent—the tendency to do homage to a class of rich men by whom necessary funds are supplied. That this evil is not worse than it is, is due to the self-restraint and sincere love of liberty which has hitherto characterised this class as a whole, but it is at best an ugly feature, and full of danger in time to come. Now, when the funds of a Church are derived from endowments or from the public purse, then every man has a right to a voice in the management of the Church, not in proportion to the amount of his individual taxation, but by virtue of the zeal, the knowledge, and the ability which he can bring to bear upon the subject. This is the very essence of democracy. And growing out of this there arises a realisation of the Christian, as connected with the Democratic, idea, in more ways than I can stop to point out. The liberty of the teacher, the equality of the taught, the democratic idea of union in one body instead of division into warring sects,—all these are characteristic of an Endowed Church, and are still in some considerable degree preserved for the world in the Church of England. When, for instance, Mr Goldwin Smith affirms that he respects the Church of England but detests the Establishment, it may with some reason be replied that the very things on account of which his respect is paid are precisely those which are due to her position as an Establishment.

The second part of our proposition, that the working classes have no affection for the Established Church, requires but little proof, though, on the other hand, we must beware of exaggeration. It seems to me, as far as I can gather from the general attitude of the men, and still more from the studiously moderate and tentative tone which Mr Bright uses when speaking on this question, that they have a lingering respect for the Establishment, and an instinct that, whatever it may have come to be, it is still in its essence a popular institution. The Conservative section of the working classes, on the other hand, make the maintenance of the union between Church and State a prominent part of their political programme. Of course, in those too many cases in which the claims of the Established Church are on one side, and the interests of liberty on the other, working men may readily be inflamed into antagonism, or even induced to take the side of the Voluntary Churches in the quarrel; but then they do not speak with quite the same contempt of the Church of England as they do of other English Churches. Nor, to the best of my knowledge, has the Reform League ever hinted at a crusade against the endowments of the Church. Still an alienation amounting almost to positive dislike is a palpable fact; and the reasons for this it is our business to discuss and to point out under their respective heads. At present they may be summed up in two main facts. First, the policy of the Church itself has been such as to turn her into a denomination. She has not thoroughly realised her duties, not so much to members of other communities, as to the

The Church and the Working Classes. 371

same persons regarded simply as citizens of the State with which she is connected. The proposal to exclude Dissenters who do not pay voluntary church-rates from the vestry (so far as concerns ecclesiastical matters), the refusal to undertake to educate children* unless they will learn all the formularies prescribed by the Church, the jealousy of the State tribunals, the eagerness to support the Voluntary principle in the colonies, and the general attitude maintained towards other English branches of the Church universal—the attitude of an irritated rival rather than of a friendly elder sister—are painful evidences of this spirit of denominationalism, against which the very notion of a National Church is a perpetual protest. And, again, the Church has become—to coin a word—intensely *middle-classy*. The democracy has stood aloof from her, just as they have done from the army, the internal politics, and the foreign policy of the kingdom. The clergy on their part have got to take the upper-class view of things, and, not without sturdy resistance, have allowed the Church to become a Conservative catchword. Politically and economically they have been against the working classes, and without, to their honour, engaging actively against them, have let it become known that their sympathies, their interests, their predilections, were (naturally enough, perhaps) on the other side. In fact the Church may be said to have taken up, as regards the working classes, the position not of rational justice, but of complacent benevolence. The middle class, on the other hand, has dominated since the Reform Bill in the Church, exactly

---

* I did not foresee how speedily the Church would be converted by stern necessity to acquiesce in a universal conscience clause.

as it has in the country, and has impressed its own ideas upon her worship, her constitution, and whatever reforms have been accomplished. This will appear more clearly as we proceed, but I adduce two facts in illustration of it now, because their full force and meaning is not always rightly comprehended.

The middle-class theory of life is, that out of a number of persons starting in rivalry and competition together, a few should be specially successful, the most just enabled to live, and a fair proportion fail so completely as to require to be supported by charity—say, in almshouses built by the money and for the glorification of their successful brethren. The working-class theory is, on the contrary, that every man, whatever his industry or ability, should succeed or fail alike. Now, without discussing the relative value of these theories, which I have purposely stated in exaggerated terms, it is very evident that this description of the middle-class theory applies without any exaggeration at all to the English Church. It is expressed, almost caricatured, in the writings of Sydney Smith as the great principle upon which the patronage of the Church should be distributed. By it a few men succeed enormously in their profession, which success, again, is administered by the hands and shared by the *protégés* of the aristocracy. The mass are barely enabled to live, while many remain "poor parsons," suitable objects of pity and worthy recipients of old clothes. This consideration explains at once the outspoken indignation of the working men at the poverty of the clergy and the inequality of benefices. It is by no means a sentimental or partisan complaint, but rather the existence of such abuses is intolerable and inexplicable to an ordinary working man, who would starve for a month sooner than allow an unfortunate brother to receive less wages than himself. That the labourer is worthy of his hire, and is not to be put off with old clothes, is a very great truth indeed with him. And as he has not the faintest chance of making his voice heard in the matter, he can, at least, utter a practical protest against a religion of this kind, and refuse to darken the doors of an institution that permits a state of things in his view plainly immoral and unjust.

The second instance is connected with an abuse that, perhaps as much as any other topic, excites the indignation of working men—I mean the sale of livings.* The ordinary Englishman regards a living simply as a piece of property; and as property is the most sacred thing in the world, the owner has clearly a right to do what he pleases with his own. Need we wonder that the working classes protest energetically against such a view of the matter? Perhaps there is hardly an instance in which the rights and duties of property come into more direct collision than in the sale of livings; and when we have on the one hand the claims of the owner sanctioned by law and custom, and on the other an increasing protest upon moral and perfectly unselfish grounds from the heart of the democracy, we seem to discern a source of unpopularity and weakness to the Church of England, which hardly admits of a remedy at present, and a difficulty which hardly anything short of a revolution can remove.

Whether or no this revolution will come to pass, or what form, supposing it to be inevitable, it will assume, is a

* Since the above was written not one single step has been taken to overthrow this crying scandal.

question upon which it is vain now to speculate. One of two things appears ultimately certain: either the Church must become really national—that is, comprehensive—or else she must cease to be established. The former alternative, which is at least possible, would remove that alienation of the democracy of which we have been speaking. Those who deprecate the latter as a real calamity both to Church and State, may however acquiesce in, with a view to make the best of, the inevitable, especially if vanquished in fair fight by opponents who would have, as Nonconformists, real, though I for one believe thoroughly mistaken, grounds of opposition and dislike. But it is difficult to think with ordinary patience of that large and increasing number within the Church who, in their childish impatience of what they deem "bondage," are beginning to welcome the idea of disestablishment. It is melancholy to think that the ecclesiastical spirit, assuming the garb and speaking in the name of religion, has made—of all persons in the world—Churchmen disloyal to the Constitution, and comparatively careless of the interests of their country. Those who call themselves "good" Churchmen ought to be above all things desirous that the Church should stand by the State in all the troubles and dangers which are for ever gathering about the path of a country like England, and should thus be enabled to lend the full weight of her moral and religious influence to the task of alleviating and removing them. To cry out for a release just at this moment resembles nothing so much as the conduct of a wife who, when things began to look gloomy and threatening, should utter whispers about obtaining a divorce, not forgetting to warn her solicitor to look well to the terms of her settlements.

II. Attendance at public worship may surely be regarded as a faithful index of the amount of interest felt towards religion by any given class of men. In the case of individuals it is of course conceivable that persons of a certain turn of mind may be sincerely attached to the truths, as well as to the morality, of the Christian religion without feeling themselves able, or at any rate disposed, to attend services (to them) encumbered by a sermon, or conducted in such a manner as to violate their ideas of taste and order. But when certain sentimentalists appear anxious to claim the benefit of this exception for the working classes in a body, and to assert that though they do not attend public worship, their lives are nevertheless admirable examples of pure and undefiled religion, one is bound to summon common-sense into court to expose egregious nonsense. For it is very obvious that to the great mass of mankind both the practice of and the belief in religion require much external help in the way of instruction, united prayer, and outward forms. And if this be true anywhere, it must be true especially of those whose lives are spent in hard work, exposed to many coarse temptations, without much opportunity of obtaining instruction for themselves. Working men, moreover, are especially gregarious in their habits, and if they realise religion at all, will certainly do so as members of a community, with its place of meeting, its outward observances, its pledge of brotherly love and communion. But what is of more importance still, it must be remembered that religion has its devotional as well as its practical side, and that the second without the first is but a maimed and imperfect representation of the Christian ideal. A man may be a very good man, and yet be all the better for coming to say his prayers on Sunday with his neighbours and kinsfolk. And further, as working men with almost one consent do not plead this excuse for themselves, but either profess their indifference to religion altogether, or else—far more frequently—acknowledge that they "do not go to church as often as they might," it may be concluded that this fallacy is effectually disposed of. If, then, outward worship be practically a test of the interest that any given class feels towards religion, how does the case stand with the working classes? I do not believe that the ordinary account, which represents that it is as much the habit of the working classes, with large exceptions, to stay away from church, as it is the habit of the upper classes, with the same exceptions, to attend, is at all exaggerated. I speak from experience in London, which is perhaps in this as in so many other respects below the level of provincial towns; but in the east of London the failure to attract the men as a class is very marked—is, I had almost said, absolute. I have been assured by one of the most intelligent and trustworthy men I ever had the fortune to meet, that out of forty men who worked with him *one* would certainly go to church, another would if he were asked, and the remaining thirty-eight would not under any circumstances. And he added, what every one's experience will verify, that this was a fair example of the general state of things among artisans of the first class. Desperate attempts are indeed made to evade the "logic of facts," and success of a certain sort, among the emotional, the feeble-minded, and the lovers of spectacles and novelties, is adduced as a great result in "Christianising the masses." There is probably more unconscious and perfectly honest lying about the number of persons, and especially of working men, composing a congregation, than about anything else in the known world. And although the churches in the east of London may present a more deplorable spectacle than can be found elsewhere, yet it must be remembered that they are badly attended simply because the population is almost entirely composed of those classes who in the "best-worked" country parishes are equally conspicuous by their absence. The perfectly respectful, intelligent, and dexterous artisan, for whom the authorities naturally send in times of emergency to do a difficult job at the church, never enters it for any other purpose. If, then, the failure be so palpable—and some failure all acknowledge—what are the causes? Now, the causes lie far deeper than any mere defects in the mode of conducting divine service, or any objections which working men have, or fancy they have, to it. They are connected with those relations of the demos to the Establishment, the clergy, and the Christian Revelation, of which —in the two latter instances—we have yet to speak. Men in earnest about religion, and on good terms with its ministers, would not lightly be kept away from its ordinances. Of course if a man be put upon his defence, and peremptorily challenged to say why he does not come to church, he will naturally catch at the first available weapon of defence and lay the blame on something in the services themselves, especially if it be something for which the challenger is responsible. Two causes, however, there are which are of some real importance in driving the working classes away from the Church, and which I will mention as furnishing notable illustrations of the besetting sins of the

Established Church—her tendency to make herself into a denomination, and her disposition to place herself, bound hand and foot, at the feet of the middle classes.

The first is connected with the always delicate subject of the pecuniary arrangements of the Church—her method, that is, of raising money. A Church receives endowments and a legal position upon the implied condition that she is to do, so to speak, the religious work of the country. And if the revenues assigned to her be, after the most judicious and equitable distribution (an experiment that has not yet been tried in the English Church), inadequate to the task, then she must rely upon the free liberality of her members. This rule applies universally, and may be illustrated by the history of the Crimean and American civil wars, in both of which private liberality in various indirect ways came to the assistance of the respective Governments, even after large sums had been voted out of the public purse. But the one thing which may *not* rightly be done by a National Church any more than by an army, by a clergyman any more than by a soldier, is to sell the services for which he is otherwise paid. Yet this is precisely what the Church of England does in two obvious instances —fees and pew-rents, which more than anything else vex the soul and alienate the affections of the working man. In a Church endowed for the express purpose of providing for the religious wants of the community, the clergy have got themselves put into the degrading position of making a charge to the poor man.* From the cradle out of which

---

* I cannot resist quoting a story as illustrating the evil effects of this. One woman was overheard by a district visitor remonstrating with another for having had her banns put up away from her parish church. "For," said she,

he comes to be baptised, and very frequently to be charged for it, to the grave in which he cannot be laid until the claims of the parson, the clerk, the sexton, and the bellringer are duly satisfied, he is pursued by vexatious exactions, which have the additional demerit of being a sort of poll-tax levied on rich and poor at the same rate. But even this is nothing to the system of pew-rents, of which the only description that I can find at all adequate is Mr Henley's famous expression, "a device of Old Nick's to oppress the poor," and, it may be added, to destroy the nationality of the English Church. If a working man ventures into most district and many parish churches, he is thrust into "free (and uncomfortable) seats" between, as the *Saturday Review* once excellently phrased it, "two frowning phalanxes of pews;" and he is told that in this so-called National Church he has no right to any of the "good" seats unless he can afford a certain number of guineas per annum, and so become that mysterious being, the religious synonym for a ten-pound householder, a seatholder. Can any one who knows the character of the average working man wonder that he secedes from a Church which possesses such vast privileges, and assumes such a lofty air, and descends to such mean devices as these? It is to the eternal credit of the High Church party (besides being a tower of strength), and should be allowed by all liberally-minded persons to counterbalance much extravagance of doctrine and ritual,

"you have had a good deal, Mrs So-and-so" (she was a widow), "out of the parsons at that church, and I do think that when you can put a shilling or two in their way you ought."

At the same time it is obvious that marriage fees for the performance of what is an important legal as well as a religious ceremony stand upon a different footing.

that they have been the first to preach and to act up to this truth. Indeed the High Church formula, which knows no distinction in church except that of priest and people, is perhaps the nearest practical approach in England to democracy of a certain type, and if the name and thing presbyter were substituted for the name and thing priest, might exactly express the democratic theory of worship. The question of appropriation without payment rests of course upon a different footing, and might safely be left to local feeling and convenience; but the abolition, wherever practicable, of pew-rents does imply of necessity the re-establishment of the weekly offertory, which again is the true expression of the democratic idea of almsgiving, and is almost invariably popular with working men. Meanwhile it is, I think, possible to suggest a very easy palliation for evils now become too inveterate to be wholly removed. By an application of the same principle which compels the running of parliamentary trains, let every church have at least one free service—if necessary, even after the first evening service, and in lieu of the abortive afternoon one —and let all seats be let with the express condition that the holders do not occupy them at that service. This remedy is easy: I wish I could add that I felt sure it would be very effectual to heal the breach which years of pew-rents have caused and will perpetuate.

The second of the two causes for the alienation of the demos from the services of the Church is to be found in the manner in which the services are conducted. Probably there is not in all Christendom a type of service so undevout, so unintellectual, so unimpressive, and at the same time so admirably suited to British Philistinism, as the once popular, and still common, service of the English Church. Wit has almost exhausted itself on the "parson and clerk duet," the gallery singing, the beadle, and the pew-opener, but they flourish yet. Here, again, much credit is due to the High Church party for perceiving that the English service was, to put it mildly, capable of improvement. Much good, no doubt, has been effected by the reforms they have instituted; but it is to be feared that the remedy, so far as working men are concerned, is little better than the disease. The capital mistake has been committed of trying to allure them, like so many children, by a gorgeous ritual, and of defending this course by appealing to their love of processions, theatrical adornments, and so forth. Whereas the answer, if one were given, would be this, "We are not children at all, but very like grown-up men and women in other ranks of life. Like them, we have a fancy for pomp and show at our festivals, social gatherings, and demonstrations. Like them also, the great majority of us are accustomed to associate a reverence for divine things with simplicity, with an absence of show, elaborate detail, and fatiguing ceremonialism." Personally I believe that the English Service, with a very few alterations—a little shortening* perhaps, or rather dividing, of the services—is capable of being made by far the most attractive to intelligent artisans of any type of service that has been yet invented. And it is certainly founded on a true democratic—that is, congregational—idea. From first to last the Prayer-book hardly seems to recognise more than the "minister" or "priest" who is to "say" the prayers, and the "people" who are to "say" them with him. And it

* This has now been done.

seems to me a matter of indifference from the democratic point of view, whether a choir is put into a gallery at the west end of the church to sing anthems over the heads of the "audience," or railed off into a chancel at the east end to sing introits and antiphons at strange and unwonted places. The general principles upon which a service suitable for working men should be founded are briefly as follows. Churches should be as beautiful as art and light can make them, especially by calling in the aid, to an extent hitherto undreamt of, of mural painting and sculpture. All the arrangements for conducting the service should be such as to give not *effect* but *meaning* to its several portions. The aim should be to appeal far more than has hitherto been done to the intelligence, as opposed to the senses or the feelings. Nothing should be allowed, so far as it can be prevented, to come in between the people and the act of worship which they are assembled to perform. Let the prayers be read (as a preference), the people responding in their natural voices, with much singing of hymns and chanting of psalms, and we may hope to have a service in which plain simple folk can take their part and exercise their rights, being protected from the vagaries of extempore praying on the one hand, and the minutiæ of ceremonialism on the other. There are signs that the High Church service is already departing from its original congregational type.

III. The very fundamental idea of the ministry of the gospel is, that they who compose its ranks are the friends of those who may without offence be termed in this connection the poor. Ministers of Christ are charged with the duty of delivering a message intended to alleviate the sufferings and sweeten the cup of life. They are supposed to be specially connected with no single class, but to be a witness of the unity of all classes, composers of differences, arbiters between contending interests, advocates of the weak and defenceless. And in this view of their duty and position, by common consent, the clergy of the English Church are not as a class found wanting. They raise and administer vast sums in the relief of the sick and distressed. They spend many hours in visiting and consoling the dying. Their labours in the cause of education have been beyond all praise. They often stand between the poor and the tyranny of employers or of guardians. They embark in a thousand schemes for the promotion of the welfare of the working classes. And all this is, I think, fairly recognised by the men themselves, who know that after all the average parson has not a single selfish interest opposed to theirs, that he has a sincere desire to benefit them according to his lights, and that officially or personally he can do them many a good turn. This general regard shows itself, for instance, in the outward respect which, as a rule, is paid to clergymen. Of course a man whose very presence is, or at any rate is regarded, as a special notice to "be good," who wears a distinctive dress, and uses, perhaps too freely, a distinctive language, must expect to be treated behind his back with that half-real, half-affected contempt, that partly good-natured, partly sincere dislike, which is by no means confined to one class, but which finds abundantly open expression in the popular literature of the day. But otherwise a clergyman, merely as such, may be in constant intercourse with artisans and labourers without meeting with a single uncivil look or word, except from "vile and churlish" persons, who are to be found in every class of society. The same thing shows itself again in a very considerable amount of real confidence. Working men entrust the clergy with the education of their children, and with the care of their money. It shows itself once more in the readiness with which the services of the minister are welcomed at the last hour. I have stood by the death-bed of many a working man, and after the first suspicions were removed, and perhaps the dislike to the popular religiousness overcome, I have met with nothing but openness, cordiality, and affection. But here it stops. Beyond this the clergy as a body have no living influence upon the hearts and conduct of the artisan class. There is no mutual sympathy, no intelligent acquaintance with each other's views and wishes. The working man fights as shy of the parson as he can, and is not to be persuaded into familiarity or friendship. If on the one hand his dislike is mainly artificial, on the other his indifference is certainly unaffected.

Now the main cause of all this springs from the view which the clergy, as a rule, take of the working class, and of the line of conduct which that view prompts them to adopt. Only, in all fairness it must be remembered that the clergyman is not without excuse. For he sees unfortunately only the worst side of this class. He is brought into constant contact with wretched homes, beaten wives, starving children whom no persuasion of his can get sent to school. His acquaintance with the principles and transactions of trade unions is confined to his knowledge of the many "clubs" which have broken up, cheating their members, and leaving them to be maintained in age and sickness by him, or to his practical experience of the misery entailed by strikes. If he pleads the cause of some poor fellow, a hundred tales of his idleness or dishonesty are repeated by angry employers, or guardians smarting under the odium of a heavy poor rate. No wonder that he begins to take a view lamentably below the true one. To him the working classes are always, in his technical language, "the poor." They are objects of his benevolent activity. It hardly enters into the mind of, at any rate, an old-fashioned clergyman, that there are multitudes of artisans living honourable and well-to-do lives, with very strong views on things in general, and on the whole as unpromising objects for the exercise of the virtue of benevolence as can well be imagined. And growing out of this, there arises a fatal train of mistakes and perplexities in his plans for bringing religion to bear upon the "masses"—some of them almost too ludicrous to be believed. Sometimes they are patronised, with great protestations against patronage, as " my " working men. I remember hearing a dignitary of the Church of England, when speaking of a Working Man's Club, exclaim, in an outburst of triumphant Liberalism, " I *make* them manage their own affairs."

Even upon points where there might be real popularity and confidence gained, the clergy somehow or other get wrong. Here are two instances. They would meet no doubt with very considerable support and gratitude from the working classes in their efforts to preserve Sunday as a day of rest; but the men see plainly enough that the anxiety to discourage any lengthening of the hours of labour is subordinated to the desire of imposing their own views of " Sabbath-keeping " upon a class whose different circumstances demand a very different treatment. In like manner all grace is taken from the boon of education, and all gratitude from its recipients, by the ungracious and arbitrary attitude assumed towards the parents; and this is all the more provoking, because the clergy in their public policy contradict their private conduct and kindly toleration of the beliefs of others. The parents cannot but see that the education of their children is made the battle-field of religious factions. On the one hand the clergy, as represented by their own society, insist upon retaining the right to teach church doctrines, whether the parents like it or not; on the other, partisans equally resolute are determined that no religion—at any rate no doctrines—shall be taught, whether the parents wish it or no : while the simple alternative of offering religious teaching to those who will accept it, and of securing to the parent some liberty of action under the conscience clause, has but just contrived to secure a hearing. Then, again, there is a fatal habit of regarding mere external results instead of adhering to sound principles of action. Young men, for instance, are gathered into Christian Young Men's Associations, or Church of England Institutes; and when it is represented that clubs for the purpose of instruction or society, if founded upon a religious basis, would not be tolerated for an instant among the upper classes, the answer is that they "do good." As though anything could in the long run really do good that was founded upon a mistaken system. What is *seen* is the good done, or supposed to be done, to the few who belong to them; what is *not seen*, and is incapable of being measured, is the general evil effect upon the religion of the whole class. For every feeble-minded Christian young man produced at these institutions ten sturdy and independent minds, capable of leading the class to which they belong, are alienated and repelled. Nor does the attempt to win these men by purely secular means, such as clubs, avail much better, for there is at present a lurking and not altogether unfounded suspicion that the parson has some ulterior views of his own, and means to make the club a back entrance to the church. Still to this there are numerous exceptions,* as I have the good fortune to know. When once the men are convinced that the clergyman is meeting them on their own ground, they will in their turn meet him with a cordiality, a gratitude, and, in plain words, a deference, which it is often hard to deserve. But then this brings him very little nearer to what after all is his one business—the influencing them for good in religious matters; nor will this ever be accomplished, until we have understood their position, and done justice to their opinions; above all gained over their leaders, and approached them through the men and the institutions they value and support. Time, and reform, and the union of classes, and a better knowledge of each other, can alone remove the obstacles which at present stand between the clergy and the demos. Political economy, which in one of its aspects might almost be called the science of Christian benevolence, will do much towards helping the clergy in dealing with the various social and economic difficulties and miseries which are now left to the agency of a charity most well meaning, devoted, and unsparing, but very frequently misguided and ineffectual.

IV. But after all it is merely playing upon the surface of a great subject to ascribe this alienation of the demos to

* Notably the Working Men's College in Great Ormond Street.

anything short of the theological forms under which Christian truth is presented to the people. It is religious thought—that is, the doctrines impressed upon the Church by the few and accepted by the many—that must be held answerable for Christian success or failure in practice. There is, let us observe, no natural infidelity among the working classes. Some, of course, in their general revolt against everything instituted or established in the country, are as regards religion unbelievers. Many more, when pressed for a reason why they decline the outward profession of a religion which their moral convictions assure them to be true, take refuge in an insincere and pretended infidelity as the easiest and safest shelter. But the enormous majority never really think about the matter at all, and are inclined to accept as true the religious creed which they have inherited or been taught, provided it does not interfere with the daily course of their lives and conduct. That this is a fair account of the "faith" of the working classes may, I think, be proved by these facts among others: that they manifest a decided preference for a religious education, and that they sincerely respect a sincerely religious man. Nor again can it be pretended that the Christian Revelation is less suited to the demos than to any other class. It was preached by a Poor Man of the outward rank of an artisan —whom the "common people heard gladly." It soon took the form of a revolt—none the less real because not political—against the "powers that be," whether in Church or State. It comes to cheer the burden of life to those upon whom that burden presses most heavily. At this moment it is the one motive power of all the many schemes for alleviating human misery. It is anchored upon that essentially democratic virtue, hopefulness; and it claims to establish, in its own way, that equality after which democracy has toiled, almost since the dawn of history with more than Herculean labour, and less than Sisyphean success. And lastly, it is presented for man's acceptance in a form especially adapted to catch the attention and enlist the sympathies of plain working people; for it is not a creed, nor a philosophy, nor a sentiment, nor a morality, but a Person and a history which comprise all these, and yet are different from, and greater than, all these. If, then, the fault do not lie in the nature of the religion itself, or in the incapacity of those to whom it is addressed, still less, I confidently maintain, is it to be attributed to any want of zeal or energy on the part of the clergy. No picture, indeed, can be sadder than the one presented in the lives of hundreds of hard-working, unsuccessful men; unsuccessful, that is, not as compared with others, but as compared with what they feel ought to be accomplished. They spare themselves no toil—they try any and every experiment that can be suggested. But so far as the *élite* of the working classes are concerned, they are like actors playing before a listless audience, on the five-hundredth night of a drama that has outlived its popularity. The old formulæ have lost their influence upon the hearts of men, and the clergy find that nineteenth-century targets are not to be pierced by sixteenth-century ordnance. They would sacrifice anything if they could bring the personal living influence of their Master to bear upon the myriads about them, to whom in His name they are sent. And thus the waste of power is enormous. Zeal that might convert a world achieves next to nothing, because of the theological trammels by which it is fettered and misguided. Sooner or later men must come to see this. Mere ecclesiastical arrangements, or mistakes such as I have before alluded to, can never account for an alienation so distressing. The Evangelical party appear fully sensible of this, and can do nothing but pray and hope for a revival of the old Evangelical earnestness. Their rivals, while taunting them with an ungenerous bitterness fatal to the very notion of religion, are engaged in the futile task of putting the strong new wine of nineteenth century thought into bottles that were waxing old more than four centuries ago, and have not improved since that time. Though I cannot hope at the close of a single essay to treat even superficially a subject which requires—and would justify—a book in itself, yet I must at least attempt to indicate some of the principal causes of this theological failure.

1. The first that would instinctively suggest itself to any inquirer is the existence of religious divisions and hatred. This is perhaps rather a result than an instance of the corruption of religious thought, but anyhow it stands first in our melancholy list. "The Church of Rome is the slayer of souls, the mother of perdition," exclaims the Protestant. "*Nulla salus extra Ecclesiam*" is the answering war-cry thundered from the opposing barrier. In England the law-courts and Parliament itself are vexed with the cries of contending factions seeking to exclude each other from the fold. At this moment a popular cry has been—it must be admitted not until after immense exertions—raised to the effect, that if we cannot silence or banish the doctrines and the practices of a certain objectionable party, we ought at least to take their vestments from them. And all this

miserable wrangling is carried on in full view of the working man to whom religion is to be taught. He, whose circumstances and easy good-nature alike incline him to accept the lazy creed of an Epicurean universalism, is to be approached after this fashion. He may not have the gospel preached to him without at the same time being solemnly warned against some other preacher of the same gospel. "Out of the same mouth proceedeth blessing and cursing." In vain do we seek to escape from the peremptory condition of success imposed by the Founder of Christianity Himself: "By this shall all men know that ye are my disciples, if ye have love one to another;" or again: "That they also may be one in us: that the world may believe that thou hast sent me." In vain do we sacrifice everything, if we cherish our strife and hatred. In vain do we make zeal do the work of charity. Contemporary religious history is the record of the failure, and zeal does but slay itself in the impossible attempt. Our religious teaching wants the one thing that can recommend it to the demos, because it wants the one thing that recommended it to the world at first. And this one thing is not inward unity, still less outward uniformity; it is not even the cessation of religious strife and jealousy. But the one imperative reform required at our hands is this: that different communities—"all that in every place call upon the name of Jesus Christ our Lord, both theirs and ours"—should learn to regard each other as but different regiments in the army of the Church Militant: that whatever jealousies, or claims to superiority, or imputations of failure, are consistent with the unity of an army, should be subordinated to the feeling, that all are under One Commander, and have one common enemy—human ignorance and wickedness. Then the poison would be taken out of our controversies, the danger out of our divisions, and we could approach the working classes without feeling that in the most important point of all in Christianity we, its preachers, were inferior to those to whom we preached. To the promotion of this idea every Christian who calls himself a Liberal should direct his energies, and that immediately.

2. Closely connected with the above, as cause and effect, comes another failing in the theology of the day which it is easier to realise than to describe. But it may be summed up as a tendency to attach exaggerated importance to minor doctrines and small points of difference. It is, so to speak, a want of the sense of theological perspective. So long as Christianity endures, we may be sure that the historical events upon which it rests will be approached differently by differently constituted minds, whether national or individual, and will create various forms of belief, and of practice also. Mere doctrinal unity is not merely impossible, but contrary to the whole genius of Christianity as a belief in an historical revelation. But the reform which lies within our reach, and which the pressure of democratic unbelief tends steadily to produce, takes the direction of subordinating minor differences to larger points of agreement—say rather to a united belief in the historical truthfulness of the New Testament. No doctrines have played a more important part in ecclesiastical history than those concerning the nature of the Real Presence and of Justification; and yet, before another century has passed away, we may hope that they, with many others, will cease to be among the number of the things which vex the unity

of the Church. That, for instance, almost all Christians keep the Lord's Supper by command and in memory of One Master, and mainly in the way in which He prescribed (many additions and one diminution notwithstanding); that all regard it as a spiritual blessing to the individual recipient, and as a pledge of brotherly love and communion; that all "worthy" partakers are as a matter of fact morally affected and improved by it in much the same way, and to much the same extent,—will be found, when confronted with general unbelief, to be facts of such surprising and vital importance, that different opinions about the mode of Christ's presence, or the working of the moral influence, or the proper ritual observance, will seem comparatively insignificant. Most true it is that time was when disagreement upon these points implied, or accompanied, opinions of religion and theories of human life and nature, the importance of a right decision as to which cannot be exaggerated. But it is necessary now that Christian people should see that this has passed away. The sea indeed tosses, but the gale has blown itself out. Protestants may indeed affirm that Rome remains the same, but it is equally true, and more to the purpose, that her power of working injury is departing from her. The progress of liberty, of science, and of confidence in human progress, is neutralising her influence. The moment that a Church ceases to be able to coerce (I am very far from asserting that this is yet as true of the Church of Rome as it ought to be*), and is obliged to enter into free competition with

* It is true now of the Church of Rome since the fall of the temporal power. It cannot be too much insisted upon that if persons accept the doctrines of that Church no state interference can save them, or ought to try and save them, from the consequences. They that would be free must themselves strike the blow.

other religious communities, her doctrines lose the only power that Liberals need recognise as dangerous. And on the other hand, it is not from Roman doctrines alone that the present reaction is taking place, but from much of what is called distinctively Protestant theology. The Thirty-nine Articles fare in these days but little better than the decrees of the Council of Trent. It is not that they are untrue, but that they are obsolete. They cannot breathe in the intellectual atmosphere which science creates. They, and similar Protestant Confessions of Faith, belong to a period of thought, a scheme of divinity, and a school of philosophy, all of which are yielding to a new order of things, and the removal of which has an intimate relation to democratic progress. Therefore it is that religious truth presented under these conditions wears a singularly unreal and unimpressive aspect to the working man, who has no sympathy, and indeed no acquaintance, with the state of things from which they come. A formulary like the Apostles' Creed suits his comprehension, and meets his religious wants. But disputes about the Real Presence hide away the thing itself from the sight of men's eyes. Disputes about justification by faith within the Church obscure divine truth in the case of men who are endeavouring to justify themselves by works without the Church upon a scale, and with at least a temporary success, never before witnessed. And so the effect of our religious teaching is, that we offer to the man who lies plundered and dying upon the road, not the wine and oil which are the healing balm of humanity, but some patent medicine of our own, for which we claim that it is the sole and universal remedy. This it is which makes men feel that religion as presented to them is so unreal, unpractical, inoperative, and unsuitable to their lives and temptations. This is the secret of that protest which they make in words so familiar to every minister of religion—"I have led a good life, and done no harm to any one." In that perpetual controversy between the clergyman and his poor parishioners, are we quite sure that all the truth is on one side?

3. Another source of theological weakness arises from doctrines either false, or so perverted and "petrified" as to become false to the people at large. I take first of all, as profoundly repugnant to the moral convictions of the demos, the doctrine of endless punishment as it is commonly held and taught. It is no part of the purpose of this essay to discuss what is the truth of this or of any other doctrine, merely as such, or indeed whether any view, of whatever school of theology, which pretends to give an exhaustive and satisfactory account of the moral conditions of the future state, can have any pretensions to be styled true. But I here record my emphatic testimony to the fact that this doctrine is hated, and at the same time feared, by the "common people" to an extent of which we have little conception. The good-natured and amiable clergyman who preaches it from his pulpit, and tricks it out with such rhetoric as his resources command, little knows what harm he may be doing to some excitable and attentive listener. The preacher himself holds it with a thousand drawbacks and difficulties. He knows that he must take into account the case of unbaptized children, of children baptized but left in practical heathenism, of virtuous heathen, and that (to him) hardest case of all, of men who live in the practice of excellent morality without a belief

in the Christian revelation. He knows, too, that there is at least another aspect of the future life presented to us in the New Testament. But his words fall in all their naked simplicity perhaps upon the ears of men who are easily moved by the pleadings of love; but all whose notions of manliness and dignity revolt at the thought of being coerced by fear. Or more probably they fall upon the ears of some one whom vice has converted into a coward. He goes out a changed man, full of the terrors of the unknown world. He believes himself to be in danger of hell-fire, and as it is a most awful reality to him, he must needs warn his fellow-workmen, with coarse importunity, of their common danger, and preach to them the gospel of an almost universal damnation. These know their comrade but too well, understand at once the paltry motive, the enfeebled morality, the profound immorality, of the whole; and they know that nine times out of ten he becomes within six months as much a reprobate as ever. No wonder they hate the religion of which they only see this parody; and yet they fear while they hate, because they are conscious that they are living without God in the world. When persons talk of the use of fear as an instrument of conviction, they apparently forget that in the far more numerous cases where fear does not convince it acts as one of the strongest repelling forces that exist in human nature, and passes invariably into an intensity of hatred and aversion. Certainly the defence of the doctrine of everlasting punishment as a useful "economy" is the worst possible ground to take: the individual is converted to a questionable religion, the class is alienated from the highest and purest truths. I know from experience that the instinctive dread of this doctrine shuts the heart of many a dying and conscience-stricken wretch against the gospel of love. Men must be approached, not with a definite set of theological doctrines upon such a vast and mysterious subject, but with (it is difficult to find a suitable word) an idea, in which hope predominates and fear mingles, the fear of sinfulness working out its own punishment in future ages, the hope of a work to be continued, a life to be lived out, a character to be developed, it may be a new chance to be allowed us, under such conditions as shall be prescribed by the justice of God.

4. I pass on to notice two samples of the obstacles to the spread of Christian truth arising respectively from the intellectual and moral faithfulness of its advocates. Both are so well known, and so frequently denounced, that I need do no more than indicate the effect they produce on the religious instinct of the demos. We know that the popular sentiment of the Church, disguising a profound faithlessness under the garb of orthodoxy, has ever desired an outward infallibility, by which it has sought to "conclude" all theological progress. Instead of spreading out her sails to meet, and escape by meeting, the approaching gale, the ship of the Church, freighted with the precious cargo of religious truth, has been anchored upon a lee shore by a single cable—the infallibility of Popes, or of Councils, or of the Bible. In our own day and country we see the result of this timid policy; the doctrine of plenary inspiration has broken like pack-thread before the rising gales of scientific discovery and historical research, and in a moment the good ship is tossing amid the breakers, "with much hurt and damage not only of the lading and ship, but also of our own lives." In plain words, the mass of mankind has been

taught to believe that the Bible was not only incapable of error, but was a sufficient guide in matters relating to natural science; and when first the real truth dawns upon them, there is naturally a terrible revulsion. Men who know at least as much geology as is contained in the pages of Hugh Miller, or who have heard and taken note of the story of Galileo *contra Ecclesiam*, are enabled to hold and even to preach this doctrine without much harm to themselves. They are compelled to acknowledge difficulties, to reconcile varying truths, to make allowances, to fall back on metaphor, or visions, or that last resource of theologians in distress, the poetic genius of the Hebrew language. But the men to whom this doctrine is preached have received it in all simplicity of heart, and are incapable of understanding the refinements by which it is explained away. To us it may seem astonishing that difficulties about the scientific value of the book of Genesis should injure a Christian's faith in the revelation contained in the New Testament; but an infidel street lecturer, as I myself know, is perfectly aware that if he can start some such difficulty by questions to us so absurd as "Who was the wife that Cain married?" he has seriously damaged the belief of his bewildered hearers. Practically careless as they may be about religion, they have nevertheless certain "idols," such as the infallibility of the Bible or Sabbath-keeping, and if these are broken, almost the last tie that binds them to Christianity is broken also. And yet broken every idol in the long run must be, because it is the creation of a timid faithlessness, that regards merely visible consequences, takes refuge in the letter rather than in the spirit, and believes in the past without daring to hope for the future.

5. Closely allied with this is the moral defect to which I have alluded. The one danger to which theology has always been exposed, and to which it has not seldom succumbed, is the temptation to divide religion from morality in the supposed interests, and to meet the pressing wants, of the former. At this very moment popular theories as to the Atonement, the usual defence for the conduct and character of the heroes of the Old Testament, much of the ordinary views of religious graces and virtues, the hateful expression " mere morality," the unnatural and " inhuman" aspect in which the history of religion in the Bible and in the Church is presented to us, are painful evidences of what I am asserting. " You seem to me," said a working man, " to make God act like a very bad man." It is easy to say that we can see at once the real disingenuousness of this remark, and the obvious want of any searching interest in the subject which it evinces. Still these are the men we have to deal with, and this is what they think and say. And however much the fault may be theirs, that does not take away our responsibility. We assume towards them, as we are bound to do, the position of teachers, and we preach to them a religion which is the sternest rebuke of their lives and beliefs. We must therefore be prepared to meet the jealous scrutiny with which they will inevitably test our claims upon their allegiance, and the fatal accuracy with which they will fasten on the weak points in our teaching. And because morality is common ground to us and them, therefore by such morality as they possess they will try the religion which professes to be the expression of the divine goodness. And thus, as ever, may we hope that the very seriousness of the danger which menaces Christianity will

prove its safeguard. For the alienation of the demos will compel us to examine closely into the defective parts of our system, in order that the people themselves may then take their place in the Church, of which they have first of all compelled the reformation.

The mention of the word reformation suggests one closing remark. It is sometimes applied with perfect propriety to describe the religious change through which we are now passing. For there are two conditions necessary to a religious reformation on a large scale: in the first place, a deep-rooted alienation of the people, or of some powerful section of the people, from the religion of the day, such as was witnessed in the eras of Tetzel and Hoadley; and, in the second place, the rising of a new force from without calculated powerfully to affect religious thought, such as the revival of learning which preceded the Reformation, or the triumph of civil and religious liberty which made the Wesleyan movement possible. At this present moment there is, as we have seen, a distinct alienation of the demos from Christianity; but as this does not now proceed, as it did in the days of Luther and Wesley, from the popular protest against moral corruption or practical infidelity within the Church itself, we shall find that the new Reformation, though equally searching and thorough, will nevertheless assume a comparatively peaceful and gradual form.* The second Reformation will be to the first much what the Reform Bill of 1867 was to its predecssor of 1832

---

* I am not sure of this now. At the close of the Franco-German war I ventured to predict that the next war might possibly be a religious one, and things have been tending in that direction ever since. Moreover, the morality of the Churches may be as much below what is *now* possible for mankind as it was before the Reformation.

Nevertheless, the "scientific mind," together with all the other elements of progress, will kill many old dogmatic formularies as effectually as the Hellenic view of life and thought slew the mediæval theology. The present "Catholic" reaction in the Church of England will avail ultimately to stem the current in England, just as much and just as little as the Catholic revival, of which Ignatius Loyola stands as the representative, did on the Continent. Protestants and Catholics may indeed, and a sad sight it is to see, continue their ancient controversies and try to breathe life into worn-out disputes, but a power greater than both is threatening to absorb them. When, for instance, men of recognised ability and high official position speak of the danger to which our "beloved Church" is exposed from the doctrines or practices of the Ritualist party, we seem to see that the instinct of statesmanship is departed from the English Church. Israel and Judah persist in fighting out their ancient border feuds, while the armies of Assyria and Egypt are gathering upon the frontiers. Let us hope that this somewhat ill-omened comparison may not be further illustrated by a Babylonish captivity, as the last method of reuniting the Church and taking away her idols.

We will however turn rather to the brighter side, and proclaim that the religion of Christ is essential to the future welfare of the democracy. I am as little disposed as any man to regard with forebodings the great change of 1867, or to speak with anything but confidence of the future. Nevertheless, no man, not absolutely a Liberal fanatic, can disguise from himself that we are about to try an experiment, new in the history of our country, new moreover in the history of the world. We are about to intrust the destinies of this nation to a democracy composed of "working men," as different as possible from the Demos of Athens or the Plebs of Rome. Hard manual labour, the ceaseless toil for daily bread, brings with it, questionless, many restraining and ennobling influences, but it brings with it also many palpable and most dangerous temptations. Men whose lot in life is so disposed have but little time for self-education, for the exercise of quiet thought, for elevating and purifying recreation. There is an inevitable tendency to coarseness, to impatience of spirit, to degrading amusements. All the ancient beauty of thought and feeling that hallowed the commonest occupation, that made princesses do the work of housemaids, and swineherds act the part of gentlemen, has long ago vanished; and labour, while growing in worth, in power, and in earnestness of purpose, has lost much of its ancient grace in men's eyes, and something of its elevating and beautifying association. And therefore God in His providence has given us the Christian religion, that a moral influence more powerful than poetry, or art, or freedom itself, may be brought to bear upon the "sons and daughters of toil;" may cheer and alleviate their lot, may sanctify their daily work. These considerations will suggest to us the direction in which the new Reformation should be guided. By teaching religion as obedience to a living Person whose work and character have been revealed in history, we can appeal to the best instincts of the working man, his susceptibility of personal influence, his enthusiastic loyalty towards those in whom he trusts, an imagination easily interested, affections readily enlisted by

The Church and the Working Classes. 403

the account of noble things well done and bravely suffered. We must proclaim that Christ is Head and King not merely of the Church, but of the world; that He has a direct interest in scientific as in religious progress, in civilisation as in evangelisation; that, in a sense of which a timid religiousness never dreamt, the kingdoms of this world are become the kingdoms of God and of His Christ. We must insist upon the truth that work is part of the religion which man owes to the King of men. We must hallow the occupation of manual labour, just as the professions of medicine or justice are hallowed, by a thousand Christian associations. We must vindicate for mechanical toil the same intimate connection with religious ideas that has ever bound together religion and the calling of the shepherd or the farmer; and we must see in the factory, no less than in the vineyard or the corn-field, a true picture of the eternal relations between God and man. And we must look forward, in however remote a future, to a state of things in which it shall not seem unnatural or absurd to think of the Church as having discovered America, or of the world as having built Westminster Abbey.

Very vain and visionary as these dreams of the future may appear to practical men, they are nevertheless akin to the views that animate all the healthiest practical working of the present day. Science, for instance, of whose arrogance divines speak so confidently, would be crushed by the sense of its own ignorance in comparison with the problems to be solved, if it were not sustained by the hope of discovering the last secrets* of life and force. And

---

* So far as they can be discovered by human faculties. The limitation of discovery in this life is an intimation of immortality.

exactly the same thing may be said of the spirit of the age as seen in one who is in England its foremost representative. We can see that Mr Mill's sense of the folly and weakness of human nature, his insight into human depravity and wickedness, would afflict him with a mere blank despair if he had not realised to himself a condition of society towards which mankind is fitfully progressing; and it is precisely because of this that the philosopher of the nineteenth century can dedicate his time and thoughts to the commonest practical questions, to the merest details of legislation. Surely every consideration that Christian men hold dear should impel us to the same practical work in the same hopeful spirit. We are the " children of the prophets," heirs of the boundless future in which their spirits dwelt, of the gladdening and encouraging hopefulness by which their hearts were consoled and animated. When all the world is hoping, Christians must not—dare not—set the example of despair.

THE END.

www.ingramcontent.com/pod-product-compliance
Lightning Source LLC
Chambersburg PA
CBHW022108290426
44112CB00008B/598